DETERMINING PROJECT REQUIREMENTS

DETERMINING PROJECT REQUIREMENTS

HANS JONASSON

Auerbach Publications
Taylor & Francis Group
Boca Raton   New York

Auerbach Publications is an imprint of the
Taylor & Francis Group, an **informa** business

Auerbach Publications
Taylor & Francis Group
6000 Broken Sound Parkway NW, Suite 300
Boca Raton, FL 33487-2742

© 2008 by Taylor & Francis Group, LLC
Auerbach is an imprint of Taylor & Francis Group, an Informa business

International Standard Book Number-10: 1-4200-4502-4 (Hardcover)
International Standard Book Number-13: 978-1-4200-4502-4 (Hardcover)

Library of Congress Cataloging-in-Publication Data

Jonasson, Hans.
   Determining project requirements / Hans Jonasson.
      p. cm. -- (ESI international project management series ; 3)
   Includes bibliographical references and index.
   ISBN 978-1-4200-4502-4 (alk. paper)
   1. Project management. I. Title.

HD69.P75J66 2007
658.4'04--dc22   2007012581

Visit the Taylor & Francis Web site at
http://www.taylorandfrancis.com

and the Auerbach Web site at
http://www.auerbach-publications.com

Contents

Foreword

When I discuss the state of project management with corporate and government executives around the world, it is increasingly evident that organizations are wasting millions of dollars every year on failed projects. At ESI International, when we looked into the root causes of project failure, we found that one of the key reasons was poor or incomplete requirements definition. Project teams had no members whose sole job it was to nail down the requirements at the outset. Rather, the function was diffused throughout the team; in short, this critical role was given short shrift. We realized we needed to address this critical piece of the project puzzle to enable our clients to be successful in their project endeavors.

Accordingly, in 2003 we decided to augment our proven project management training with a comprehensive curriculum in business analysis, a rapidly growing discipline whose primary focus is on the tools, techniques, and approaches in requirements engineering. In this curriculum the focus is developing the skill set of the business analyst to make sure that we know what the customer needs rather than developing what we think the customer is asking for.

Given the positive response to our curriculum, it was obvious that this was something the industry had been longing for. The interest in the curriculum was immediate and a little bit overwhelming. The interest is still growing, even more so with the growth and increased maturity of the International Institute of Business Analysis (IIBA™), an organization which seems destined to do for business analysis what the Project Management Institute® (PMI) did for project management some 30 years ago.

Our success in the business analyst curriculum is due, in large part, to the experienced consultants with whom we work. One of the first consultants we certified was Hans Jonasson. Hans had 20 years of industry background when he first started working with us in 1999. In addition to his work with us in project management training, Hans had, and does to this day, a successful consultancy including presenting his own JAD (Joint Application Development) classes to government and industry, including PMI. Not only does he have mastery of the subject, he has the ability to communicate those concepts to a global audience. After teaching the business analysis curriculum for over three years to hundreds of business analysts, Hans is now in a unique position to be able to present these topics in an easy-to-follow manner.

Although it is always tough to predict what the future will hold, I am confident that this profession, and the importance of it, will continue to grow. Already there has been an increased desire to formalize the profession through certifications like the ESI International and George Washington University Professional Certificate in Business Analysis and the IIBA Certified Business Analysis Professional program. The book that you now hold in your hands will not only help you achieve such certifications, it will also make you a better business analyst.

J. LeRoy Ward
Executive Vice President, ESI International

Acknowledgments

This book is the result of a request by LeRoy Ward of ESI International, who was looking for subject matter experts interested in writing a book. I want to thank him for that opportunity, for his helpful advice, and for writing the foreword for the book.

Thank you to Glenn Brule, who is responsible for the international chapters of the International Institute of Business Analysis® (IIBA), for kindly agreeing to review the book and provide comments for the book cover.

Bonnie Roche helped with in-depth reviews of both content and format and greatly improved the material. Thanks, Bonnie!

From the initial contact with Richard O'Hanley, many e-mails with the senior editor John Wyzalek, and working with Jessica Vakili on the production plan as well as with Karen Simon for editing, this has been a great learning process for me. Thanks to them and all the people at Taylor & Francis, my publisher, for being very supportive through the process and answering endless questions.

Many thanks to my friends and family. You have all been great with interest, support, and (sometimes) advice.

My love and special thanks to my daughter Lisa, who designed the book cover and created some of the graphics, and to my son Erik, for his encouragement.

More than anyone I want to thank my wife Jan for her hard work on the book. She has spent many hours doing endless editing, putting material together, reviewing both content and format, and bringing many ideas for improvement to the book. All of it has been greatly appreciated. I love you.

About the Author

Hans Jonasson, PMP, founder of JTC Unlimited, has more than 25 years of experience in the areas of project management, business analysis and professional development training. He started his career with Volvo LTD in Gothenburg, Sweden, in 1980 as a systems analyst/programmer. In 1984 he moved to the United States to work on new development projects for EDS and General Motors. He has managed all aspects of software development projects for the automotive industry whose budgets have ranged from $100,000 to $10 million.

He has taught introductory and advanced-level courses on project management, requirements gathering, CMMI® and process development, to more than 10,000 professionals at companies that include IBM, EDS, Ford Motors, DaimlerChrysler, General Dynamics, Citibank, and JP Morgan Chase.

Since 1996, he has been a Project Management Professional (PMP®) and member of the Project Management Institute (PMI®), as well as a frequent presenter at PMI events in North America and Europe for the last eight years. He is a member of the Great Lakes Chapter of PMI and the International Institute of Business Analysis (IIBA™).

Chapter 1

Introduction

If you don't know where you're going, chances are you will end up somewhere else.

— Yogi Berra

In the last ten years I have taught project management and requirements gathering to over 10,000 people worldwide. In most of those classes there has been a discussion about why projects, especially IT projects, fail. Inevitably the number one reason always comes back to unclear requirements or changing requirements. When organizations try to address these problems, they often try for quick fixes such as buying new tools or hiring a consultant. The message conveyed in this book is that it takes more than that. Good requirements do not come from a tool, or from a customer interview. They come from a repeatable set of processes which take the project from the early idea stage through to the creation of an agreed-upon project and product scope between the customer and the developer. This repeatable set of processes, and the tools and techniques that help to execute them, are what I want to address by writing this book.

This chapter sets the stage for the rest of the book by getting you familiar with the format, the writing style, and the purpose of the book. Each chapter has a similar structure and format that are used throughout the book. The content is based on certain choices in regard to what standards to use and what techniques to include. These choices were made by me and are explained in this chapter through a review of the history of systems development and the evolution of today's standards. One of the primarily goals in this chapter is to let you know how the book is organized, what it is covering, and what is expected of you afterward. This is very much in line with what is recommended when creating a good requirements document.

1.1 Objectives

- Explain the purpose of the book.
- Introduce how to use the book.
- Review the target audience of the book.
- Introduce the professional domain of business analysis.
- Review the evolution of business analysis over the last few decades.
- Review the standard-setting forces in the industry today.
- Introduce the project which will be used throughout the book as an example.

1.2 Overview

This book is designed to be used for multiple purposes:

1. Reference book: Any person involved with gathering requirements can utilize this book to discover best practices and learn useful techniques, as well as tools and templates, to improve the requirements gathering processes within their organization.
2. Self study: A business analyst needing more guidance on requirements gathering techniques, or one who is preparing for any certifications in business analysis can use this book as a study guide. The book contains exercises and sample solutions to demonstrate how to deal with different situations that may be encountered in the requirements gathering process.
3. Course book: Study groups, internal corporate training, and consultative training can use this book as a textbook, with built-in exercises, best practices, tools, and templates. Because it also contains comprehensive solutions to the activities, a warning is warranted. The solutions are "a solution," not "the solution." Because there are no real customers being interviewed, there will be assumptions made, so there is likely to be some difference in what the book solution is versus your solution.
4. Provide templates: Two different examples of a Business Requirements Document have been included in Appendix B of this book. The first is a comprehensive template, provided courtesy of ESI International, the second a simpler template, suitable for smaller projects. Review them, customize them, and introduce them into your organization.

This book is not intended as a tool book, nor an advocate of any special methodology or technique. Its purpose is to give a broad overview of a multitude of business analysis issues and to provide enough information about tools and techniques to select the best approach for different types of projects. It is a generalist book, not a specialist. For the key areas where an organization may invest a significant amount of time and effort, more comprehensive training should be considered.

To evaluate the current state of the industry and gather pertinent information on the challenges facing the business analysts of today, I conducted a study with a group of business analysts and project participants who had previously attended my training seminars. While not a large or comprehensive study, it served its purpose well by exploring the role of the business analyst in different organizations, the difficulties in capturing requirements, as well as information about the tools used by practitioners to assist in the analysis process. This study is referenced and discussed throughout the book.

One of the questions asked on the survey was "What are the main difficulties with gathering and documenting requirements?" The top five responses were:

1. Lack of time/availability on the part of the customer
2. Lack of customer knowledge
3. Lack of buy-in to scope
4. Lack of skilled business analysts
5. No repeatable process from which to learn

These problems, and others, are explored throughout the book. However, at a high level, it is striking that the first three areas all deal with customer issues. Is that because most people responding to the survey were developers, and it is easier to blame the customer? Or is it because customers truly have challenges in the areas of communication and perhaps in their understanding of what the business really needs? It's likely a bit of both. Either way, it clearly shows the importance of the customer's role and competency in requirements gathering.

1.3   The Early Days

In the early days of computer systems most applications were geared toward solving a specific problem. The customer was often personally known by the developer and had a relatively clear understanding of what was wanted, and the biggest constraint was typically the capabilities of the computers themselves. Hardware was expensive with limited capabilities. It is always an amazing journey to review what computers were capable of 30 years ago versus what they are able to perform today. And although the capacities continue to improve, the computer's capability is rarely the limiting factor anymore. Back then, computer systems were viewed as tools, like an adding machine or telephone, with no real vision of how the tool could drive organizational change or move the business in new directions. Integration and interoperability was crude at best. Life for the developer was easy, because customers were not very picky and normally were quite happy with any tool that would help them in their day-to-day work. It is interesting to draw a parallel with the early days of television: the programming was sparse, the picture quality low, and many of the shows crude (at best), but in general, people were happy with it because expectations were low and not difficult to meet. Today, with hundreds of channels and digital quality, it seems like most people still have a hard time finding anything they like. Expectations have changed.

Although there were several systems development methodologies around in the mid-1980s, they all tended to have a strong focus on the systems side, often at the expense of understanding the real business need. The creation of the system, or the programming of the same system, was typically the starting point of the project followed by a multitude of trials and errors. Many projects were cancelled and even more were not received well by the customers. There was little or no attention paid to making sure that the developers understood what the actual business problem was that they were trying to solve. Although this was understandable because there was limited precedence in the way of system solutions, customers were often faced with not knowing how to describe what they needed and quite often took the "I'll know it when I see it" approach.

Gradually throughout the 1980s and 1990s, this started changing. Systems rapidly became more complex, and business more competitive and global, leading to a shift from struggling with what technology could do to struggling with what the business was trying to accomplish. One of the first projects that I worked on after moving to the United States in 1984 was a common accounts payable system for General Motors (GM). Prior to that, the projects I had seen at Volvo Ltd. in Sweden were mostly single-user, relatively non-integrated applications. At GM, there was a stronger emphasis on capturing what the customer needed, trying to get consensus between different organizations to build "common" systems, as well as trying to closely integrate the accounts payable function with receivables and purchasing (Figure 1.1).

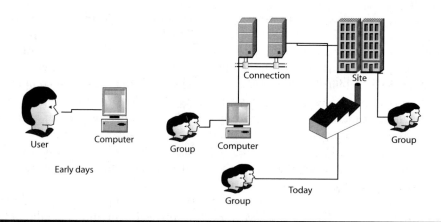

Figure 1.1 Evolution of systems.

To be successful in that environment (and because the system is still running 20 some years later, I think one could argue that the project was successful), it took a different skill set than that of the traditional system developer. Although technical skills are still important, systems development now becomes more and more about communication, facilitation, negotiation, and basic people skills. There were many very good technical people that didn't enjoy this new environment, resulting in many issues between the developers with their minds on the solution and the users with their minds on what the business needed.

> Although technical skills are still important, systems development now becomes more and more about communication, facilitation, negotiation, and basic people skills.

In an attempt to try different ways to improve communication between the developers and the customers, some organizations created account teams made up of analysts responsible for interfacing with the customers, gathering their requirements, and making sure that they were satisfied. Instead of the customer talking to the developer, it became the account team's responsibility to make sure the development team understood the customer's requirements. Unfortunately, people put in those positions often did not have a strong business background or didn't have a good understanding of what the developers needed. Based on the lack of tools and training, the business analysts were struggling with this dual communication role — talking business to the customer and systems to the developers. It made projects more complex by requiring coordination between developers, users, and go-betweens. It made the need for good project management practices even more critical than before.

1.4   The Project Management Institute®

In the late 1960s, the Project Management Institute (PMI®) was started. Although its impact was gradual in the beginning, by the mid-1990s PMI had become a driving force in the area of establishing standards for project management. Their *Guide to the Project Management Body of Knowledge,* currently in its third edition, has been instrumental in establishing a common language and a concentration on the planning aspects of a project.

So with the help of PMI and various development methodologies, by the late 1990s there were good development practices and good management of the development process in place, enabling the development teams to develop something faster. However, that still left a big void. PMI's domain is how to take an idea and implement it. The product description (in whatever level of detail it is available) is an input into the project management processes. But who creates the product description? How does the developer make sure that the right product is developed? Obviously, it is nice to develop a solid product and to do it in an organized fashion; however, if it is the wrong product, there is still a big problem. Some people feel that PMI could have done more to define standards for this, but there is really a need to separate the role of the project manager and the role of the product developer. They have conflicting roles and conflicting goals. In addition, the product definition aspect tends to be very dependent on the industry for which the work is being done. Product definition for information technology (IT) projects is not the same as product definition for construction. The process of requirements development was rightfully left to other organizations by PMI. There have been various training companies and toolmakers concentrating on tools and processes for the requirements development aspects of a project, but there has not been an industrywide, non-tool-specific approach … until now.

1.5   The International Institute of Business Analysis®

In 2003, the International Institute of Business Analysis (IIBA) was started in Canada with the goal of improving the working environment for people who are involved in analysis for systems, business, and process improvement. The IIBA's first few years had rapid growth and they have been hard at work on *A Guide to the Business Analysis Body of Knowledge* (BABOK®) with their latest version that was released in the summer of 2006, version 1.6. It is the intention of this book to stay consistent with the material covered in the BABOK.

IIBA has had a lot of immediate success and has been embraced by a large number of practitioners, often based on faith alone, which is the way it must be in the beginning. There has been a feeling among business analysts that there has been too much attention paid to the project plan and the system design and not enough to defining the product being delivered. The processes and methodologies used have often been rooted in a tool, or connected with a specific vendor. IIBA is likely to be a key driver in establishing the framework of the professional domain that is being called business analysis.

> There has been a feeling among business analysts that there has been too much attention paid to the project plan and the system design and not enough to defining the product being delivered.

Throughout the time period described earlier, the role of the business analyst has evolved. Initially being a part of the developer's job, the role has been known as systems analyst and requirements analyst. It has been a job where the job duties have varied greatly depending on the organization they worked for and the tools that were used for development. Now it is evolving into a value-added position, serving as a communication link between the developers and the customers. The language of development can often be cryptic and full of acronyms. So is the language of the business. What the organization is looking for in the business analyst is the ability to effectively communicate with both the business and the developing organization. This has become an even larger issue with the offshoring of IT projects. The communication problems traditionally faced by customers and developers, who may be located on different floors and use different terminology, get multiplied when complexities such as time, language, and cultural differences are added. Because globalization is likely to be a trend that is here to stay, there will probably continue to be an increased need to deal with these issues in the future. The job of the business analyst is secure and appears to be moving in the direction of increased importance and stature. It is actually one of the more difficult jobs to offshore because there is a need to be close to the customer. This by itself may explain, at least partially, the increased interest in business analysis not only from organizations, but also from the individual practitioners.

The job of the business analyst is secure and appears to be moving in the direction of increased importance and stature.

1.6   The Role of the Business Analyst

In the survey mentioned earlier in this chapter, the respondents were asked what the role of the business analyst is in their organization. It was clear from their responses that there is not yet a universally accepted industry standard for this. Examples of responses include:

- Create a document.
- Work with end users to define requirements and then with developers to ensure that those requirements can be translated into code.
- Facilitate meetings.
- Approve test plans and test cases.
- Develop process and procedure documentation.
- Create project plans.

- Low-level liaison between customer and IT.
- Train user.
- Create designs for offshore positions.

As can be seen from this, the business analyst is sometimes an entry level position, sometimes a senior person, so be aware that the definitions used in this book are reflective of where the industry is heading, not necessarily where it is today.

If the analyst works in a large organization, assigned to a significant project, he may very well be a full-time business analyst. However, that is typically not the case for most business analysts. In addition to gathering requirements, they manage projects, design systems, build customer relationships, and may even make coffee in the morning. Chapter 2 more closely defines what the current thoughts are on the role delineation of the business analyst. For now though, keep in mind that when the term business analyst is used in this book it is not describing a person, it is describing a role in the business. It may be 20 percent of a person's time, or it may take three people 100 percent (or more) of their time to fill the role (Figure 1.2).

Job
Gather requirements
Manage project
Design system
Test
Do performance feedback
Train users

Business Analyst

Role

Gather requirements
Analyze requirements
Document requirements

Figure 1.2 Business analyst role versus job.

The level of formality involved with the processes used by the business analyst will also vary greatly based on the tools used, the size of the organization, and the project, as well as the type of project that is being worked on. Naturally, if the project is a large, enterprisewide initiative, the analyst will spend a lot of time analyzing the business, doing enterprise modeling, planning for organizational change, etc. However, if the project is to modify an existing report in a current system, there will likely be very little time spent on analyzing enterprise goals (or the customer will question the competency of the analyst).

As with most business activities, there is no "one size fits all." Using this book, just like with the IIBA standards and any methodologies used for requirements gathering, evaluate what is applicable to the organization and project. Maybe there is a need to develop a plan for the analysis phase of the project. If so, read more in chapter 4. Chapter 7 can help if it is necessary to implement new best practices on requirements-gathering techniques. If an introduction to modeling techniques is needed to pick one for an upcoming initiative, Chapter 8 is intended to do just that (Figure 1.3).

Business Analyst Skill	Chapter where covered	IIBA knowledge area
Understanding the business	3, 9, 10	Enterprise Analysis
Plan and manage requirements gathering	4	Requirements Planning and Management
Select a development methodology	5	Requirements Planning and Management
Gather requirements	7	Requirements Elicitation
Modeling	8	Requirements Analysis and Documentation
Documenting requirements	6, 8, 9	Requirements Analysis and Documentation
Validating requirements	7, 8, 9,10	Solution Assessment and Validation Requirements Communication

Figure 1.3 Focus areas of the book.

In addition to IIBA, there are other organizations that have influenced the evolution of the business analysis profession, including the large toolmakers, training companies, and other standard-setting bodies such as the Institute of Electrical and Electronics Engineers (IEEE), the Software Engineering Institute (SEI™), and others. One that deserves a bit of extra attention is the SEI. Started in the early 1980s, SEI initially targeted the software industry and looked at defined processes needed to successfully run a software project. Today's SEI goes beyond just software and is looking at engineering practices, but a lot of their standards still have a software feel to them. They did, early on, put a special emphasis on requirements practices, and they did it before many other organizations had caught on to it. Some of SEI's definitions will be explored in Chapter 2.

1.7   Where Is It All Going?

Although IIBA is doing a great job developing the framework for business analysis, it is a moving target. The domain that IIBA has taken on within their borders of business analysis is very large, a lot larger really than the domain that PMI took on with project management. Part of the reason for this is that PMI chose to deal with generic project management, processes that should be applied to all projects. On the other hand, IIBA appears to be going into a greater level of detail when exploring development methodologies, modeling techniques, quality assurance, and organizational involvement. As an example, the business analyst is involved pre-project, during the project, and post-project, and not only at a cursory level. The business analyst has significant roles and responsibilities in all three areas; the project manager, on the other hand, is primarily responsible for the project.

Business analysis is also more immature than most other domains. Systems development has only been done for about 40 to 50 years, and business analysis in this context even less than that. This may seem like a long time, but compared to manufacturing, construction, and other disciplines, it's new. This means that there likely will be significant changes in the body of knowledge for many years to come. That's OK; the basic concepts of lessons learned and process improvements apply here as well. As the industry is changing, the practitioners need to change with it. This is an industry where tools, methods, and best practices are changing, and changing drastically. Just look at a topic like agile development (which will be further explored later): ten years ago few people had heard of it and virtually no one had used it. Today, most organizations have incorporated some aspects of agile development approaches in their projects.

1.8 Book Project

To give examples of the different techniques and tools discussed throughout the book, a fictitious project, called the Prescription Interaction Project, will be used. The decision to make it a fictitious project rather than a real one is based on many reasons. First, any real project is likely to get into unique details for a specific industry, which while interesting, is not the purpose of this book. Second, no project would use all the techniques and tools discussed in this book, meaning that even a real project would need some fabrication to accomplish this. Third and most importantly, there is a need for the project to be simple and intuitive, so that the main concern is on the business analysis portions, not the business itself.

The Prescription Interaction Project is a project being done by a large drug store chain, C.V. Green. They are traditionally U.S.-based, but are slowly expanding into Asia and Europe. C.V. Green has a vision of minimizing negative interaction between different drugs prescribed to their customers, and wants to aggressively identify any potential drug interactions as early as possible. They have been leading the effort to standardize drug interaction reporting and are working with a consortium to create a shared database where potential drug interactions can be identified, while still safeguarding the rights of the individual customers. That is the starting point and the framework for the examples found in the following chapters.

Separate from the book project theme, there is also a case study project. This is the creation of an inventory and ordering system for Swede-Mart which will be used for most of the case study activities found at the end of each chapter. The detailed description of the Swede-Mart case study is in Chapter 11.

1.9 Summary

Business analysis is still a relatively new discipline. Although there are many emerging standards in the industry, to a large extent it is still up to each organization to pick the tools, processes, and definitions that work in their environment. This book uses the IIBA° Body of Knowledge (BABOK) as the main reference for the framework of business analysis. The goal of this book is to get an organization, or an individual, started on the path toward a formalization of business analysis processes, and also to help as a study guide for individuals looking for certification in business analysis.

1.10 Activity

- What are the biggest blockers to successful requirements gathering in your organization(s)? Either brainstorm as a team or by yourself. Create a list of eight to ten factors.
- Prioritize them based on the importance for project success and then select the top five. For those top five blockers, document one or two things that your organization can do to minimize the blockers and one or two actions that you as an individual can take to minimize them.
- Discuss these in an upcoming team meeting to educate the organization and to start toward the path of a more repeatable process for requirements gathering.

Chapter 2

Laying the Foundation

In theory, there is no difference between theory and practice. But, in practice, there is.

— **Jan L.A. van de Snepscheut**

This chapter reviews the standards that will be used as a foundation for the rest of the book. While many organizations strive toward implementing standard processes, this is often not as easy to do as it sounds. There are many organizations defining standards, and these standards are often different from each other. How to select the "best" standard? In this book the selection of which standards to use was based on what seems to have the strongest following today, as well as what I believe will be the dominating standards in the future. In addition, because this book was written in the United States, the standards will be U.S.-centric. Regardless of which standards are used in your organization, it is important that the whole organization has the same definitions and the same processes. If not, business analysis (and project management) will be almost impossible to do in an efficient manner.

2.1 Objectives

- Define what a life cycle is.
- Define what a Body of Knowledge does.
- Review standards from the Project Management Institute™ (PMI).
- Review standards from the International Institute of Business Analysis® (IIBA).

- Review standards from the Software Engineering Institute (SEI).
- Compare and contrast the standards defined.
- Identify key skills needed for a business analyst.

2.2 Overview

While this book considers the IIBA and the *Guide to the Business Analysis Body of Knowledge*® (BABOK) as the primary sources for requirements gathering and product definition standards, numerous other organizations such as PMI and SEI are also involved with defining standards in this domain and will also be recognized and discussed in this chapter. It is vital for the understanding of business analysis, and IIBA, to realize that there is not necessarily a consensus on what the business analysis Body of Knowledge should contain. It is likely, over time, that the industry will move toward agreement on these standards. Even PMI, having been around for a long time, does not have industrywide agreement on what project management is. Over the years, though, they have been moving the industry much closer to a prevailing view.

In recent years standards have also become more important for a different, and probably more powerful, reason. The customer demands it. More and more organizations are using standards such as SEI's Capability Maturity Model® Integrated (CMMI), PMI's Organizational Project Management Maturity Model (OPM3), and International Organization for Standardization (ISO) certifications to assess an organization's process maturity. Although the intent of many of these efforts was toward internal process improvement, there has been more of an external drive behind them in the last few years. Many customers, especially in the government, will not even allow a vendor to bid on business unless they can show the proper pedigree (or certifications). This often causes an organization to invest heavily into attaining the certification, sometimes at the cost of adding unnecessary overhead. The demand for certification appears to be growing globally and will probably be one of the main drivers for standardization. Although process implementations and improvement efforts are desirable, they need to be done at a pace that the organization can absorb. In other words, if too much change is introduced too quickly into an organization to reach some certification, then the certification often becomes the purpose of the effort rather than a help in improving product development. This tends to lead to any certification results being short lived and lost within a few years.

These standards, when implemented and followed, can greatly improve the success of any project, but only if they are used by skilled business analysts. So this chapter will also review some of the key skills required to make a business analyst successful.

2.3 Life Cycle Definitions

Most projects use two different life cycles to create an IT product. The first life cycle, the project life cycle, deals with the standard project management process groups of initiating, planning, executing, monitoring and controlling, and close-down. These processes are concerned with standard project issues like budget, risk, schedule, and procurement. They are done for all projects in a fairly identical way regardless of what the organization's business is, and are typically controlled by the project manager.

The second life cycle is the product life cycle, often called the systems development life cycle (SDLC). This life cycle is unique to the product being developed; IT typically has life cycles different than the construction or pharmaceutical industries. This life cycle describes the product development activities such as design, prototyping, testing, etc., that are done to develop a product. The ownership of these activities often resides with business analysts, systems analysts, or other subject matter experts.

To complicate matters further, there is not only one standard SDLC in existence for IT projects, there are many. Some of the various SDLC's will be discussed in Chapter 4, but for the purpose of establishing a base for the material in this book, a standard, simple, old-fashioned waterfall life cycle like the one shown in Figure 2.1 will be used for this book. So when this book discusses analysis, it may be what other life cycles call definition, or requirements documentation. The intent of the phase is the same in all of the life cycles: to document the product.

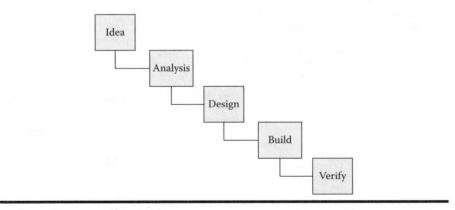

Figure 2.1 Standard life cycle.

It is easy to see why this is called the waterfall approach and why it is preferred from a management view. Everything is flowing logically from the beginning of the project to the end.

The main deliverables from each phase in the SDLC and the roles and responsibilities for those deliverables are shown in Figure 2.2.

When matching up the project process groups with the product life cycle, it helps to view the project processes as iterative in nature. The project will perform these processes for the whole project, but also for each individual phase of the project, which is shown in Figure 2.3.

Phase	Key Deliverables	Responsibility
Idea	Feasibility study Initial business case	Business owner
Analyze	Requirements document	Business analyst
Design	Specification	Systems analyst
Build	Product	Programmer
Verify	Test results Sign off	Quality assurance Business analyst

Figure 2.2 SDLC phases, roles, and responsibilities.

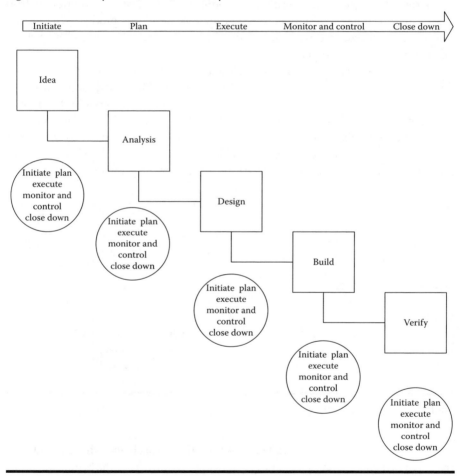

Figure 2.3 Standard life cycle and project management processes.

As shown in the figure, while each project must be initiated, planned, executed, monitored and controlled, and closed down, the same is true for each phase of the project. Analysis, design, and other product development phases should be treated as their own dependent mini-projects with initiation, planning, execution, controlling, and close-down. In addition, although the project manager oversees the project at a top level, frequently it is more efficient to have the business analyst or system analyst function as the sub-project manager for the individual SDLC phases.

2.4   What Is a Body of Knowledge?

A Body of Knowledge, be it IIBA's or PMI's, strives to define all the knowledge that is pertinent within a profession, discipline, or specialty. That does not mean that every professional within the profession must be expert in all areas. It is desirable for the professional to have an understanding of all areas and may be an expert in some of the areas.

It is important to understand the boundaries of the knowledge area being explored. For PMI, that is project management; for IIBA, it is business analysis. It reflects what is currently considered best practices in each respective domain. Note that PMI and IIBA publish a *Guide to...* each Body of Knowledge, which really means an introduction to the topic, a definition of terms and boundaries, and an outline of key processes. It does not mean that the *Guide* contains everything that must be known to be successful.

There are many unique specifics, variations, tools, and implementations for each organization. The *Guide* shows the framework, the "what." It is still up to each organization to define the "how." An example of this is modeling. The BABOK discusses many types of modeling and also gives examples of detailed modeling techniques. That does not mean that those are the only techniques to be used. Rather it means that the business analyst should consider modeling requirements (both data and process), and that the techniques shown are some of the more common ones.

Some people have already been concerned that it may appear that IIBA is promoting object-oriented modeling because it has a dominant role in the BABOK. That is probably more a result of the people writing those sections having more knowledge in those areas and it should eventually have a more even distribution of what is used in the industry. Keep in mind that this is a moving target. The BABOK should reflect current practices and in an industry as dynamic as Information Technology, current practices are likely to keep changing.

2.5   Overview of PMI Applicable Standards

PMI's *Guide to the Project Management Body of Knowledge*, third edition (PMBOK™ Guide), is currently viewed as the main standards document for project management. The PMBOK definition (on page 5) of a project as "a temporary endeavor undertaken to create a unique product, service, or result" is today accepted by most project management organizations around the world.

With the nine knowledge areas and five process groups from the PMBOK, it outlines what is, and in some cases what is not, project management. PMI's nine knowledge areas are:

- Integration Management: Handling the integration of the different components of the project plan. This is an overall knowledge area which sits on top of the other knowledge areas, making sure that they are well integrated. It also makes sure that the scope of the product is synchronized with the scope of the project. This knowledge area is where the project manager and the business analysts synchronize their effort. Any change to product or project scope will impact the other.
- Scope Management: This is where the project scope is defined, meaning what is the work that needs to be done to deliver the desired product or service. The product scope or product description is an input and the business owner (often through the business analyst) uses that to define the functions and features of the end product.
- Cost Management: Estimating the effort and cost involved with creating the deliverables for the project. While PMI does talk about life cycle costing and business cases, the PMBOK Guide mainly covers project budgeting.
- Time Management: Determining the detail of activities and the duration of them to create a schedule for the project. This is the traditional project management area with Gantt charts and network diagrams.
- Risk Management: Identifying, analyzing, responding to, and monitoring the project risk. Although product risk is also brought up here, the project manager is not typically the owner of product risks; that should reside with the business owner (again, often through the business analyst).
- Human Resource Management: Finding the resources for the project and building them into a productive team.
- Procurement Management: Deciding on what to procure, going through the solicitation process, selecting a vendor, and then managing the vendor relationship through the project.
- Communications Management: Defining the communications plan, and collecting and disseminating information and status reporting for the project.
- Quality Management: Identifying the applicable quality standards for this project. Determining what activity to do for quality inspection and quality assurance.

It is important to note that although these are the key project management-related knowledge areas, they do not represent all the skills needed by a project manager (PM) to be successful. The PM must also possess general management skills, application area skills, and leadership skills. However, the knowledge areas highlight the unique PM skills for a project. Although not all projects will have a procurement portion, the other eight knowledge areas would be represented on all projects to some extent.

The PMBOK also shows the five process groups that any project most go through. How they are done may vary, but they must be done at some level of detail:

- Initiating: Starting the project or phase and getting buy-in to the activities.
- Planning: Creating a plan for how to create the project or phase deliverables.
- Executing: Performing the actual work outlined in the product development life cycle.
- Monitoring and Controlling: Evaluating and comparing actual performance to planned performance and taking corrective actions when needed.
- Close-Down: Finishing the project or phase and getting acceptance of the deliverables.

The output from the work of the business analyst, the Business Requirements Document (BRD), is actually what PMI refers to as Product Description, and is largely an input into the project management processes.

On many projects the business analyst also becomes a project manager for the analysis phase of the project; thus, for the project management portion of the analysis phase, many of the tools and techniques defined by PMI can be used. The knowledge areas of Scope Management, Time Management, Human Resource Management, Quality Management, Risk Management, and Communications Management are especially relevant. In Chapter 5, it is shown how those standards can be adapted for a typical (if there's such a thing) business analysis project.

Project management and business analysis are disciplines which tend to interact heavily. Although they are clearly distinct domains, it is important for the practitioners of each to be aware of deliverables and processes in the each others areas.

> On many projects the business analyst also becomes a project manager for the analysis phase of the project; thus, for the project management portion of the analysis phase, many of the tools and techniques defined by PMI can be used.

PMI has rolled out its OPM3 as a way of measuring an organization's project management maturity. Although not a major force in the industry yet, it is likely to grow in acceptance as PMI improves and enhances it.

2.6 Overview of IIBA Framework and Standards

The IIBA issued BABOK version 1.6 in July 2006. It defines business analysis as "the set of tasks, knowledge, and techniques required to identify business needs and determine solutions to business problems." BABOK continues to state that this includes "systems development and sometimes process improvements or organizational change." This is an important distinction. It means that the business analyst must go beyond just the development of IT systems and be involved with the impact those efforts have on the organization as well. IIBA simply defines the role of the business analyst as "someone that performs business analysis."

When it comes to defining what a requirement is, IIBA borrowed the base for it from IEEE Std 610.12-1990, but did enhance it to better suit today's environment. The IIBA definition:

A requirement is:
 (1) A condition or capability needed by a stakeholder to solve a problem or achieve an objective.
 (2) A condition or capability that must be met or possessed by a system or system component to satisfy a contract, standard, specification, or other formally imposed document.
 (3) A documented representation of a condition or capability as in (1) or (2).

When dissecting these statements it becomes a bit clearer. A requirement is something that is needed to solve a business problem [as in (1)] or to deal with an outside constraint such as a corporate standard or a government regulation. Item (3) adds that it must be written down. It does not count as a requirement if it is just a mental note. It has to be documented for traceability and for change control.

IIBA has identified six knowledge areas and two additional topics that are all a part of the BABOK:

- Enterprise Analysis: Business analysts must understand the business and organizational environment in which they are working and recognize that a project does not operate in a vacuum, but rather is interacting with the rest of the enterprise. For the business analyst to successfully document requirements, the business, its goals, visions, business rules, and mission must be documented as well. This knowledge area also deals with feasibility studies and evaluation of business cases for different projects.
- Requirements Planning and Management: This deals with the planning of the requirements gathering activities, analyzing stakeholders, and getting buy-in to the requirements gathering efforts. It also outlines how change control and traceability of requirements will be dealt with.
- Requirements Elicitation: Different projects need different approaches to capture requirements. Sometimes it may be a survey, sometimes an interview. This section documents best practices and identifies pros and cons with each approach. It is the job of the business analyst to select the best technique for each stakeholder on each project.

- Requirements Analysis and Documentation: After requirements have been elicited, they must be organized, analyzed, and documented. This may be in text format or in models, or a combination of both. Conflicting requirements should be identified and the set of requirements should be evaluated for priority and completeness.
- Requirements Communication: Requirements must be effectively communicated to the users, the developers, and all other stakeholders. The means of communication will often vary depending on the audience. Effective communication will lead to buy-in to the requirements and a correctly developed product.
- Solution Assessment and Validation: The business analyst must trace the requirements through the product cycle and ensure that the product being designed and developed matches the requirements given by the stakeholders. This includes verifying that the customer is satisfied with the product after implementation.
- Complementary chapters of the BABOK deal with fundamental skills of a business analyst, such as facilitation and negotiation. It also contains a glossary to promote a common language for the industry.

> Business analysts must understand the business and organizational environment in which they are working and recognize that a project does not operate in a vacuum, but rather is interacting with the rest of the enterprise.

The IIBA standards are among the most recent additions to the fields of standards. That probably means that they are likely to change the most. At this point in time they have been developed by a group of dedicated and competent people receiving some feedback from the community. It is likely that as the exposure of the standard increases, there will be more diverging views on what should and should not be a part of the BABOK. Over the next few years there will likely be more changes and new versions of this standard versus the others reviewed in this chapter. So does that mean that an organization would be better off waiting until the standard is more well-established? There are both positives and negatives with either approach.

If an organization waits until a standard is fully developed it runs the risk of losing years of working with a very good, albeit not perfect standard, as well as losing the chance of impacting the direction of that standard. By getting on board early, the organization is more likely to be viewed as innovative and an industry leader. However, the organization does need to be flexible and able to deal with change. It is also worth looking at what the expectations are from the organization investing in the standards. If it is to learn best practices and a standard approach to business analysis the organization will need patience; if the expectation is to provide a competitive advantage by moving staff toward certification, then the earlier the effort to get up to speed on IIBA concepts begins, the more benefit there will be.

2.7   SEI-CMMI and Applicability

In the early 1980s, the Department of Defense (DoD) was looking for a way to evaluate systems engineering vendors to see which ones had mature development processes and, as a result, were more likely to meet their time and cost estimates with good quality. The DoD funded the Software Engineering Institute (SEI), located at the Carnegie Mellon University in Pennsylvania.

SEI has defined a requirement as "something that the product must do or a quality that the product must have." This definition is much simpler to understand than the IIBA definition and, as such, probably more usable in real life. This definition can be shared with the customer and easily understood.

SEI developed a maturity model evaluating the capability of an organization to implement repeatable development processes. The current version is called CMMI version 1.2. It identifies five levels of maturity for an organization from ad hoc fly-by-night to being totally obsessed with process improvement. It identifies a number of activities that need to be performed to reach each level. Two of the key activities identified, as they relate to business analysis, are requirements management and requirements development. Every key activity in CMMI is associated with goals for the area and key practices for the successful implementation of it.

2.7.1   Requirements Management

The Software Engineering Institute states that "The purpose of requirements management is to manage the requirements of the project's products and product components and to identify inconsistencies between those requirements and the project's plans and work products."

This implies a concentration on managing the requirements after they have been identified and documented. It is interesting to note that SEI actually sequences this activity before the actual activity of capturing requirements from a process viewpoint. The thought is that unless there is a formal approach to getting buy-in and reviewing the requirements with key stakeholders, there is not much point in formalizing what the process should be for capturing the requirements. The approach make sense, but most organizations out there appear to spend much more effort on eliciting the requirements than what is spent on validating them.

The goals and key practices for the requirements management area:

Goal 1:   Manage Requirements
   1.1   Obtain an understanding of requirements.
   1.2   Obtain commitment to requirements.
   1.3   Manage requirements changes.
   1.4   Maintain bidirectional traceability of requirements.
   1.5   Identify inconsistencies between project work and requirements.

Goal 2: Institutionalize a Managed Process
   2.1   Establish an organizational policy.
   2.2   Plan the process.
   2.3   Provide resources.
   2.4   Assign responsibility.
   2.5   Train people.
   2.6   Manage configurations.
   2.7   Identify and involve relevant stakeholders.
   2.8   Monitor and control the process.
   2.9   Objectively evaluate adherence.
   2.10   Review status with higher level management.

At first glance, these practices appear almost obvious: understand requirements, manage changes to requirements, and establish traceability. However, these are the areas that tend to cause projects to fail, largely because these processes are not performed consistently and with discipline within many organizations. The focus here is on repeatability and consistency. If an organization establishes traceability between business need, requirements, and the product, gets organizational commitment to the requirements, and handles changes in the requirements in an organized approach, many of today's project frustrations would be eliminated.

2.7.2   Requirements Development

The Software Engineering Institute states that "The purpose of requirements development is to produce and analyze customer, product, and product-component requirements."

This is where the requirements are actually captured and analyzed. Once that is done, the requirements can be managed and controlled, thanks to the processes implemented earlier in requirements management.

Goal 1:   Develop Customer Requirements
   1.1   Elicit needs.
   1.2   Develop the customer requirements.

Goal 2:   Develop Product Requirements
   2.1   Establish product and product-component requirements.
   2.2   Allocate product-component requirements.
   2.3   Identify interface requirements.

Goal 3:   Analyze and Validate Requirements
   3.1   Establish operational concepts and scenarios.
   3.2   Establish a definition of required functionality.
   3.3   Analyze requirements.
   3.4   Analyze requirements to achieve balance.
   3.5   Validate requirements with comprehensive methods.

Goal 4:   Institutionalize a Defined Process
   4.1   Establish an organizational policy.
   4.2   Establish a defined process.
   4.3   Plan the process.
   4.4   Provide resources.

These goals and practices are more comprehensive than those seen for requirements management. That is partly due to the fact that requirements development emphasizes best practices much more and is a much larger domain than just requirements management. That also matches the different CMMI levels. Level 2, where requirements management resides, is about project management and discipline. Level 3, where requirements development is, deals more with systems engineering and defined processes.

2.8   Which Standard to Use?

All the standards described have different specialties and different strengths. In addition to those discussed here, there are numerous other standards that have been developed which are excellent, such as Six Sigma and Total Quality Management. It is more important that the organization uses a standard and uses it consistently than the specific standard the organization has selected to use. In the IT industry in general there tends to be a focus in three dimensions:

- The project
- The product
- The development process

Figure 2.4 shows these three dimensions and the main focus for each standard. So what does that mean? Should an organization pick all three? Just one?

One good approach is to select a foundational standard. If the primary concern of the organization is to train the organization on requirements gathering, then IIBA can serve as a foundation. If the goal is to implement solid processes for software development, then SEI-CMMI may be the best, keeping in mind that it does

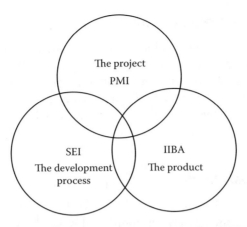

Figure 2.4 The standards and their strengths.

require a significant organizational commitment. If the main issue is getting the job done, resource planning, scheduling, and budgeting, then PMI can help with the groundwork. While learning from all, it is best to start with one; otherwise, there can be confusion and lack of buy-in from the organization. Probably the most commonly heard complaint about implementing a new process initiative is that it is new, inconsistent with other standards, and adds overhead and bureaucracy. Although that is often true, the impact of it can be significantly less if the organization picks one standard and then stays with it. The main benefit from adopting standards is down the road, when they become second nature. So be patient and don't move from SEI to PMI to IIBA (with some Six Sigma thrown in) in a short time period. Also, if the organization is adopting multiple standards, then create a map that shows the intended use of each standard and how they interact with each other.

2.9   Comments on Tool Standards

As a part of the job of the business analyst it is likely that some (or all) of the requirements will be documented in some package or tool. This can be something simple as SmartDraw™ Visio™, or something more sophisticated like Oracle™ Designer or Rational. All of these packages have standards built into them, and the more sophisticated the package, the more rigid the standards. It does make sense to attempt to follow these standards as closely as possible. Trying to circumvent the standards in a package tends to lead to extensive extra work and a result that is less than optimal. Most tools try to be consistent with PMI and standards like that, but the tools don't always keep in sync with changes to the standards. When looking at what tools to use, review what expertise the organization already has. It is much more important that a tool is selected where the expertise already resides within the project team then to pick a "neater" tool that no one knows how to use.

2.10   Business Analyst's Skills

One of the areas in the BABOK which needs the most augmentation right now is the Underlying Fundamentals. The current version of the BABOK contains a list of some business analysis skills, but there is no elaboration or detail to describe the skills. Although many of them are fairly obvious it is important to look at them in the light of business analysis rather than just regular soft skills. Some of the key skills from the BABOK list are outlined here.

2.10.1   Analysis Skills

This may seem too obvious to be stated because it is built into the name of the profession, but the business analyst is not just a documenter or an interviewer. The business analyst needs to be able to organize and analyze a variety of information for conflicts, impacts, and priorities. This includes structured analysis, root cause analysis, and impact analysis.

Structured analysis techniques, like the ones covered in Chapter 8 of this book, allow the business analyst to take abstract concepts, complex scenarios, and disjointed customer wishes and put all of that into a structured document which can be used by the developers as a basis for developing a system.

Root cause analysis is another skill at the core of the business analysis profession. The customer will often bring problems, or sometimes even just symptoms of problems, to the business analyst and expect a solution. It is up to the business analyst to work with the customer to figure out what the root cause is. A key help in root cause analysis is to ask why. Why is this a problem? Why is this happening? Any solution which does not address the root cause is likely to be incomplete and short lived.

Finally, what is impact analysis? The customer must understand what the impact is of introducing the solution to a problem into an organization. Although customers normally understand the benefit of getting rid of the problem they have, they may not be clear on the impact of the solution. Looking at the Prescription Interaction Project from Chapter 1, the customer likes the thought of being able to identify and stop dangerous drug interaction from prescriptions used by different family members; however, the customer may not like the potential privacy breeches that may result from sharing this data between family members. In this case the customer may be trading one set of lawsuits for another set. The business analyst must be evaluating and bringing those types of issues to the customer's attention.

2.10.2   Business Knowledge

The business analyst must understand the business of the customer, the marketplace, the products, and the competitive position of the customer. The analyst must also understand the business processes and the systems which currently support the business. Although business analysts can come from the IT side or from the business side, it does appear that more of them are from the business side today than what was the case only ten years ago. There may be many reasons for that; my personal view is that there are two primary drivers:

1. Knowing and understanding the business can be harder than understanding the IT area. It is often easier to teach a savvy business person enough about systems to be successful than to teach a systems person about the business side. Although this certainly depends on the environment, usually the business drives technology and not the other way around. There are exceptions, such as a global data-mining operation, where technology is actually driving and changing the business.
2. The business is realizing the importance of IT solutions and is no longer comfortable delegating to the IT department the responsibility of determining how to best take advantage of systems.

> Although business analysts can come from the IT side or from the business side, it does appear that more of them are from the business side today than what was the case only ten years ago.

Regardless of the background of the analyst, they must receive continual training and exposure to the business environment.

2.10.3   IT Knowledge

Although the mind-set should be on "what" and not "how," business analysts cannot be successful unless they understand the systems and technologies that are supporting the business. They may not need to be able to write a computer program, but must understand what is needed by the developers to write a good program. Difficulties in communicating with the developers can usually be traced to a poorly defined Business Requirements Document (BRD). The content and level of detail included in the BRD must be predefined and this activity, assuming that the project will be an in-house development, should be driven by the development team. The development team is the primary audience of the document, and if there is not enough information in it for the team to develop from, then the efforts have failed. So make sure that the BRD template is developed as a joint effort by business analysts and developers where the balance of power resides with the developers.

2.10.4 *Meeting and Presentation Skills*

The business analyst's job, unlike the programmer's, is not a solitary one. Most of the business analyst's time will be spent interviewing, meeting, and presenting to stakeholders. Solid time management skills, the ability to stay on target, and the ability to logically guide a group of people though elicitation, validation, and buy-in is key for the business analyst.

Most of the presentations and meetings that the business analyst will facilitate will be to discuss or review information which comes from other stakeholders. It takes a certain talent to be able to present this in a neutral and unbiased manner, while still being enthusiastic about the project. The mind-set should always be "Here's what the stakeholders have decided" rather than "Here's what I have decided."

Although this skill can be enhanced by training and practice, some of it is based on personality as well. The business analyst profession is like many other professions: a person with the right personality and characteristics is much more likely to be successful.

2.10.5 *Decision Making/Negotiation/Conflict Resolution and Escalation Skills*

Business analysts are not traditionally viewed as decision makers, at least not from a product view. However, they must be decisive when it comes to the process, the meetings, the commitment, and getting stakeholder buy-in to both process and product. The ability to effectively accomplish these tasks requires strong negotiation skills. The analysis phase of the project is full of negotiation opportunities. There will be negotiation about time and resources for the analysis activity, about which stakeholders can be interviewed, about the approach to gathering requirements and the best way to document those requirements, and much more. The analyst must be aggressive as far as getting what is needed for the work, but also realistic. There are competing priorities in all organizations. Make sure to always keep the project objectives in the forefront of any negotiation. Ask: "How will the outcome of this negotiation impact the project's abilities to meet the objectives?"

Conflict resolution has a number of applications for the business analysts. There can be conflicts with the customers, with other analysts, and with developers, just to name a few. Part of conflict resolution is also to know when to escalate. Business analysts must understand the organizational culture and know the individuals well enough to be able to decide when to solve the conflict versus when to escalate it. This escalation can be to the project manager, to the customer, or to the sponsor. Normally though, the business analyst should work through the project manager with most issues needing escalation.

2.10.6   *Questioning Skills/Systems Thinking and Logic*

A person can be great at regular conversation, but fail as a business analyst. To get requirements from a customer, the business analyst must provide a structure and a flow to the discussion during the collection of information. A conversation may gain significant information, but it is likely to have holes and lack detail. An interview will be structured to go from high level to details, from general to specific. It will provide a systems thinking and a logical flow to the session. Requirements classifications, which will be covered in Chapter 6, help with this by starting at the top level, understanding what the business needs, and gradually decomposing that understanding into user requirements and eventually into system requirements. The business analyst must facilitate this flow by preparing and asking the right questions at the right time.

This is a skill which can be learned and improved, but for some people this type of systems thinking comes more naturally. Those people are good business analyst candidates in any organization.

2.10.7   *Leadership Skills*

Although business analysts are not necessarily managers of the tasks performed, they must be able to lead a diverse group of people through the analysis phase. As leaders, they must provide the context of the activities, in other words, why the activities are being done. If the participants don't see the value of root cause analysis or process modeling, then it is unlikely that they will put their best effort into them. And in many cases business analysts will lead a group of other analysts, developers, and users in capturing requirements and building a consensus for a solution.

2.11   Summary

No organization can be successful in the long run without a common language and an ability to have the whole organization moving in the same direction. That is the purpose of implementing standards. It allows the participants on a project to know what is expected of them, to identify standard deliverables, and to ensure that lessons learned from past projects are implemented on future endeavors. With all the standards available it is more and more common that different parts of an organization are adopting different standards. This can cause confusion throughout the organization and often leads to a feeling of each initiative being the "flavor of the month," rather than something that has full management commitment behind it. However, the standards will not substitute for skilled business analysts. A skilled business analyst will get better with good processes. An unskilled business analyst will struggle with or without processes.

2.12 Activity

Take inventory of what standards, certifications, and processes exist in your organization. These standards should include what training is being done, the forms and templates that exist in the organization, and the tools being used. Even if there isn't a book sitting somewhere called "Standards," by asking around and talking to experienced practitioners a base of tools can be discovered.

Document them in the following table:

Organization	Standard	Process Owner	In Use Since

Chapter 3

Enterprise Analysis

Seek first to understand, then to be understood.

—Stephen Covey

Enterprise analysis is perhaps the fastest growing area of business analysis. It provides the context and the link between projects and the business. Although most of the business analyst's work tends to reside within the project boundaries, there are parts of the job which take place before and after the project. This section deals with most of the pre-project activities, such as feasibility studies and industry benchmarking. It is often the most difficult part of the business analyst's job because it can be highly political, complex, and unchartered. The pre-project activities tend to give the analyst the most organizational visibility through dealings with the upper levels of the organization. If the business analyst is successful in this area, it can be a great career enhancer; if unsuccessful, it will be noticed.

3.1   Objectives

- Understand the importance of the business analyst having a strong understanding of the enterprise.
- Review ways of documenting and understanding the business.
- Identify business vision, goals, and objectives.
- Identify prerequisites to requirements gathering.
- Identify how a project maps to the enterprise.
- Document an enterprise analysis for the case study.

3.2 Overview

The International Institute of Business Analysis® (IIBA) defines enterprise analysis as the knowledge area "that describes the business analysis activities that take place for the organization to (1) identify business opportunities, (2) build the business architecture framework, and (3) implement new business and technical systems solutions" (BABOK release 1.6). In more common terms it means to develop and document the functions, processes, and tools that the business needs to successfully meet its objectives, to identify opportunities with the business, and to work on implementing business and systems solutions to meet those opportunities.

The key processes outlined by IIBA for enterprise analysis are:

- Creating and Maintaining the Business Architecture
- Conducting Feasibility Studies
- Determining Project Scope
- Preparing the Business Case
- Conducting the Initial Risk Assessment
- Preparing the Decision Package

This chapter reviews these areas and also discusses the skills the business analyst must have to accomplish this work. It is important to note that this knowledge area may be the one to change the most over the next few years. Enterprise analysis is not the traditional role for the business analyst, and the type of work done here varies greatly from organization to organization. Right now the domain of the business analyst overlaps in areas with project management, program management, and business architects. As the domain of business analysis becomes more refined over the next few years, some of the overlapping areas will become clarified and some will not, requiring each organization to customize its definition of the business analyst. This tailoring process is still going on within most project management organizations even after more than 35 years since the Project Management Institute™ (PMI) was formed, so it will take some patience for IIBA as well.

> Enterprise analysis is not the traditional role for the business analyst, and the type of work done here varies greatly from organization to organization.

Although the primary role of the business analyst is to function as a communication link between the customer and the developer in relation to defining the requirements of a product or service, the role is expanding in many organizations. Clearly, the business analyst must have a solid understanding of the overall business environment in which the customer operates. The business analyst is often assigned to do competitive benchmarking against other companies, evaluating best practices and, in general, keeping up on trends in the industry. This naturally makes the necessity for a strong business background an increasing demand on future business analysts.

Some areas of involvement for the business analyst, in addition to the areas outlined by IIBA, may be:

- Benchmarking: This can be part of a feasibility study, but can also be a stand-alone activity. The purpose of benchmarking is to evaluate where the customer's competitors are. Who is considered to be "Best in Class," who is improving rapidly, and what new trends are emerging in the customer's area of business. For the C.V. Green example started in Chapter 1, this involves researching what the competition is doing. Creativity is a good skill here. It may be obvious to check out the pharmacies that are in the same business. But also look beyond the obvious and see if there are other industries which do similar work. There could be lessons learned from order entry projects or from medical billing.
- Identifying and analyzing new business opportunities: By attending conferences as well as being aware of and up to date on new technology trends, the business analyst can actually be the instigator of new opportunities. A business must continuously evolve and change to stay competitive and the business analyst can be a catalyst in that process.

3.3   The IIBA Key Processes

The processes listed in the previous section and presented below are the key processes introduced by IIBA for the knowledge area of enterprise analysis. Each organization must determine which is applicable and to what level of detail each will be explored. Clearly, some organizations already have existing functions and professionals that have done this work for a long time and with great results. They may be the owners, the strategists, or the executives of the organization. That's great! All the business analyst needs to do is to trace the project objectives back to the deliverables, which may be the strategic plans, the tactical initiatives, or the company vision. However, for the organizations that currently do not have a good handle on these activities, the business analyst may be the natural person to start taking on these responsibilities.

> ... for the organizations that currently do not have a good handle on these activities, the business analyst may be the natural person to start taking on these responsibilities.

Enterprise analysis should not be viewed as a "one size fits all" approach. There should be established ground rules regarding the level of effort needed for different types of projects and organizations. This customization may be driven by project size, risk, complexity, visibility, or any other parameter that makes sense to the business. As an example, if the customer submits a request to change a report or to implement a minor change in an existing system, there is probably no need to do extensive enterprise analysis. On the other hand, if the organization is switching to a new enterprise resource planning (ERP) system, then the enterprise analysis may be more extensive than the actual projects.

For many of the IIBA key processes the inputs come from customers, government, or executives during one-on-one interviews as well as documents such as the strategic plans and goals of the business, the problems and opportunities which the business is facing, and regulations which the business must follow. Although sometimes these documents are identified at executive offsites and at a level of the organization where the business analyst does not normally tread, it is a good idea to have the business analyst as informed and involved as possible in these events. A strategic plan will lead to tactical initiatives within the organization. These initiatives potentially will lead to many projects, which will need to be prioritized based on their ability to meet the strategic plan.

So what is the business analyst's role in creating the strategic plan and documenting the strategic goals? Most organizations will primarily use the management team and often some consultants to facilitate and drive these efforts. However, this is an area where IIBA appears to be visualizing a bigger involvement in the future for the business analyst. Once the organization develops business analysts with a strong understanding of the business along with good communication and facilitation skills, those analysts can become very effective in leading the sessions where the strategic goals are set. Because the analysts will become heavily involved with the implementation of the strategic plans, at least at a project level, the skills and knowledge obtained in this early effort will not be lost. However, sometimes strategic sessions will not be taken seriously if they are facilitated by an internal analyst. There is an old saying that no one is a prophet at home. If there are any concerns about this, then the organization would be better off bringing in an independent consultant to lead the activity. Even in this case, it is desirable to have the business analyst involved, either as a scribe, observer, or subject matter expert (SME).

An especially value-added role for business analysts in the creation of the strategic plan, regardless if they are actually in the sessions, is the creation of score cards and metrics. Any good strategic plan or set of strategic goals must be measurable to be effective. So what are the metrics needed to measure a strategic plan? They could be cost or profit related. Most strategic goals have at least some financial ties within them. They could be related to market share, market position, or anything else related to the goal. C.V. Green wants to be the "premier pharmacy." What does that mean? Highest market share? Most revenue? Most customers? Most satisfied customers? The business analysts are not the ones to answer the question; rather, their job is to find the person who can answer the question, and then document the answer.

Without a clear understanding of this linkage between, and importance of, the different components of the strategic plan it would be hard to recommend potential improvements to the business. Returning to the Prescription Interaction Project, the strategic goal for C.V. Green is to become the premier pharmacy chain in the world through superior service and competitive cost. One tactical initiative is to minimize harmful effects of drugs. This would provide benefits to both the competitive cost picture and the superior service objectives. The project of checking for prescription drug interaction (the project used as an example in this book) fits nicely here. By doing this trace and understanding how the project fits within the bigger business picture, the analyst can identify benefits, ask the right questions, and assist in getting stakeholder buy-in for the effort.

By learning about the global aspect of the goal of C.V. Green and the desire for superior service, it is likely the analyst will pay more attention to how to identify drug interaction on a global basis as well as how to maximize the customer safety issues versus just staying legally compliant. For instance, if the project had a purely legal driver, the focus would be narrower and only consider how the pharmacy can limit drug interaction based on best-available information. If the goal is primarily customer satisfaction and service, the business analyst may go out and look for what information could be obtained by working with other pharmacies, or by looking for drug interactions from drugs that the customer's family members have bought.

This ties in well with the topic of validation, which is discussed in more detail in Chapter 10. The purpose of validation is to make sure that the product or service that is eventually developed will solve, at least partially, the business problem or opportunity that caused it to be started. Naturally this is hard to accomplish unless the organization as well as the business analyst clearly understands that problem or opportunity.

3.3.1   Creating and Maintaining the Business Architecture

Business architecture is not yet an expression used in most organizations, at least not by the business analysts, but there is an increasing need to put more emphasis on and resources in making sure that the business environment, vision, goals, and objectives are known and understood before a significant project is undertaken. Clearly, for many business analysts, this is beyond the scope of the work they do, but for the ones that do get assigned to the large, enterprisewide, high-visibility-type projects, the knowledge of this area is crucial. In many organizations this activity may primarily involve digging for information. The strategic goals and tactical initiatives are often already documented at a corporate level. The link between these and the projects done at the operational level is part of the traceability needed to justify the existence of a project. Figure 3.1 is an example of a model of those relationships.

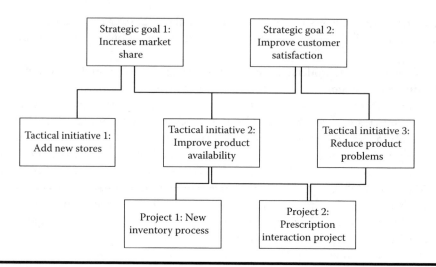

Figure 3.1 Strategic goals and tactical initiatives.

The executives may have an annual strategic session or there may have been consulting studies done on where the company is heading and its vision and mission. SWOT (strengths-weaknesses-opportunities-threats) analysis is a tool often used to show the status of a business. Figure 3.2 shows an example of a SWOT analysis.

The SWOT analysis will often be a foundation for business strategic goals and plans. An aggressive business will focus on taking advantage of its strengths and exploring its opportunities. On the other hand, a risk-averse business may be more focused on protecting against its weaknesses and defending against threats. By reviewing Figure 3.2 in more detail it can be seen that a key strength for C.V. Green is a superior technology integration process. However, a weakness is a limited global presence. A business would need to decide whether to focus on capitalizing on strengths or defending against weaknesses. Although it is quite possible to do both, in many cases this will lead to a dilution of effort with the possible result that neither action is successful. What is the right approach? That is one of the many "it depends" questions asked in business analysis. The main driver is often the maturity of the organization and the personality of the decision makers. Is their attitude to utilize strengths and conquer? Or is it more of defense and survival? Those are the types of questions that may be answered during the review of a SWOT analysis.

By having this type of information available when going into the requirements-gathering effort for a project, the business analyst can ask the right questions and be able to trace the decisions made for the project back to actual business needs. In addition to SWOT analysis, other articles included in the business architecture are:

- Policies and Business Rules: Explains what standards the business has for certain actions. Policies and business rules tend to be overlapping. They both deal with actions that must be taken or rules that must be complied with by

Strengths What are your competitive advantages What are your strongest skills What do you do well	Opportunities How can you leverage your competitive advantage How can you utilize your skills How can you take advantage of what you do well
• Superior technology integration • Strong product line • Good industry reputation locally • Strong sales force	• Streamline and integrate business processes • Create local partnerships with global partners • Leverage current sales force globally
• Limited Global Presence • Lack of high tech networking • High cost of inventory	• Competitor may have better global contacts • Communication between regions may be unreliable • Inventory cost may increase further with global expansion
Weaknesses Where are you lagging the competition What skills do you lack Where are your problem areas	Threats How can the competition hurt you Where can the competition surprise you Where is the competition stronger than you

Figure 3.2 SWOT analysis.

the business in response to certain conditions. Examples include "The company will not accept a prescription unless payment is made or a pre-approved drug plan is given," or "Pharmacist must verify doctor's signature before issuing a prescription."

- Procedures: Shows how certain key activities are done within the business. Examples of procedures can be "Prescription Refill Procedure," "Drug Interaction Verification."
- Competencies: Shows what the business should be capable of doing. They can include competitive advantages or unique skills such as "Ability to refill prescription from any store in the network," or "Offer generic equivalents for 75 percent of all prescriptions."

Although these articles are needed for the business analyst to be successful, it is important not to get them confused with actual requirements. A business must be able to follow its policies, procedures, and business rules and utilize its competencies within the developed system, but the system itself does not explicitly have to enforce them. As an example, there may be a business rule stating "A pharmacist must check for drug interaction before filling a prescription." When the analyst is gathering requirements, this business rule should trigger some questions:

- Should this check be automated within the system?
- What information does the pharmacist need to be able to decide if there is harmful drug interaction?
- Does the pharmacist just need to check for it? If there is potentially harmful interaction with other drugs, what action should the pharmacist take?
- Are there any reporting or data requirements for this business rule?

A business must be able to follow its policies, procedures, and business rules and utilize its competencies within the developed system, but the system itself does not explicitly have to enforce them.

It is easy to understand the value of having the business rules, policies, procedures, and competencies known when going into the analysis phase of the project. If they are not readily available, the business analyst may need to be a part of documenting them. This is part of the overall "AS-IS" documentation. In the Business Requirements Document (BRD) template shown in Appendix B, the business rules and other similar artifacts are documented in the AS-IS portion of the BRD. This section may not always be present in a BRD template because the AS-IS documentation often exists within other business documents or existing system documentation. In those cases it is sufficient just to reference the source documents. Do not create duplicate information by copying information into the BRD.

There are existing modeling techniques available to describe a business. One that is mentioned by IIBA is the "Zachman Framework for Enterprise Architecture," as shown in Figure 3.3. This framework looks at different views of the business; for example, Business Model, Technology Model, and System Model. It then describes what, how, where, who, when, and why for each of those models, and identifies a specific deliverable going along for each intersection. As an example, the "why" for the Business Model is documented in the business plan, and the "what" for the System Model is contained in the Logical Data Model. It provides a very structured view of the business. There are, of course, other techniques besides Zachman, taking different approaches. The more a technique is used within an organization, the more comfortable everyone will be in viewing and analyzing the information. Rather than trying to find the perfect model, pick one that is usable

Figure 3.3 The Zachman Framework for Enterprise Architecture.

and train the organization on how to use it. Figure 3.4 shows a Business Model for the pharmacy C.V. Green, tying back into the Zachman Framework from above.

Zachman Framework	What	How	Where	Who	When	Why
Business Model	Global Presence	Prescription Interaction Project	Europe	Headquartered in the US	Largest pharmacy in the world by 2010	Become Premier Pharmacy
	Customer Safety	Inventory management initiative	Asia	Regional offices in London and Tokyo		Stay cost effective
	Efficient Purchasing		North America			

Figure 3.4 C. V. Green business model.

The "why" for C.V. Green is "premier pharmacy" and "cost effective." This can be looked at as the vision of the organization. The "what" is then at the mission level, including areas such as "efficient purchasing," "global presence," and "customer safety focus." "Where" just shows the business's geographical locations and "who" shows the organizational structure. "When" deals with business cycles and key business events, and "how" is what will link to the projects and initiatives going on in the organization. While obviously being a simplification, it shows the basic thought process needed for an enterprise analysis and understanding of the Business Model.

The activities of enterprise analysis will necessitate the business analyst interfacing with executives and other stakeholders who are not necessarily impacted by any project being contemplated. If tasked with documenting the AS-IS situation for the business, the business analyst should start by doing a stakeholder analysis. It does not matter if a stakeholder analysis has already been done for the project. Describing the AS-IS situation of the business may need to go beyond the stakeholders already identified by the project manager. The question here is not just who will be impacted by the project, but rather who has information that may help the analyst understand the business. The marketing department at C.V. Green may not be involved directly with the Prescription Interaction Project; however, it does play a role in identifying the enterprise architecture within which the project exists.

An important skill set for doing this work is the business analyst's communication skills and ability to have clear and concise conversations with upper management. Although some people do this naturally, for most analysts this will be something that takes both education and practice. Training in negotiation, communication, and facilitation will be helpful. There is a need to be well prepared, have clear questions, and a clear goal in mind of what the interview with the executives should produce. Although there is no need to be intimidated, there is a need to be focused and respectful of the time commitment given. In large organizations with many business analysts, there is probably someone in the group who is more capable than the rest at interfacing with the executives. Select these analysts and prepare them well. Perform some practice sessions before going in front of the executives. Because it often makes people nervous to speak in front of upper management, it is important to come prepared with a lot of questions and have the pertinent facts at hand. When presenting a business case, an impact analysis, or a feasibility study, make sure that there is information to back up all numbers that are shown. Even if it is never used, it will make the analyst more comfortable, knowing that the information is there if needed. It will also increase the likelihood that the executives will buy into the presentation. It only takes one missed fact or one "I don't know" to leave a trace of uncertainty which may take a long time and a lot of effort to erase.

3.3.2   Conducting Feasibility Studies

Most businesses have a constant need to change and improve to stay viable. Even if the business does not want to change, the world around it, the competition, and the marketplace are changing, driving a need to change and improve the business. That means a continuous update of vision, mission, goals, and objectives. To implement these changing directions, there is a constant need to assess what the organization is capable of doing, and a feasibility study is a way of helping with that. A feasibility study looks at feasibility from an organizational view. By evaluating different potential solutions to a business issue, a determination can be made to see what the impact is on the organization and also on the outside world. Feasibility doesn't necessarily mean "is it doable?" It may just as often mean "based on our current situation, is this option reasonable?" Many feasibility studies are initiated based on the SWOT analysis reviewed earlier in this chapter. The SWOT analysis lets the business know its strengths and weaknesses, opportunities and threats. The feasibility study uses these areas as inputs into an evaluation of what the business can do. Does the organization have the capability to overcome a weakness? How realistic is it to capitalize on the organization's strength?

Treat the feasibility study like a project. As with most projects, there are dependencies on other projects and the study may or may not lead to other efforts in the future. But for now, the feasibility study is a project in itself and, as such, should have requirements, deliverables, and a project plan. There is often a narrower question to answer in a feasibility study than the generic "is this feasible?" It could be a technical view, it could be a globalization view, or it could be an evaluation of the skills of the organization. The more precise the initial question asked is, the better defined and, by extension, well executed the feasibility study will be.

> ... the feasibility study is a project in itself and, as such, should have requirements, deliverables, and a project plan.

The key steps when performing a feasibility study are:

- Identify the problem or opportunity. Always start by understanding why this effort is being made. Whether traceable back to a SWOT analysis or initiated by some legislative change, understanding the drivers behind the request will help in understanding what areas to concentrate on. For example, if the feasibility study involves evaluating the possibility of sharing prescription information with other pharmacies for the purpose of evaluating drug interactions, it would help to know if this is undertaken to enhance the competitiveness of the organization or if this is done to minimize lawsuits.
- Understand the current situation. This can tie into understanding the previously discussed business architecture. Are there any partial solutions in place with this organization or anywhere else in the market? What infrastructure is already in place? What is the competitive situation and how will that change if we do, or do not do, the effort? A feasibility study is largely an analysis of "Where are we?" and "Where do we want to be?", determining what the gap is between those two, and how the gap can be filled. Understanding the current situation gives the answer to "Where are we?"
- Define a vision of the solution. Following the thread from the previous bullet, this answers "Where do we want to be?" At this point don't get bogged down with reality or constraints or requirements. Here the main objective is to define what the world will look like when the opportunity has been realized or the problem solved.
- Determine alternative solutions. Be creative! If the first idea that comes up gets selected, there is a chance that eventually someone will think of a better way, which can cause major rework to the project. Alternative solutions not only help coming up with a better solution, they also help reviewing and rejecting undesirable solutions early on in the process, which will save time and effort revisiting these later.
- Recommend a solution. Evaluate the alternatives and pick the one (or ones) that best address the original business problem. This can be done objectively, using financial data when available, or it can be done subjectively, by customer voting or the sponsor making a decision.

A big portion of feasibility is evaluating the risks associated with each of the alternatives. It is often necessary to take high risks to be successful and it is true that a high risk may equal high pay-out, but for the decision makers to make a well-informed choice they must be aware of what the risks are. Conceptually many of the techniques used for risk assessment are similar to the ones discussed in Chapter 4 as well as later in this chapter in Section 3.3.5, but at this level the focus is more on the organizational risk rather than the project risk. Capture both negative risks (threats) and positive risks (opportunities). In the end, the feasibility decision is largely based on comparing the value of the opportunities and the value of the threats, and if the opportunities are worth more, then the project will get a nod of approval.

The business analysts involved with doing feasibility studies must have broad business and IT knowledge. They must also have a good financial analysis understanding. For this type of effort, the analyst must be a person who can hone in on the important areas, the areas that will make a difference from the capabilities and financial standpoints. They must be able to understand the size of the investment needed and when it is needed, and to compare that to the benefits that will be achieved and when those benefits will be realized. This will include comparing the cost of developing a product in-house versus purchasing a ready-made product. This type of decision is often based more on the financial viability of each option versus looking at what is the "better" solution. Maybe building a product is cheaper and will provide what the customer wants, but by buying it off the shelf the customer can start realizing the benefits earlier, which makes this effort financially viable.

3.3.3 Determining Project Scope

There must be a link between the business architecture, the evaluation of conceptual solutions, and the project itself. If the business analyst does not clearly understand that link, the project is less likely to hit the target. So how can that linkage be captured? Most of it has probably already been captured in the general project request or project selection process and it may just be a matter of discovering that information. But often the information needed is inside of the customer's head, which can be a scary place to visit. One of the key problems brought up in the business analyst survey discussed in Chapter 1 was scope creep. The initial definition of the scope is the place to lay the foundation to avoid scope creep later on. A well-defined scope definition will clearly show the boundaries of the project. A poorly defined scope will lead to continuous evaluation of what is inside of the project and what is outside.

If the business analyst begins gathering requirements from the stakeholders before the purpose or basic constraints of the project are determined, it is likely that the end product will be something very different than what the customer expected. Some of the key things to define to set the stage for the project are:

- Business goals and objectives
- Assumptions
- Constraints

- Scope statement
- Impacted organizations

If the business analyst begins gathering requirements from the stakeholders before the purpose or basic constraints of the project are determined, it is likely that the end product will be something very different than what the customer expected.

3.3.3.1 Business Goals and Objectives

Here we are trying to answer the "why" question. Why are we doing this project? What is it that we want to have happen as a result of the project? This could be traditional business goals like increase profit, reduce cost, increase revenue, but could also be to meet a new government regulation or respond to competitors. Whatever it is, it's key for the project manager to have a strong understanding of the true business need, and the business analyst can be the best person to assist the project manager in getting that understanding. It is sometimes said that a very good project manager who doesn't understand the business goals can very effectively deliver the wrong product. So make sure to have clear business goals and objectives for the project. All project objectives should be traceable back to a specific business need. Again, the project scope definition is owned by the project manager, but it is also vital information for the business analyst.

In an ideal world, the business analyst would be involved early in the process and be a part of developing the initial project documents such as the project charter, scope documents, and project plans. If that has not been the case, the business analyst must become familiar with these documents. Not understanding the context of an initiative will often lead to asking the wrong questions or asking the right questions of the wrong people.

3.3.3.2 Assumptions

Because much information is unknown at this early stage of the project, the business analyst will need to make some assumptions for planning purposes. This is mainly a CYA (cover your assets) to make sure that everyone is on the same page. For example, if the customers assume that the product will work globally and the developer assumes that it'll only work in Iowa, there will definitely be problems later on. Typically, in the beginning of a project there will be a large number of assumptions. As the project life cycle progresses, there should be a discovery that these assumptions are proven right or wrong, resulting (if they were wrong) in a replanning of the project. Typical assumptions on an IT project may deal with:

- Customer availability for sessions and approvals
- Technology availability
- Project priority
- Resource skill sets, availability, and geographical placement

All of these assumptions should be documented.

3.3.3.3 Constraints

The project team must understand the limitations under which the project is operating. Constraints are things that limit solution options, and the project team must live within these limitations. Constraints often deal with budget, resources, and schedules. It is important to remember to accept the constraints once they are agreed on by the sponsor and customer. They basically define the box within which the project operates. "Low skills," for example, would typically not be a good constraint. It is probably something that should be dealt with by hiring a consultant or sending people to training. "Low skills" would more likely be categorized as an issue. More common constraints for an IT project may include:

- Existing infrastructure
- Preferred vendor lists
- Schedules (both internal and external).

3.3.3.4 Scope Statement

The scope is often high level this early in the cycle, but needs to consider all key deliverables to the customer. The customer should be able to read it and say, "Yes, this is what I want." This is really a mix of project and product scope. It should contain elements of product scope, such as features included and excluded, but it should also contain project scope elements such as timing, budget, and release schedules. At this level the focus is on the boundaries. The concern should be about what is included or excluded, not about the details of any feature. Those details will be captured as the analysis phase gets started.

3.3.3.5 Impacted Organizations

This is the start of the communication plan. It tells which organizations to talk to and which ones to actually include on the project team. Although not all stakeholders are equal, they should all be considered. Much of the impact from other organizations can be documented in a context diagram. This shows areas that the project interfaces with and key information going to and from those areas (Figure 3.5).

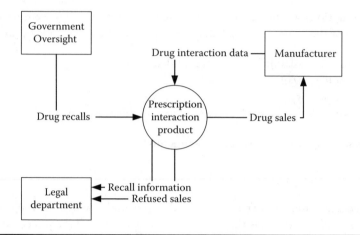

Figure 3.5 Context diagram.

The context diagram, sometimes called the Level 0 Data Flow Diagram, consists of three main parts:

1. Scope Area: Represented by a circle in the middle. This can be a business area such as order processing or accounts payable, but it can also be at a much lower level such as "Order prescription drug" or "Pay a bill," the point being that everything inside of the circle is part of the scope.
2. External Entities: Represented by a rectangle. These may be people, organizations, or other systems that will either send information to or receive information from the scope area.
3. Data Flow: Represented by an arrow. This represents a packet of information going between an external entity and the scope area. These data flows should be key business concepts and are typically easy for the customer to recognize. They can be items such as Order, Shipping notice, Invoice, Receipt, or Prescription.

Start the drawing of the context diagram by creating the center and labeling it. Then identify outside organizations, people, and systems that the product must interface with. By asking the customer, "Who will the system receive information from, and what information will it receive?" and "What information will this system need to provide for the outside world, and where will it be sent?" the business analyst should be able to identify most of these external entities and data flows. It is an activity that should be done together with the customer. The visual representation serves as a catalyst for the customer to think of more interfaces and more data flows. In addition to reviewing this with the customer, it should also be reviewed with the application owners within IT. There are often interfaces needed between systems that customers are either unaware of, or just don't think of when they are interviewed. Systems development today is so integrated that very often most of a project's budget is spent identifying and implementing interfaces, with less being spent on the core functionality the customer is looking for. This can lead to the customer questioning why everything takes so long and costs so much. Communicate these interfaces to customers to ensure that they have an accurate understanding of the complexity. Sometimes customers may decide not to do a project once they realize how severe the impact is on the rest of the enterprise.

All of this information may have been documented already in the project charter, the statement of work, or a request for service. If those documents don't exist or are not detailed enough, work needs to be done to create or enhance them.

3.3.4 *Preparing the Business Case*

Before a project is initiated, there must be a business case made for why the organization should spend money on this project. In its purest form this would simply be a financial evaluation based on comparing benefits to cost. If the benefits are higher than the cost, the project has value to the organization. However, because most organizations have limited resources and there may be multiple projects that are valuable, a comparison between projects is necessary to evaluate which one (or ones) the organization should invest in. There are many factors impacting this, such as cost to the organization, when the benefits will be realized, when the cost will occur, as well as other non-financial considerations. There may be regulatory reasons as well as market reasons which would cause one project to look better than another. A good business case includes both quantitative information (dollars and time) and qualitative (image, gut feel, preferences). When making these estimates, both of cost and benefits, the analysts must attach a rating for each factor indicating how comfortable they are with the numbers. Some costs may be known exactly and should be presented that way. Other numbers are good-faith estimates or, in some cases, wild guesses. The numbers must be included either way, but the decision makers deserve to know whether or not the numbers are solid. This will drive their risk analysis. If all the costs are solid and all the benefits are guesses, then this will be a high-risk project.

Business analysts are not typically responsible for the development of the business case, but they can be participants in the process. By having a good understanding of the business, the business analyst can pinpoint areas of the business that will be impacted by a solution. The business analyst may also be involved with estimating some of the cost factors not only for development of a solution, but also for re-engineering the organization. It is a common mistake when doing business cases to be too narrow in the definition of both benefits and costs. Job satisfaction, reduced staff levels, and global presence may be large benefits that are overlooked, just as maintenance, training staff, and turnover represent costs that are often missed.

By having a good understanding of the business, the business analyst can pinpoint areas of the business that will be impacted by a solution.

Clearly identify who will be involved with creating the business case as well as who will approve it. The finance organization, the IT group, and the business owner are all likely to be involved with the estimation of the costs and most of them will also help estimate the benefits. Before starting the effort to create a business case, the business owner must describe what is required and the format of the case. A business case can be as easy as a benefit and a cost number or as complex as detailed estimates, labor rates, currency exchange rates, and calculations of net present value and internal rate of return. These calculations are normally beyond what the analyst is responsible for.

One of the assumptions that may need to be made while working on the business case is to consider if this will be an in-house development project or if there is commercial off-the-shelf (COTS) software available. A COTS project may be faster and can reduce risk because a working product already exists. However, COTS projects also tend to be underestimated in the area of business impact. Most packages are designed to work within a certain set of business processes. If the customer wants to run the business differently, then there may be a need for extensive customization; if the customer is willing to run the business like the package is envisioning it, then there can be a large organizational impact to update procedures and policies and to train the staff. These are the types of issues that the business analyst can assist both in identifying as well as in quantifying in the process of developing the business case.

3.3.5   Conducting the Initial Risk Assessment

The initial risk assessment is intended to find out if the risk tolerance of the stakeholders is high enough to do this project. All projects are risky; that's part of the definition of a project. A project is unique, temporary, and that leads to high risk. For some organizations, that is good: they live and succeed by being able to overcome risks and being able to deliver products in a high-risk environment. For other organizations risk can be dangerous. If margins are slim and capabilities are low, then risk can push a business or project over the edge and make it unsuccessful.

For the initial risk assessment there is a set of main questions to be answered by the business:

- How likely is it that we can successfully deliver this product?
- How likely is it that the organization will be able to reap the expected benefits from this project?
- What will the impact be to our business once the product is successfully implemented?
- Is it likely that our business or the marketplace will change by the time this product is implemented?

When doing the risk assessment and recommendation, it is important to look at all these aspects combined. Most organizations are primarily focused on whether or not the project can be successful, and secondarily if the benefits can be achieved once the project is implemented. It is equally important, sometimes maybe even more important, that the business evaluates the total impact to the business, both positive and negative, and does a realistic assessment of where the business and market will be by the time the product is implemented. As an example, a business may invest in a new order processing product, streamlining the order processing function and integrating it with inventory control. By the time the product is developed the business may find that the market has changed and the competitors have gone to an E-commerce model, so the product just developed is obsolete as soon as it is rolled out. Clearly, these trends are not always easy to see or predict, but it is important that the questions are asked, and the initial risk assessment is a good place to ask them.

Risk assessments are done continuously throughout a business cycle and many of the tools and techniques are the same, regardless of when in the cycle they are performed. Chapter 4 has a more detailed examination of the risk management process. At the stage of enterprise analysis, the main risk focus will be on impact to business, capabilities, and organizational readiness. As risk is assessed further and further into the project, the more detailed it will be. During the enterprise analysis, most risks will need to be negotiated with management. Later in the project, the project manager will own more of them.

3.3.6   *Preparing the Decision Package*

There is always someone who will need to make a decision on each idea to determine if it deserves to move on to a full-blown project or if it should be put on the shelf. This may be an executive committee, the business owner, or a product manager. Regardless, the decision maker will need some information to make a good decision. Sometimes this may be an informal briefing, but often for large initiatives there should be a more formal decision package prepared. The business analyst can be a significant player in creating and documenting this package.

1. Problem Description
2. Project Description
3. Project Background
4. Project Benefits
5. Projects Costs
6. Risk of doing project
7. Risk of not doing project
8. Alternative solutions
9. Recommendation

Figure 3.6 Decision package table of content (sample).

The main components of this package are items already discussed in this section:

- The feasibility study report
- The business case
- The project scope
- The initial risk assessment

A good decision package is more than just a summary of these deliverables. It needs to understand the stakeholders making the decision, along with how much information they need and the level of product understanding they already have. The decision package should be a clear and succinct summary of the enterprise analysis, with recommendations to the decision maker. Figure 3.6 shows an example of a table of contents for a decision package targeting a medium-to-large initiative in an organization requiring formal approaches.

Although much of the decision package may have been prepared by the business analyst, it would normally be presented to the decision maker by either a project sponsor or by the project manager. This is a key milestone for any project and the way the proposal is presented can be just as important as what is presented. It needs to be presented with confidence, using strong executive presentation skills.

3.4 Understanding the Business

Although business analysts must have a good overall understanding of the customer's business, they are not expected to be the subject matter experts. The business analysts should understand the main drivers of the business such as business goals and objectives, key competitors, and the customer's market position. They must also have a good understanding of how existing systems are used in the customer's environment.

Some of the most common ways to gain an understanding of the customer's business include:

- Selecting business analysts from the business side. Although it is still more common that the business analyst comes from the development side, more and more organizations are now selecting customers with strong IT understanding to be business analysts. That gives the analyst a strong base business understanding, plus it often provides a network of people who already have a working relationship with the business analyst. And, as will be mentioned many times, relationship building is a key to success for the business analyst.
- Co-locating the analyst with the customer. When working next to the customer, the analyst tends to get more involved with the day-to-day operations of the business as well as building a more personal relationship with the customer.
- Reviewing trade journals, attending conferences, being part of industry organizations. This adds the benefit of not only understanding the customer's business, but also learning about industry trends and seeing what the competition is doing. It is likely that the business analyst's role will keep expanding more and more into trend analysis and identification of new technologies and solutions.

Whatever methods are used to educate the business analyst, it is important to the success of the requirements gathering effort that the analyst understands the overall business picture and can relate how the specific project objectives support or fit in with that business.

In addition, business analysts must view themselves as members of the overall team. Although a business analyst may not have the full knowledge needed, that knowledge often exists within the organization. Knowing who to ask and building a network of people such as project managers, business owners, technical experts, and industry experts will greatly help the business analyst to become successful.

3.5 Business Models

In addition to the context diagram, the SWOT analysis, and the Zachman Framework already discussed in this chapter, there are also a number of other models which may be used to help describe and understand the business. Many of these are detailed models from the Zachman Framework, and some are documents which exist in most businesses at some levels, but which may not be readily available to the business analyst. The ones to be discussed here are:

- Organization charts
- Infrastructure models
- Business Location models

- Business Events
- Business Entity models
- Business Process models

3.5.1   Organization Charts

Although sometimes overlooked as a model, the organization chart is something that most organizations have and is often easy for the business analyst to access. Traditionally the organization chart is viewed with a number of hierarchically organized boxes, with a name and a title in each of them. However, an organization chart can be much more than that. A good example that is available on the World Wide Web is the organization chart of the United Nations. The web link is www. un.org/aboutun/chart.html and a print-out of it has been included in Appendix C. The value-added portion of this chart is that in addition to illustrating the basic structure of the organization, it also describes what each department or sub-area does. Applying this to a business organization, there could be information behind each box stating the vision and mission of each organization, the current initiatives, and a description of the functions of the organization. This information is invaluable for the business analyst when working on documenting and understanding the enterprise. If this type of organization chart is not available, it may be good for business analysts to start creating it; but even if they just have access to the basic, traditional organization chart, that will give them a starting point to go to for more information.

3.5.2   Infrastructure Models

To understand the capabilities of a business, it is often necessary to understand its infrastructure. This can be through a model of worldwide facilities, or a model of networks and computers. For the purpose of this discussion the attention will be on network and computers, but the concepts are valid for any infrastructure.

Figure 3.7 shows the Infrastructure model for C.V. Green. By reviewing this model, it is notable that although each global region appears to have some level of internal communication, there is no global network linking all areas. These types of findings are important to the business analyst. Some of the questions that need to be asked:

- Are there plans for a global network?
- Is communication between regions of the world part of the scope of this project?
- Are there legislative or cost issues prohibiting a global network?

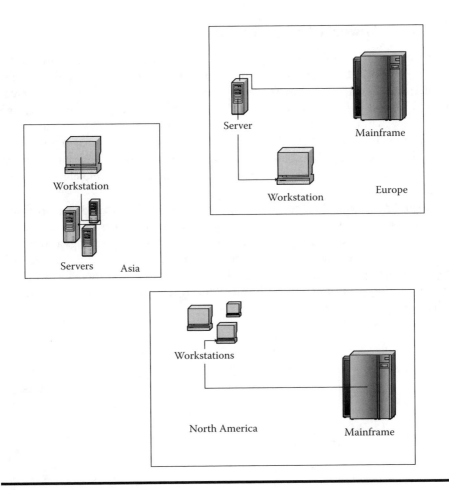

Figure 3.7 Infrastructure model.

Most organizations have some form of documentation supporting their Infrastructure model. This will often be held by the IT organization so there may be a need to do some digging around.

This model has a dual purpose. At this time, when trying to understand the AS-IS situation it provides a good picture of existing capabilities. It will also be useful for the system analyst, who eventually will be designing a technical solution. Much of the information found in the Infrastructure model will convert to being constraints of the solution. Although it is certainly possible that a key corporate project can modify and add on to the existing infrastructure, for most projects the flexibility will be minimal and it will need to live within the existing capabilities. Combining the Infrastructure model with the high-level business case can give an indication of how likely it is that significant infrastructure investments will be made.

3.5.3   *Business Location Models*

There may be overlaps between the organization chart, the Infrastructure model, and the Business Location model. The purpose is a bit different though: here the model shows geographical locations in which the business operates. The intention is to find information about local laws, different languages, cultures, and customers well as local infrastructure (buildings, utilities, etc.). Why should the business analyst care? These things may in many ways drive what solutions are possible. If this is a global solution involving three continents and ten countries, it may be difficult to find an enterprise solution which can be implemented in all locations.

Figure 3.8 shows a Business Location model for C.V. Green. As seen, any global solution would need to incorporate standards from countries as diverse as France, India, and the United States. There are likely to be differences in things as simple as power sources and building codes to areas as complex as trade regulations regarding local content and language issues. The Business Location model can help in understanding what parts of the business must be regionalized or localized and what parts must be centralized.

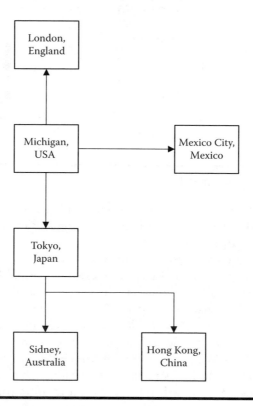

Figure 3.8 C. V. Green business location model.

3.5.4 Business Events

Much of what a business does is driven by events, sometimes cyclical, sometimes random. Identifying and analyzing these events often leads to a greater understanding of the business and what drives it. The events modeled should be things that require a response from the business, and events that have a significant impact on the business. Good examples of key business events for C.V. Green are:

- FDA approval of new drug
- FDA warning of drug interaction
- Manufacturer warning of drug interaction
- Drug recalls
- Legislative change on drug disclosure

The identification of events helps when discussing the business with the customer. It helps frame and focus the conversation. Instead of asking what the customer does, the questions should be:

- What are key events in your business?
- How do you respond to these events?

Event models work well together with creating business scenarios. Rather than abstractly reviewing with the customer what actions are taken when the FDA issues a drug interaction warning, pick a specific case and walk that through to completion. For example, "FDA just identified a harmful drug interaction between drug A from manufacturer X and drug B from manufacturer Z." Building this scenario will give a better understanding of the business process as well as help identify key decision points in the process. Questions such as "Does it matter if the drugs targeted by the warning come from the same company or from two different ones?" should be asked. These types of conversations tend to be less ambiguous and more valuable for both the customer and the business analyst.

One advantage with Events modeling is that the customer seems to relate to it. Most customers look at their business in the context of responding to things, normally from the outside, but the events could also be based on time such as "month end" or "tax deadline," so this form of modeling is likely to engage the customer in the process. Be aware that not everything the customer does is in response to an event. Things like "price increase" and "take inventory" are both actions which may be taken without being initiated by any specific event.

3.5.5 Business Entity Models

Business Entity models can be done at multiple levels (Figure 3.9). For example, they can be looked at within a business to see how departments are relating to each other, or they can be done between companies to understand the organizational interfaces. Viewed from an internal focus, as in the example of C.V. Green, the Business Entity model can show what other areas of the business the pharmacists deal with. Do they need to get information from Accounting? How is inventory determined? Are they interfacing with Legal? Looking at it from the external viewpoint, the focus is on business impacts on the outside world, and outside impacts on the business. Business entities could be "customer," "vendor," "FDA," or "drug manufacturer."

An example of a Business Entity model is shown in figure 3.9. The arrows going back and forth between the business entities and the organization show the main flow of information or products. This model is helpful in gaining a big-picture understanding of what outside organizations provide products, services, or information. That does not mean that these organizations will all be interviewed, but their impacts will be considered. A business analyst starting to gather requirements for the Prescription Interaction Project may not understand that the pharmacy gets some of its information for drug interaction problems directly from law suits and that any good solution to the problem must include capturing law suit information as early as possible. This type of information can be caught by reviewing the Business Entity model prior to planning the requirements gathering efforts.

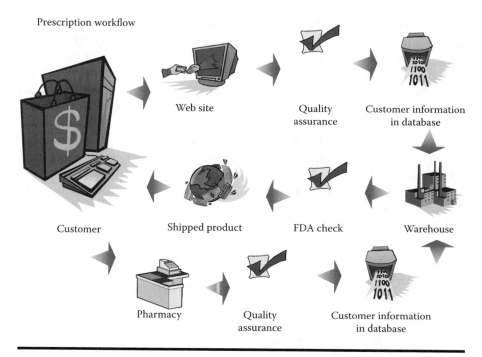

Prescription workflow

Web site

Quality assurance

Customer information in database

Customer

Shipped product

FDA check

Warehouse

Pharmacy

Quality assurance

Customer information in database

Figure 3.9 Business entity model.

3.5.6   *Business Process Models*

Perhaps the most common set of models used to describe the business are Process models. There are many types of Process models including workflow, flowchart, and swim lanes, just to name a few. Some of these will be discussed in Chapter 8 as a part of requirements documentation and modeling. In the context of this unit, they are being reviewed at a higher level, as an approach of understanding the business. An example of a Business Process model is shown in Figure 3.10.

Looking at the model, it is easy to see that there are many steps in identifying interacting drugs and some of them reside outside of C.V. Green. This will help determine the scope of the undertaking and how feasible the whole effort is.

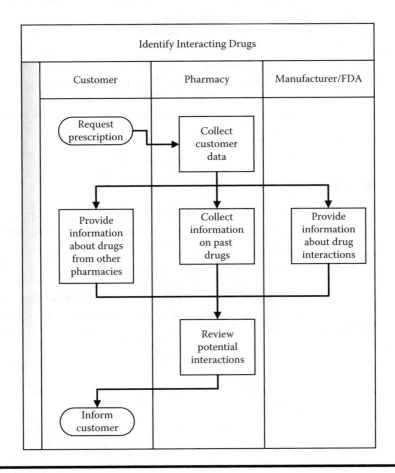

Figure 3.10 Business process flow.

In this case, there will need to be considerable cooperation with businesses and organizations from outside of the immediate organization, with which there is usually little communication. Therefore, if the business wants to take on this endeavor, it must be prepared for a large undertaking.

Other types of Process models include hierarchical process structures, Input-Process-Output (IPO) models, and Business Use Case models. Hierarchical models include Functional Decomposition Diagrams (FDD), and IPO models can be Data Flow Diagrams (DFD), both of which are covered in Chapter 8. Business Use Cases are similar to use cases as covered in Chapter 8, but take a business view rather than a systems view. Business Use Cases take an external view of the business. What does the outside world want to do with this business? Using FDDs and DFDs takes an internal view, looking at what the business does, not what the customer wants it to do. This difference in approach should be considered when selecting which technique to use. Will this project primarily focus on an external customer view of the business, or is it being driven by internal needs?

Most projects will deal with impacting business processes in some way so there is always a need to understand those processes. Make sure that the business is heavily involved with creating these models. If they are IT-related, then they tend to put too much emphasis on what the technology does, and while that is important, it is not where the focus should be at this time.

3.6 Summary

The business analyst typically works on projects which are supporting the enterprise in some way. Understanding the business drivers behind the project and ensuring that the business analyst has a solid understanding of the customer's business will greatly enhance the chance to successfully elicit and document the right requirements. Hopefully much of this work has already been completed by the business, but if not, it should be done at the beginning of the analysis phase. On a small project or on an enhancement project, little effort may be spent in this area, but for a large, enterprisewide initiative, this area deserves serious attention up front.

3.7 Activity

Review the Swede-Mart case study in Chapter 11 and fill out the charter for the project:

Project Charter	
Project Name:	Customer:
Project Manager:	Project Sponsor:
Business need/issue:	
Project justification:	
Critical success factors:	
Key product deliverables and milestones:	
Organizational assumptions:	
Organizational constraints:	

Chapter 4

Creating a Plan for the Requirements Phase

In preparing for battle I have always found that plans are useless, but planning is indispensable.

—Dwight D. Eisenhower

Project management is a more mature discipline than business analysis, and the standards set for project management have been well defined by the Project Management Institute® (PMI). There is nothing contradictory to those standards in this chapter; project management for a business analyst is conceptually the same as any other project management. With that said, what this chapter emphasizes are the areas of project management that are most likely to be of interest to a business analyst, and to look at some of the unique challenges that the business analyst may face during the analysis phase of a project.

4.1   Objectives

- Review the role of the business analyst in project planning.
- Identify the components that may be a part of a Requirements Plan.
- Provide a template for a Requirements Plan.
- Review project management practices within the context of the analysis phase.
- Understand the importance of stakeholder analysis.
- Create a Requirements Plan for a sample project.

4.2   Overview

The business analyst is typically responsible for the planning of the requirements-gathering effort. Although the extent of these responsibilities varies greatly from organization to organization, there is a drive toward having the person with the most knowledge about the activities performed also being the person planning them. For the analysis phase of the project, that person is the business analyst, and for the design phase, it may be the systems analyst. It is important to note that the responsibility of this planning effort is delegated from the project manager, meaning that approval, status reporting, and escalation should typically be done through the project manager, rather than directly with the customer, sponsor, or other stakeholders. Therefore, from a planning standpoint, the business analyst should regard the project manager as the customer. This is an important distinction. If the business analysts are not clear on exactly what authority they have and how they should communicate with the project manager and the customer, it is likely that there will be some conflict and frustration during the project.

> From a planning standpoint, the business analyst should regard the project manager as the customer.

If there are multiple business analysts assigned to the project, one should be designated as the coordinator or planner. That person functions as a team leader for this phase and coordinates, assigns tasks, and interfaces with the project manager from a management standpoint. The other business analysts may still be planning their individual activities, but there should be a lead analyst coordinating the whole analysis phase. Of course, on many projects, especially small ones, the project manager may retain all planning responsibilities, meaning that they actually take on the analyst's planning role as well as the overall project planning role.

In the survey of business analysts mentioned in Chapter 1, it was clear that the biggest difficulties in gathering requirements was lack of process focus, lack of time, and lack of buy-in to scope. All of these areas can be enhanced by good planning practices.

4.3   Why plan?

I often ask this question in my classes: why do you plan? It seems like such an obvious activity that the participants often struggle to come up with meaningful answers. Common answers include:

- To create a schedule.
- To find out what it'll cost.

- So we know what to do.
- To give us a baseline.

These are all correct answers; however, the two answers that most often are missed are stakeholder buy-in and negotiation. And these two may be the most important ones for the success of the project.

1. Stakeholder buy-in: For a business analyst, getting access to users and other stakeholders is vital. If the customer is invited to a two-day requirements-gathering session and is only given a one-day notice, it is unlikely that the customer will send the best people to it. However, if there is a well-documented plan and the customer has three to four weeks notice prior to the session, the likelihood of customer commitment is greatly increased. So, plan early and involve the stakeholders in the planning process. Many projects fail because of poor requirements, and one of the root causes for poor requirements is often that the right people were not involved. Lack of customer availability is the number one mentioned difficulty when gathering requirements.
2. Negotiation: Most (if not all) projects have resource constraints. There will be pressure to cut costs and schedule out of all project phases. If the estimate for the analysis phase is based on gut feeling and intuition, it is unlikely that the decision makers will be convinced that all the time and money asked for is truly needed. However, if there is a detailed plan with well-defined tasks and deliverables, the discussion will focus on which task should or should not be done, rather than the quality of the estimate given for the project. In negotiation, the person with the most information will always have a clear advantage.

A plan is a stake in the ground against which progress is measured. There is no such thing as a perfect plan, at least not once the project is underway. The focus should be on creating a plan that all parties are comfortable with, and then deal with any variance to the plan through corrective actions. So decide how much time and effort should be spent on planning for each specific project. If the business analyst and the customer are co-located and both parties are experienced and understand both the business and the systems environment, then the planning effort can be fairly minimal. But there still must be a plan!

> If the business analyst and the customer are co-located and both parties are experienced and understand both the business and the systems environment, then the planning effort can be fairly minimal.

Manage the plan whenever possible. After the project has started and there is a need to update stakeholders on status, that update will largely consist of documenting actual progress and comparing it to the planned progress. If the discrepancy between the plan and the actual result gets too large (what project managers call a significant variance), there may be a need to re-baseline, meaning re-plan the project. This is not a preferred approach because it tends to lessen accountability; however, it is preferred to running by a plan that is widely considered to be unreachable. However, the first choice should always be to take a corrective action to bring the project in line with the plan. There is often a significant organizational commitment to a plan, and if the plan keeps changing, the organizational commitment is likely to wane.

4.4 Roles and Responsibilities

All work done by the business analyst in the project planning arena is viewed as a subset to the overall project plan that is managed by the project manager. The business analyst is viewed as a sub-project manager, at least on large projects. Thus, the tools used by the business analyst here should be the same tools (and templates) that are being used for the overall project plan. In Figure 2.2 in chapter 2, the responsibilities for each project phase were defined. That definition determines who the sub-project manager is for each phase.

On large projects there will often be multiple business analysts working together. Some can be doing documentation, some facilitation, while others are taking a lead and a planning role. It is that lead role that will focus in on creating the Requirements Plan. It is a "best practice" to define the roles of all the team members up front. It will save a lot of duplication of effort and avoid tasks being forgotten. A study of responsibilities of the business analyst found the following roles (this is just a subset):

- Facilitator
- Modeler
- Technical writer
- Tester
- Test case writer
- Planner
- Interviewer

Although the International Institute of Business Analysis® (IIBA) gives us a good definition of the role of the business analyst, which was explored in Chapter 2, most organizations have their own twist on this topic. If the organization has a quality assurance department, their roles can sometimes overlap with the business analyst.

4.5　User Profiling

Before any realistic plans for the analysis phase can be developed there must be an evaluation of the scope of the elicitation effort. Some projects may only need to interview one customer; others need to build consensus among thousands of users over multiple continents, speaking different languages and having cultural difference. These differences will drive not only the timeline and the costing of the analysis activities, but they will also determine the skills needed by the business analyst and the necessary organizational involvement.

Users can be categorized in many ways, including:

- Primary/secondary user
- Experienced/novice user
- Full-time/part-time user
- Organizational entities
- Internal/external user
- Language and cultural differences
- Geographical differences

There are many other ways as well. One good approach is to sit down in the beginning of the project and have a brainstorming session to determine who will use the system, and then review the result of that session as a starting point for the user categories.

The result of user profiling will not only drive the planning of the analysis phase, but also the actual elicitation, documentation, modeling, and communication of the requirements. It may even necessitate different solutions for different users. So the information covered on the next few pages will serve as a basis for many of the following chapters. The different categories will be reviewed in the context of the Prescription Interaction Project, described in Chapter 1.

The result of user profiling will not only drive the planning of the analysis phase, but also the actual elicitation, documentation, modeling, and communication of the requirements.

4.5.1　Primary/Secondary User

If the user's job is prescription entry clerk, then they will be a primary user when a prescription entry system is developed. They cannot do their job without the system, or at least it is an integral part of the core job functions. This group normally comes to mind first when identifying users because they will usually be the ones spending most time using the system. For the Prescription Interaction Project, this is primarily the pharmacist and pharmacy assistant. However, make sure to expand the thinking when looking for primary users. If the intention is for the customers to be able to enter prescription information online themselves, then that would make the customers primary users as well.

So who would be the secondary user? It could be the actual customer who wants to get a prescription filled. Or it could be the manager who needs to measure prescription entry performance or the doctor writing the prescription. Secondary user does not indicate less importance or less interest in the outcome. Obviously the customer presenting the prescription may have more interest in a well-executed order than the person entering the prescription. Secondary just means that the system itself is not a primary part of the person's job. To identify a list of potential secondary users, ask the following questions:

- Who will be impacted by the system?
- Who will impact the system?

4.5.2 Experienced/Novice User

Experienced users tend to be good at giving big-picture views. They understand the process, and they often understand how their role fits into the overall business. But sometimes they struggle with the detail requirements. Because they are experienced they tend to make a lot of assumptions about the business analyst's understanding and the basic functionality of the product. The pharmacist who has been working for 15 years filling prescriptions is doing many of the mundane steps, such as verifying past prescription, without thinking about it, and they may forget to tell the analyst about the detailed steps.

Novice users know what their struggles are, like what steps in the process are difficult, where the bottlenecks are. They struggle with things that the experienced user has already discovered workarounds for. At the same time they have little knowledge of the big picture, such as why something is being done or who is dependent on the process. The newly hired pharmacy technicians will typically have a written set of instructions which they follow, even if they don't fully understand why they need to do it. Their ability to visualize a new solution is probably also more limited than the experienced user's.

So when planning for the analysis phase there must be a plan for including both experienced and novice users, and each probably should be handled using different elicitation techniques: job shadowing for some, facilitated sessions for others, and surveys for still other users. There is a more detailed discussion on each technique as well as their pros and cons in Chapter 7.

4.5.3   Full-Time/Part-Time User

This is not referring to the work status of the users. Instead it is looking for how much of their time they spend using the product. A user who spends most of the day using a system will be focused on efficiency and speed, but a user who only spends a few hours every month will tend to look for intuitiveness, forgiveness, and general ease of use. Some pharmacies may have a dedicated person doing nothing but entering prescriptions. At smaller pharmacies, there may only be one person doing all job functions, so entering prescription may only be a relatively small portion of that person's day. If the business analyst captures requirements from one but not the other, the system will be poorly received when installed.

4.5.4   Organizational Entities

If the project is to develop a prescription interaction system, it would be obvious that the Pharmacy department must be interviewed. In addition Accounting, Purchasing, Legal, Marketing, and others must be interviewed as well. The other entities may not have the same interest, but they are likely to be impacted or have on impact on the project. If the current marketing campaigns state that the organization allows for seamless transfer of prescriptions, it is likely to have an impact on the requirements for this project.

4.5.5   Internal/External User

Some systems are used both by people from within the organization as well as by people outside. If the prescription is entered in the pharmacy by the pharmacy staff, they will have requirements. If the prescription is entered online by a doctor or a customer, their expectations may be different. Also, the external user's environment will be much harder to control as far as hardware, operating system, etc., which must be considered by the business analyst.

4.5.6   Language and Cultural Differences

This can be looked at from two different viewpoints: (1) differences in the people who will eventually be using the product, and (2) differences in the people giving the requirements. Both scenarios will have an impact on the approach used to gather requirements. For language differences among the end users, the difference may lead to multilingual support, help functions, and different auditing functions. It can also lead to a more graphical user interface with a stronger focus on pictures than on words.

For the people giving the requirements it may lead to different approaches in eliciting, reviewing, and validating requirements. Brainstorming sessions are often difficult to do when the participants are speaking different languages, so one-on-one interviews or surveys in the users' primary language may be an option. For the pharmacy this can be a difficult issue. At the headquarters location, where most of the requirements are likely to be gathered, there will often be a primary language used, but in more rural pharmacies the language could be different.

4.5.7 Geographical Differences

Some geographical differences may be overlapping with the language and cultural issues discussed above, but it can be also be related to legislative differences between different countries or even within a country as well as issues with network, power structure (electrical power), and availability of technology. There also tends to be a very different price sensitivity for product pricing in different parts of the world: what is considered affordable in Sweden may not be viewed the same way in India.

4.6 Elements of a Requirements Plan

On a large, complex project there needs to be a comprehensive plan for the analysis phase; for a small project most of the plan may be Post-It® notes on workstations. Project planning is not a "one size fits all" activity. By using a repeatable process and predefined templates, the planning process will be less painful, but any process selected must still be customized to fit the specifics of each situation.

> By using a repeatable process and predefined templates, the planning process will be less painful, but any process selected must still be customized to fit the specifics of each situation.

The following shows a sample Requirements Plan template (see Appendix B) with the key sections and a brief description of each. After that follows a more detailed review of each section:

1. Project overview and background: This provides context and background for readers.
2. Scope and deliverables: This shows scope and deliverables from the viewpoint of a business analyst.
3. Stakeholder analysis: Who is impacted (or impacts) the project?
4. Communications plan: How will project status be taken and distributed? What types of meetings are needed?

5. Project activities: Identifies the work that needs to be done on the project. This could be in the form of a Work Breakdown Structure (WBS) or in a list format, and will be input into detail scheduling and estimating.
6. Roles and responsibilities: Who will do what on the project?
7. Resource plan: What resources are needed for the completion of the analysis activities? This includes human, tools, software, and equipment resources.
8. Requirements risk plan: What are the requirements/product-related risks?
9. Manage changes to requirements: How are changes handled?

Some organizations may have more sections such as a Quality Plan, a Procurement Plan, and others. Negotiate with the project manager to determine what is needed for the project.

4.6.1   Project Overview and Background

This is not intended to be a duplication of the project information that the project manager has collected. The general project information may be referenced here, but should not be copied. Duplication of information tends to cause confusion and should be discouraged. Rather, this section should focus on how the developed product fits into the overall enterprise. How was the original need identified? How will it fit into the product portfolio? What is the long-term vision of the product? A lot of the information covered here would be developed or captured during the enterprise analysis described in Chapter 3. Think of including:

- Origination of the project idea
- Previous attempts to develop this product
- Competitive forces
- What will success do for the organization?
- What will failure do for the organization?
- Initiatives that this project is dependent on
- Other initiatives that are dependent on this project
- Key business integration point

This section may have many uses, but one of the main purposes is "lessons learned." When future projects try to learn from this effort and evaluate what worked and what didn't, this section will help put things into perspective. It is also a good training tool for new people joining the project. It gives them an idea of the history behind getting to where the project is today.

4.6.2   Scope and Deliverables

The project scope will be documented in the Charter, Statement of Work (SOW), Work Breakdown Structure (WBS), or other documents, depending on the process used. This section is an extension of previously completed documentation into areas that are of significant interest to the business analyst. Typical deliverables are a Business Requirements Document, a Requirements Plan, a User Acceptance Plan, and others, depending on the specifics of the project. This is intended for establishing boundaries, what is included and excluded from the scope of the project, again with a focus on the analyst's viewpoint.

Examples of good areas to explore for inclusion/exclusion are:

- Geographic locations: Is there a need to talk to stakeholders from multiple locations/countries? Will the users all speak the same language?
- Staged deliverables: Will this be requirements for the final product, or just for a portion of that product?
- Integration to other areas of the business: Whose responsibility is this? Does each area need to define the impact on their systems?

Also look for responsibilities of the business analyst that may go beyond the analysis phase. Who will train the user? What is the business analyst's involvement with testing? What kind of follow-up is needed after implementation? These are all activities that need to be planned by their owner. It actually may mean that the business analyst's scope goes beyond the project scope. The project scope may end when the system is implemented, but the business analyst often has tasks going past implementations. Examples include:

- Assess customer satisfaction
- User training
- Quantifying improvements

4.6.3   Stakeholder Analysis

There are many drivers of the Requirements Plan, but the most important one tends to be the stakeholders that are involved. If this is a single-user environment with a well-defined business process, the plan should be very simple and straightforward. However, if the customer has locations on multiple continents, is operating under a new business model, and is not sure what they are really looking for, then a more detailed plan is needed.

Start the stakeholder analysis by documenting the categories of stakeholders. These categories can be overlapping (one stakeholder can be a part of multiple categories), such as a sponsor may also be a user of the product, or they can be hierarchical (one stakeholder can be a subset of a different stakeholder category) such as data entry clerk being a category of user. Regardless, the stakeholder identification must be as complete as possible. A stakeholder overlooked at this early point of the project can lead to a significant rework or even failure of the project later.

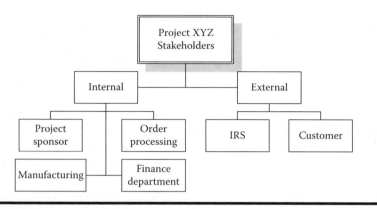

Figure 4.1 Stakeholder hierarchical view.

Figure 4.1 shows an example of stakeholder categorization. This stakeholder diagram should be reviewed with all the stakeholders identified, if possible. The government, as an example, may be a stakeholder, but reviewing anything with the government may not be realistic. In the review the analyst looks for buy-in that the stakeholders are agreeing to participate in the project and also for identification of potential stakeholders that may have been missed.

Once a list of stakeholders has been documented and reviewed, the stakeholders should be prioritized. Each stakeholder's role and priority must be documented. Prioritizing the stakeholders may sound like a political activity, and it definitely can be, but it is also necessary. Not every stakeholder has the same influence over project decisions, and the business analyst must know, going into requirements sessions, who the key players are. The priority decision should be made by the project sponsor or the paying customer.

Why is this important? A personal example from earlier in my career was the development of the computer systems for the Saturn automotive dealers. Some of the key stakeholders were the Saturn Corporation and the actual Saturn dealers. They would often have different thoughts on what the product should (and should not) do. There was a lot of discussion on control, privacy of business information, and what can be required of an independent business. Those were questions far beyond the job description of a business analyst, and they had to be decided on by the customer up front.

In this specific case, it was eventually determined that the priorities were different, depending on the part of the system we were talking about. For any functionality that was dealing with cross-dealer communication and communication with corporate, Saturn corporate was the lead. Any functionality dealing with operations of the dealership were decided on by the dealer group. If this had not been realized and agreed to, it is likely that the developed product would not have satisfied either party.

Also make sure that the stakeholder's role is well understood. Many of them may be passive, they need information from the product, or they provide information to the product, but they have no real interest in what the product does. Others may be severely impacted in how they do business and may experience cascading impacts, causing new projects in their area as a response. Their role also often depends on the person or persons that are selected to represent them. A strong, competent representative tends to ensure that the organization's interests are looked out for; a weak, uninterested representative can be a disaster for the stakeholder and potentially for the project. Always try to influence which stakeholder representatives are selected for the project by defining what their roles will be and what type of person is expected. Be aware of the person available. When the stakeholder states, "You can have Joe over there in the corner as our representative, he doesn't really have anything else going on," it is time to start negotiating. There's an old saying: "If you want something done, look for a busy person," and that is equally true for requirements gathering. Find a representative who speaks for the organization and is well respected.

Figure 4.2 shows an example of a completed stakeholder analysis. As seen when reviewing the form, there must be some judgment used regarding what to put in this document. Decide how it will be used. If this is private documentation, there can be more items included on the form. If this is a project form, visible to everyone, be more restrictive. In either case, naturally, don't put any inappropriate information in the form.

<table>
<tr><td colspan="2" align="center">**Stakeholder Analysis**</td></tr>
<tr><td>**Project Name:** XYZ Project</td><td>**Date:** Jan 1, 2007</td></tr>
<tr><td>**Project Manager:** John Jones</td><td>**Project Sponsor:** Jans Smith</td></tr>
<tr><td colspan="2">**Stakeholder organization:**
Finance</td></tr>
<tr><td colspan="2">**Stakeholder name and contact information:**

Linda Williams, VP Finance
(121) 555-1212</td></tr>
<tr><td colspan="2">**What will this stakeholder provide to the project?**

Will provide initial funding by month.
Will approve/reject change requests that requires increased budgets</td></tr>
<tr><td colspan="2">**What will the project provide to this stakeholder?**

Timeline for expense
Cost/Benefit analysis</td></tr>
<tr><td colspan="2">**What is the impact to this stakeholder if the project succeeds or fails?**

If this project fails Linda will be responsible for finding other areas of the organization that can make up for the shortfall</td></tr>
<tr><td colspan="2">**Hot issues for this stakeholder**

Solid estimates
No padding at project level. She will set a management reserve</td></tr>
</table>

Figure 4.2 Stakeholder analysis.

4.6.4   Communications Plan

The Communications Plan is partly an extension of the stakeholder analysis. It focuses on status reporting to the project manager, customer, management, and others as well as information needed to create the deliverables. It contains the following columns:

- What: What is the content of the communication? Is it a status report? Is it approval? Is it a document? Create and show templates for the communication when possible.
- Who creates: Who is responsible for creating and distributing the communication?
- Who receives: Who will be the recipient? Verify that it is really wanted/needed.
- Why: Is this really needed? What is being accomplished with this communication? The reason for the communication should be understood by all.
- When: When will this happen? Once? Weekly? At the beginning of a phase? When a milestone is reached?
- Where: Location for meetings.
- How: In person, videoconferencing, over the Web.

Figure 4.3 shows a partially filled out Communications Plan. The Communications Plan serves two main purposes for the analysis phase. First, it's a to-do list and, like any plan, it is a trigger for what to do and when. Second, it lets everyone else on the project know what is expected and assists in getting them to buy-in to communication. If the Communications Plan states that the customer will approve the Requirements Document within 15 days, and the customer signs off on the Communications Plan, the chances of approval actually happening increases dramatically. Project management and business analysis are both communicative responsibilities. The Communications Plan lays the foundation for that communication.

What	Who (Responsible)	Who (Audience)	Why	When	Where	How
BRD approval	Business Analyst	Customer, developer, sponsor	Go/ No-go decision for the analysis phase	April 10, 2007	Executive conference room	In Person

Figure 4.3 Communications plan.

4.6.5 Project Activities

The process of identifying the activities needed for the analysis phase lays the foundation for estimation, scheduling, sequencing, and overall planning. But more than that, it greatly increases the business analysis team's understanding of what the phase is actually all about. In a number of the classes I teach, the students are asked to create a WBS or a task list. Inevitably, it becomes somewhat frustrating, they don't have enough information, and they are not subject matter experts in the business areas used in the classroom. Even so, it forces them to think about the work to be done, to make assumptions, and to ask questions. It is relatively easy to understand a one-line scope statement, but it is often very hard to take that statement and create a detail activity list. Figure 4.4 shows an example of a WBS for the analysis phase of the project.

When creating the WBS, involve as many of the team members in the process as possible. Utilizing the diversity and experience of the whole team will create a more complete and accurate WBS. If the organization follows a standard process for the analysis phase, use that as a starting point. If there is not a standard process, try to find a similar project that the organization has done in the past and use that as a starting point.

Most plans should be developed using progressive elaboration as a guideline. This technique recognizes that in the beginning of a project (or a phase of the project), there is limited knowledge and a lot of unknowns that will be hard to plan for. By using progressive elaboration the areas that are well understood are planned at a detailed level, while areas that need more work can be planned at a higher level. This is definitely a "best practice"; however, in some organization, where the plan

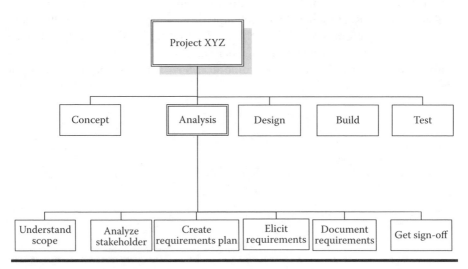

Figure 4.4 Sample WBS for the analysis phase.

must be 100 percent complete and shared with the customer at a detailed level, this approach may not be allowed. Unfortunately, the estimating process in those organizations tends to result in more contingency (and padding) of estimates.

By using progressive elaboration the areas that are well understood are planned at a detail level, while areas that need more work can be planned at a higher level.

4.6.6   Roles and Responsibilities

If there is only one business analyst on the project, defining roles and responsibilities may be an easy task, but on large projects this becomes more complex. Responsibility Matrixes (such as the one shown in Figure 4.5) can be done at multiple levels.

Task \ Responsible	Project Manager	Business Analyst	Project Sponsor	Technical Writer
Analyze stakeholder	A	R	I	
Create requirements plan	A	R	I	
Elicit requirements		R	A	I
Document requirements		C	A	R
Get Sign-off	R	I	A	I

R= Responsible, A=Approve, C=Concur, I=Inform

Figure 4.5 Roles and responsibility matrix.

Early in the process the tasks will be relatively high-level and can often be assigned to an organizational unit or to a job classification (such as the business analyst or the facilitator). As the project moves along the path of progressive elaboration, the plan will go down into more detailed tasks and eventually should get an actual name assigned to each task.

A Responsibility Matrix must be approved by the organizations and people who have tasks to perform. "Approve" may be strong word, but they must at least acknowledge that they are aware there is a task for them on the project. Remember that a lot of the tasks done in the analysis phase may be done by the customer. Those tasks must also be documented in the roles and responsibility matrix and the customer must buy into their involvement. There is not much point in the business analyst creating a survey if the customer is not committed to filling it out.

4.6.7   Resource Plan

Creating the schedule, figuring out skills needed and assigning responsibilities is good progress. The Resource Plan is where it is shown how this will actually happen. Identifying the people needed, when they are needed, and for how long, is not an easy task. It requires communication and negotiation skills. Also, the task of identifying nonhuman resources such as the tools, the software and hardware, and the facilities needed is often a time-consuming and contentious activity.

Most projects today operate in some type of matrix organization. That means that although the business analyst will have responsibility for the analysis phase and will be held accountable for tasks in that phase, the resources will typically be reporting to someone else. Being in a matrix organization probably also means that the resources for the analysis work will not be assigned to the project on a full-time basis.

Start early with the Resource Plan and keep communicating with the organizations that will be providing resources. Common resources needed for the analysis phase are data architects, quality assurance specialists, testing groups, business process owners, facilitators, and support staff. By involving their management early on and keeping them up-to-date on project progress, the project is more likely to get the right resources at the right time. Be aware of what the project's priority is within the organization and periodically assess if that priority is changing. Although it is fairly easy to acquire resources for a high-priority project, if that priority decreases, the availability of resources tends to decrease as well.

4.6.8   Requirements Risk Plan

PMI's *Guide to the Project Management Institute's Body of Knowledge, Third Edition* (PMBOK) defines risk as "… an uncertain event that, if it occurs, has a positive or negative impact on at least one project objective … ." Although that is certainly a good definition, for this book the concentration is on the risks that have a negative impact. The positive risks or opportunities are more of interest to the business owner, even though the business analyst definitely has a role in identifying them. It is also fair to say that opportunities are looked at more during enterprise analysis, which is normally where the full benefit of an opportunity can be realized.

Software development is risky business. For the project manager there are risks that deal with new and unproven technology, changing technology, lack of knowledge about capabilities of the organization, and lack of trained people. The risk plan covered in this section focuses on the risks that the business analyst is most concerned with.

For the business analyst there are two main areas for risk management: (1) risks associated with the actual requirements gathering process and (2) risks associated with the product being developed. Risks associated with gathering of requirements are more temporary in nature and are primarily dealt with by the analyst during the analysis phase. Risks associated with the product are addressed throughout the project life cycle, and these risks are really owned by the business owner, although the business analyst should be heavily involved as well. Based on the different audiences for these risks, it would normally be good to track and report on them separately. Typical requirements gathering risks to consider are:

- Customers not knowing what they want: This is more often a question of not being able to clearly express what customers want, often based on not speaking the techie's language.
- Business analysts not understanding the business: Traditionally most business analysts come from a technical background, but this is changing. An increasing number of business analysts are now from the business side, which should help reduce this risk.
- Lack of skills on toolset: There are more tools available for requirements gathering than ever before. This is good once the business analyst is up to speed on the tools, but until that happens, the tools can actually slow down the process.
- Customers not willing to dedicate enough time for requirements process: Most customers actually have a regular job to do. It is often hard to find time to meet with the business analyst.
- Customers defining solution, not requirements: Customers often see something similar to what they want. Instead of describing what they need, they describe what they perceive as the best solution. The business analyst needs both skills and tact to push back on this.

Typical product related risks are:

- Product not meeting business need: It may meet the requirements, but the requirements don't solve the problem.
- Users not accepting product: This is especially common when only a subset of the user population has been involved with giving requirements.
- Product pricing not competitive: The product is great, but no one can afford it.
- Product too complex for user: May meet the functional requirements, but too complex.
- Technology outdated by the time product is released: State of the art changes fast. If leading edge is needed, the project needs to be short.

A general risk approach which can be applied at enterprise analysis, requirements gathering, or any other analysis activity is discussed later in this chapter.

4.6.9   Manage Changes to Requirements

The end result of the analysis phase is the Business Requirements Document (BRD). This is the ultimate definition of the product scope. As such, it must be controlled throughout the rest of the project and any changes to it should be evaluated to assess their impact on other project and product objectives.

Even though the discussion here talks about the BRD as one document, it is really a composite of many documents. Change control is initiated at a point in time when a document is being baselined. The different sections of the BRD should normally be baselined at different times. For example, the executives' requirements should be captured and baselined before the user requirements are finalized, and the user requirements should be baselined before the system requirements. So part of the change control process should be to establish what documents the project will track change control on and when those documents go from being "work in progress" to "baseline." Many organizations baseline the whole BRD at one time and although this sometimes works fine, it is not consistent with a progressive elaboration approach. The approach to baseline or "freeze" different parts of the requirements document at different times does add complexity to the change control process, but on a complex project it minimizes the chance of scope creep as you go from one stakeholder type to the next.

In line with this approach, there must be a decision up front in regard to who can approve what type of change. A change that has a cost impact only may be approved by the customer, but a change that will delay the schedule may also need approval from the project office (to evaluate impact on other projects which may need the same resources). Establish responsibilities up front and follow a repeatable process that is known to all. It would typically look similar to this:

- Submit change request.
- Assign for analysis.
- Evaluate impact of change.
- Forward request with recommendation to Change Control Board.
- Approve or reject.
- Track changes.

Successful change control is largely about discipline. All changes must go through formal change control. This does not mean that the customer will be charged for all changes. Billing is a business decision; impact analysis is an awareness issue. Successful change control will ensure that changes that are made are needed, wanted, and meet the objectives of the project. Despite customers feeling that they are being hindered by all this paperwork, it is really there to protect them from changes that are not desirable to the organization (even though they may be wanted by a stakeholder).

4.7 General Guidelines for the Requirements Plan

The next few sections will delve into more detail on specific tools and techniques creating different portions of the plan described above. The business analyst must work with the project manager to clearly define which of these tasks should be done by the analyst and which will be kept by the project manager. The tasks here are project management tasks which may (and often should) be delegated.

4.8 Risk

The risk process recommended for the analysis phase is very similar to the overall risk management process as shown in the PMBOK. It has been simplified here to account for it being a subset of the overall risk process. The main steps in the process are:

1. Develop the risk management approach.
2. Identify risks.
3. Assess risks.
4. Respond to risks.
5. Monitor and control risks.

4.8.1   Step 1: Develop the Risk Management Approach

How much time should be spent discovering and dealing with risks? The easy answer is "it depends." But on what does it depend? A large project tends to be more risky than a small one. A product that may jeopardize the company's future will also deserve a higher focus. Some people are gamblers, some are not. So the following areas are worthy of research when determining the risk approach:

- Project size and complexity
- Precedence: Has anything like this been done before?
- Skills with tools and technology
- Maturity of the business
- Impact if project succeeds/fails

On a low-risk project the project team may spend less than 10 percent of the project time dealing with risk and contingencies; on a high-risk project that can easily get up to 25 percent or more.

Develop a plan up front, define roles and responsibilities for the risk activities, and get buy-in from the involved parties. That minimizes that chance of over- or under-focusing on risk. Keep in mind that finding and reducing or eliminating risks is probably the most effective approach to delivering the right product in the right time frame for the right price.

4.8.2   Step 2: Identify Risks

Identifying risks can be a time-consuming and sometimes nonproductive activity. Although brainstorming is the most common approach to risk identification, brainstorming that is not focused often leads to a list of obvious risks or risks that are hard to address. The more structure and focus there is in the process, without stifling creativity too much, the more useful the activity will be. Some "best practices" when identifying risks include:

- Learn from the past. History has a tendency to repeat itself; the areas that have caused problems in the past can be a good starting point. Lessons learned documentation can be hard to find; some project managers may have them hidden away, in some cases they may have been thrown away. Start a new best practice within your organization. In a common area, set aside a folder called "Lessons Learned" and start filing the reports created for lessons learned in there. In a couple years that will yield an impressive starting point.
- Talk to the experts. Anyone who has done a similar activity in the past or who has seen similar efforts in other organizations can identify potential areas of concern. Experts may be past project managers, project participants, or external resources. Vendors and customers may have done similar efforts in the past.
- Categorize risk. Categorization can be done before or after the risks have been identified; either way it helps determine priorities. Categorization can help identify further risks as well as identify areas that may have been overlooked. Figure 4.6 shows a risk categorization structure.

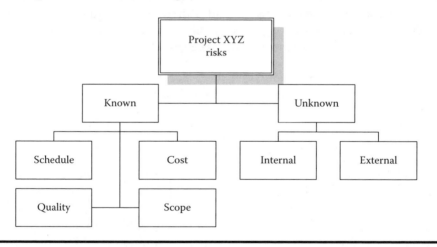

Figure 4.6 Risk structure.

- A more detailed risk structure, covering the whole project, not just requirements, can be found on the SEI Website (www.sei.cmu.edu; search for Risk Taxonomy TR06.93). This has been developed to focus on the risks associated with software development and based on industry best practices. The specific classification system used is less important than the fact that one is being used. Classification of risk helps with readability, organization, assigning responsibilities as well as with prioritization of risks.

- Document the risks in a cause-and-effect statement. "If the customer does not attend the prototype review, the final product may not be accepted by the users." Too often, risk statements are too generic to actually act on. Risk statements like "May miss schedule," "May go over budget," and "System may not work" are not really describing what the risk is, but rather what the impact of the risk will be. The cause-and-effect approach gives a much better understanding of the risk and the main impact areas.

4.8.3   Step 3: Assess Risks

Although it is a "best practice" to identify a large number of risks, it is also important to spend most of the available time and money focusing on the high-value ones, meaning that the focus should be on the risks that are most likely to hurt the project objectives. The two dimensions traditionally used to evaluate risks are probability and impact. Look at how likely is it that a risk will happen, and if it happens, what the impact of the risk is.

In this book there is a third dimension added, called controllability. This is a somewhat subjective analysis of the level of control there is over the risk drivers. For example, a risk of "Inadequate skills on the project team will lead to poor quality" is a risk that appears to be controllable. However, the risk "FDA may pass new reporting requirements, causing our project to lose resources to other projects" is a risk where the project team probably has limited control. It doesn't mean that those risks are ignored, but the thought process deciding on responses will be different. Figure 4.7 shows how the risks are positioned on the graph, giving an easily understandable prioritization.

Ideally, there is enough information to put an actual percentage and dollar amount on the probability and impact, but this is not realistic for most software projects. Good history is needed to create good numbers and for most organizations that history is just

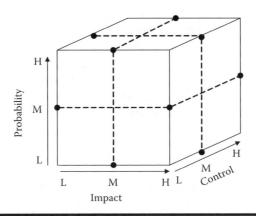

Figure 4.7 Risk prioritization tool.

not available yet. So for most projects it is often sufficient to use a high/medium/low approach to qualifying the risk, with some subjective definition of what high versus medium and low means. The controllability dimension will always be subjective so high/medium/low works well for that. Using the example risk from earlier, "If the customer does not attend the prototype review, the final product may not be accepted by the users," to classify probability the analyst may find that because in the past the customer has been attending most sessions when sufficient notice has been given, the probability is rated as a medium. The impact would be very severe to multiple project objectives so the analyst rates the impact as high. Controllability is medium, the customer is not directly under the analyst's control, but there are ways to influence the customer.

4.8.4   Step 4: Respond to Risks

There are four classic ways of responding to risk:

1. Avoid: Don't do the risky behavior. If the risk is associated with prototypes, don't use prototypes (this may create other risks, but this specific risk is avoided). Just not doing the project is another example of "avoid."
2. Mitigate: Take some action to minimize the risk. For the customer not attending the review, it could be "Have review in users office," "Send out reminder notice."
3. Transfer: Find someone to absorb all or part of the risk. Could involve outsourcing, insurance, and penalties in contracts.
4. Accept: Maybe there's nothing that can be done, or the price of action is higher than the price of doing nothing.

Responding to risks is often a mix of the approaches above. Depending on the project and on the specific circumstances there may be some mitigation of a risk; some of it can be transferred while the rest is accepted. It is important to consider all options. There is a tendency to try to mitigate all risks, but this is not necessarily the right approach. If the cost–benefit ratio of inaction is better than that of action, "accept" would be the better risk approach.

Also be aware that in most cases the response to one risk may be a source of new risks. Part of the response evaluation and documentation should be a review of what new risks have been created. This is especially true for the business analyst. The risk of the customer not understanding the requirements is mitigated by prototyping. This creates the risks of prototyping setting unrealistic expectations with the customer, which is mitigated by creating a prototype which will have no real functionality ... and on it goes.

4.8.5   Step 5: Monitor and Control Risks

Risk monitoring and controlling should be done throughout the analysis phase. Normally it can be included as a part of the regular project status reviews being done throughout the phase, but the analysis team may need to add additional checkpoints focusing on the requirements gathering and product development. It is especially important to take a checkpoint at the end of the analysis phase and document what risks are still outstanding and make sure that the development team and the project manager are aware of them.

4.9   Estimating

Earlier in this chapter it was stated that one of the main purposes of creating a Requirements Plan is to help in negotiation with other stakeholders. The more reliable and justified the estimate is, the stronger the analysts' negotiating position will be. Often in a negotiation, the person with the most facts wins. A "gut feel" estimate of "I'd guess about three months for that" will not be very credible with the stakeholders. However, a step-by-step plan outlining the analysis activities with assumptions about each of them and an estimate to go along will be impressive. It tends to shift the focus from "How do you know how long that task will take?" to "Which ones of these activities do we really need to do?", which is a great starting position.

> The more reliable and justified the estimate is, the stronger the analysts' negotiating position will be.

There are two basic types of estimates you can create:

1. Analogous estimates, often called top-down estimates: These estimates are often done early on and are based on similar activities done in the past. If the last project the organization did was similar to the current one, that project result may be used as an estimate for the current effort. If facilitated sessions are used on this project, compare it to a project where similar techniques were used. It is an estimating technique that has a high degree of inaccuracy, the main use for it should be to see if the estimate is in the ballpark. This type of estimate may be ±50 percent, but it gives an idea with regard to it being a $1-million or a $10-million project. Good solid assumptions are needed for good analogous estimates.
2. Detailed or bottom-up estimates: This requires a breakdown of the analysis phase to detail activities. This is often unrealistic in the beginning of the analysis phase, because the stakeholders are unknown and the requirements have not yet been captured. It may work for a small, well-defined project, but in most cases there needs to be quite a bit of work done before this level of detail can be reached.

As a business analyst, the estimate needs to be reviewed with the project manager, and it would normally be the project manager actually taking the estimate to the customer or sponsor.

4.10 Laying Out Tasks

Part of any good plan is to determine what activities are dependent on other activities and which ones can go in parallel. The following five activities will serve as an example:

1. Create a Requirements Plan.
2. Interview executives.
3. Interview users.
4. Document interfaces.
5. Create BRD.

The user interviews should probably not start until the executives have been interviewed, but documentation of interfaces can be done in parallel with both of those activities. So, this could look like the network diagram shown in Figure 4.8.

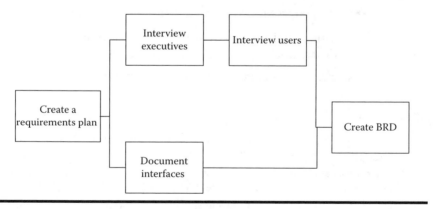

Figure 4.8 Network diagram.

The network diagram is a useful tool to analyze risks, find areas that can speed up the project, and look for resource leveling opportunities. If a more aggressive schedule is needed, PMI identifies two main ways to compress schedule:

- Crashing: Add resources to activities to make them go faster. Not always doable, and will typically increase the overall cost to the project.
- Fast Tracking: Run things in parallel which were not intended to be in parallel. This can cause mistakes and rework, and typically adds to the risk of the project.

The dependencies and constraints that are discovered in the analysis phase will often be related to customer availability and sign-off. Once the draft schedule is created, use that to review with the customers, users, and other key stakeholders to get their buy-in to constraints, assumptions, and dependencies.

4.11 Costing

Most business analysts are not responsible for the cost estimation of the analysis phase, but they will often have input into it. Different organizations count different line items as part of the analysis cost. The following is a starting point for cost items that should be considered for the analysis phase.

- Analyst time: This is normally included and tends to be the easiest cost item to identify.
- Customer/user time: This is rarely included, but really should be if there is an interest in getting to the real cost of development.
- Analyzing interfaces (even if done by other groups): Although this is often the work of business analysts, who are often working for a different department and their time, while it may be charged for, is rarely budgeted for.
- Analysis and development tools: Hopefully these tools will be used on many projects so the current project should not have to take on the whole cost. However, in many organizations the project making the initial investment is the project getting charged.
- Quality assurance: This is often an overhead function and is normally not charged directly to the project. Note that if the QA group does testing, that puts this in a different light. Then it is likely that there will be charges, even for their involvement in planning for the test.
- Process work: Improvements to development processes, roll-out, and training on processes tend to be an indirect (overhead) charges.

Some organizations are starting to outsource requirements gathering. This is likely to lead to a more competitive environment where the costs of creating the BRD will be scrutinized more than what it has traditionally been. Being cost conscious and aware of the financial impact of various approaches will make it more likely that the business analyst will come across more competitive.

4.12 Tracking and Reporting

Tracking and status reporting can be difficult in the analysis phase. Because this is the phase that most heavily relies on progressive elaboration, it is often hard to know how much else will surface down the road. Every time a stakeholder is interviewed, it is likely that more stakeholders will be discovered and that more activities will be added to the task list. There must be a balance between the need to interview more stakeholders, the need to finish the phase, and the risk associated with both. Make sure that all key stakeholders are updated and in sync with the approach and the risks associated with it. If the decision has been made that it will be too costly to interview users in other countries, then that decision must be documented and communicated to all relevant stakeholders. This will allow anyone with strong objections to raise them early on instead of having to deal with them when it is too late to change direction. If there is a lack of communication from the business analyst and it is discovered that some stakeholders were missed in the decision-making process, there will likely be dissatisfaction. However, if everyone is informed of progress along the way, it will be easier to correct any issues from missed stakeholders. It is the difference between a team's mistake and a business analyst's mistake.

4.13   Kick-off Meeting

Once a plan has been created for the analysis phase and the analyst is ready to start capturing requirements, then there is a good opportunity for a kick-off meeting. Kick-off meetings can (and often should) be held at numerous times in the project such as:

- When a significant activity is about to start
- When there are a lot of new players on the team
- When the direction of the project has changed for some reason

This kick-off meeting is more traditional in purpose, focusing on the players and processes used in the requirements-gathering effort.

Like with all kick-off meetings, the purpose of this one is to get everyone on the same page, making sure that goals and objectives are understood, and to build team morale. This one has a special additional purpose. Because the requirements gathering is about to start, this is a great time to get commitment for participation from the different stakeholders. It is a good time to review the overall approaches that will be used to capture the requirements and to make sure that everyone is comfortable with those approaches. These approaches include both what elicitation techniques the team is intending to use as well as which people will actually be involved with providing requirements to the team. This is also a good time to ask who else should be talked to during the requirements gathering process. One of the most difficult parts of requirements gathering in a large organization is to find all the right people to talk to.

A well executed kick-off meeting is started by the project sponsor and, ideally, some upper-level management from both the customer and development organization. Having the right people in the room will show the organization's commitment and will make it much easier to get the users to actually show up for the sessions, fill out the surveys, and participate in brainstorming sessions. Also allow for some team-building time. Because requirements gathering is largely a communicative process, it is important that the people involved are as relaxed and comfortable with the rest of the team as possible. Do some introductions, get some ideas about people's backgrounds and, if possible, set aside some time for socializing. Many projects today are global in nature and consist of virtual teams. It is still recommended to have the meeting in person whenever possible, but if that cannot be done, a virtual meeting can be a decent substitute.

> Having the right people in the room will show the organization's commitment.

4.14 Summary

Although the project manager is the owner of overall project planning, the business analyst should be responsible or at least heavily involved with the planning of the analysis phase. The plan created may be simple for small projects or highly complex for large projects. The plan created by the business analyst should be integrated and really be a subset of the overall Project Plan. Thus, using the same templates, tools, and processes as the main Project Plan makes sense. Also make sure that the analyst's plan is reviewed and approved by the project manager before presenting it to the customer.

Some of the Requirements Plan will actually be used after the analysis phase. Things like product risk assessments will be valid concerns to monitor for the duration of the project.

4.15 Activity

Refer back to the Swede-Mart case study information in Chapter 11. The project manager has just met with you, the business analyst, and asked you to come up with your plan for the analysis phase. Review the list below to determine what still must be developed. Remember that the focus is the gathering of requirements, not the whole project.

1. Project overview and background.
2. Scope and deliverables: Identify three examples of exclusions.
3. Stakeholder analysis: Fill out the stakeholder analysis for Joe Jones.
4. Communications Plan: Fill out with two sample communication items.
5. Project activities: Create a WBS with three layers (top layer being analysis phase) and a total of 15 to 18 activities at the lowest level.

6. Roles and responsibilities: Assign responsibilities to the activities from Activity 5.
7. Resource Plan: Create a list of potential nonhuman resources and subject matter experts you may need.
8. Requirements Risk Plan: Brainstorm four to six risks. Select the top one and create a risk handling plan.
9. Identify who will be responsible for approving changes.

Chapter 5

Development Methodologies and Requirements Impact

*The computer allows you to make mistakes faster than any other invention,
with the possible exception of handguns and tequila.*

—Mitch Ratcliffe

Development methodologies vary greatly between organizations and between
industries. The approach that is selected will depend on logical factors (skill set,
available tools, type of effort) as well as emotional factors (how cool it is, what
the latest buzz is). Selecting the project approach (or the requirements gathering
approach) is a decision that will likely have a huge impact on how successful the
project will be. That does not mean that there is a best approach. All methodologies
sometimes work. None of them work all the time. The trick is to figure out which
one will work best for a specific project.

5.1 Objectives

- Review common development approaches.
- Contrast the strengths and weaknesses of each process.
- Review when each process should be used.
- Look at methodologies both at the project level and at the analysis phase level.

5.2   Overview

Software development, and requirements gathering as a subset of it, is still a relatively immature industry. This means that processes, frameworks, tools, and techniques are still rapidly evolving. In the early days of software development, there were no processes in place. Products were simple and the entrepreneurs who developed them often worked by the trial-and-error method. There was nothing wrong with this approach. On small projects it may still make sense to try to develop something quickly, show it to the customer, get feedback and then rewrite it if needed. Some people actually call this methodology "code and fix," and elements of this approach are actually popular again in what today is called "agile" development. However, as the complexity of the product as well as the number of customers involved increases, it will soon become clear that some structure is needed.

From traditional waterfall life cycles in the 1970s, through iterative and spiral development in the 1980s, software development has now evolved to adaptive and agile life cycles for today's projects. Some of these concepts are mostly buzzwords and are implemented without true understanding of the steps involved, but most of them can add value to the development process. The most common life cycles are waterfall, iterative, and agile, all of which are further explained along with the advantages and disadvantages of each in the following paragraphs.

The continuous creation of new development approaches, tools, and techniques, makes the software development domain appear like a moving target. Part of this is due to the immaturity of the industry and part of it is due to the great differences in the types of projects to which these approaches are being applied. It is easy to see that the process and tools used to build a tree house in the backyard may not be the same process and tools used to build a skyscraper in a large city. But for software developers, there is often an attempt to fit the same tools, the same process, and the same approach to very small projects as to large enterprise efforts. As PMI states in the PMBOK, realizing that all projects are unique is a good starting point.

Most projects are a mix of multiple life cycles where some phases are run with a waterfall approach, some iterative, and often some with attempts at agility thrown in. It is important to understand that the type of life cycle used largely provides a mental picture for how the project is run. There is nothing that prevents the project from doing iterations in a waterfall life cycle, or to apply agile techniques in either of them. The methodology gives an image of how the project will be managed. It tells the stakeholders what level of formality is planned; it shows if this project is an exploratory endeavor or if it is predetermined. In short, it puts the team on the same page.

Most projects are a mix of multiple life cycles where some phases are run with a waterfall approach, some iterative, and often some with attempts at agility thrown in.

5.3 Selecting and Customizing a Process

Good business analysts (just like a good project manager) have a toolkit available to them. In this toolkit they will have processes that can be used in various situations. Some projects may just require a sit-down interview with the customer; others may need to mix in some iterative requirements sessions of gradually increasing levels of requirements detail. Yet others may work best by sitting next to the customer and working out the requirements together in a more dynamic environment. The point is that each situation is unique. The business analyst who always uses the same approach and the same techniques will become ineffective. What worked last time may not work on this project. So when starting a new project, review the methodologies discussed in this chapter, add in your own experiences, and then decide what to do for the current project.

SEI, for level 3 of CMMI, has a knowledge area called "Integrated Project Management." SEI describes this knowledge area as follows in their publication "CMU/SEI-2002-TR-012":

> The purpose of Integrated Project Management is to establish and manage the project and the involvement of the relevant stakeholders according to an integrated and defined process that is tailored from the organization's set of standard processes.
>
> For Integrated Product and Process Development, Integrated Project Management also covers the establishment of a shared vision for the project and a team structure for integrated teams that will carry out the objectives of the project.

So what does that mean? To start with, there are really three main components here. First, it means that an organization should have a set of processes and approaches that it uses for different types of projects. These processes may be internally developed, they may come out of a book, or they may be associated with a specific tool. This organizational library of processes (as well as tools and techniques) is necessary to be able to implement continuous process improvement in an organization. After each project, lessons learned should be added to the process library. This will minimize the likelihood of repeating the same mistakes over again.

Second, a stakeholder analysis and coordination effort is done. Stakeholder analysis is done for many reasons during a project and different views of that are shared throughout this book. At this time the focus is to understand what type of project this is from the stakeholders' view. If their view is that this is a global, enterprisewide undertaking where the company's future success is at stake, then a formal approach will be needed. However, if they view this as a discovery process, blazing the way for new approaches, then a more flexible, or agile, approach would be warranted.

Third, the project's vision is defined, understood, and communicated to all stakeholders. This includes an understanding of what the project itself is all about as well as identifying interfaces, constraints, and critical success factors. Without this being established, half the organization may view this as a research and development project, the other half as an operational improvement.

By the way, these steps are not done sequentially; there is really one effort with three focus areas which will impact each other. When all three are understood, then the customized process for this specific project can be established. This process may exactly follow one of the organizational processes or it may be a combination of a number of them, but this is where the project manager at the project level and the business analyst at the requirements level define what approach their efforts take.

The book will cover some specific approaches below, but at a summary level, the requirements phase can have two general approaches:

- Formal: For projects which are large and complex or for projects with stakeholders spread over many locations and where consensus building is needed. This approach is also good for when the customers have a good understanding of what they want and there is a desire to avoid scope creep.
- Flexible: This is for projects where the end result is not yet well understood. It works best in an environment where stakeholders are co-located and where the projects are either small or can be decomposed into smaller, well-defined, sub-projects.

5.4 Waterfall

The waterfall life cycle at the project level was introduced in Figure 2.1. In this chapter the attention will be on the analysis phase and the waterfall approach as it applies to this phase. In Figure 5.1, the approach of going through the analysis phase one step at a time and finalizing each step before moving on to the next step is shown. This is the key premise of the waterfall.

Step 1 is to understand project and product scope. This means establishing how the project fits inside of the enterprise, what strategic goals it will help accomplish, and what dependent projects there are in the organization. A large portion of this effort is to understand the AS-IS situation in the business: what the problem is, and what the root causes, the organizational constraints, and the critical success factors are.

Step 2 creates the requirements plan (actually the step that was covered in Chapter 4). This step will let everyone know what approach to take for gathering requirements and achieve buy-in from the stakeholders. In a waterfall life cycle, this is based on the assumption that the project team has a good understanding of who the stakeholders are and what the business problem is. That allows us this clean step-by-step approach.

Step 3 captures the requirements using whatever methods were selected during the planning step. This is often the step that the business analyst starts with in a less-mature organization. The project has started and the analyst is asked to go to the customer and ask what's wanted. However, if the two previous steps are not

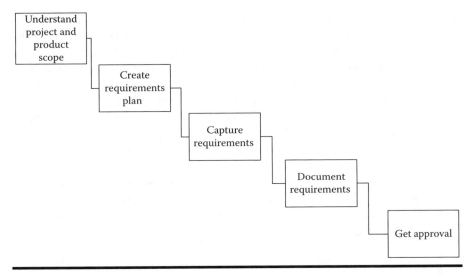

Figure 5.1 Waterfall requirements.

completed, there will be no clearly established boundaries for the requirements gathering and it will be hard to get stakeholder buy-in to the whole process.

Step 4 documents and validates the requirements. Part of the International Institute of Business Analysis® (IIBA) definition of a requirement is that it is documented. In this step the requirements are written down, which can be done using models or text, and then reviewed with the stakeholders to make sure that the requirements were understood correctly. In this book this document is referred to as the BRD (Business Requirements Document). A sample template is included in Appendix B.

Step 5 then gets approval from the stakeholders. Auditability and traceability require formalizing this process. Stakeholders are often uncomfortable with actually signing off on any deliverables; they would like to retain flexibility. This tends to lessen over time if the sign-off is done consistently and if it is a part of the original plan. This step signifies the official end of the requirements-gathering phase and the start of the design phase.

When creating a task list for an analysis effort, all of these can be further decomposed into more detailed tasks such as schedule an interview, conduct an interview, and follow-up on interview results. This process of creating a Work Breakdown Structure (WBS) is discussed in Chapter 4. For the purpose of discussing waterfall as an approach, the level of detail used above should be sufficient.

As shown in Figure 5.1, it is a very distinct process, with clear tasks building on the result of the previous. In its purest form, there is no overlap between the steps; rather the output of each step is an input to the next. It's a manager's dream approach — clean, clear, and manageable. It is an excellent approach when dealing with well-known products and customers that clearly understand what they want. If that is not the case, if the requirements gathering is more of a discovery process, then waterfall can be cumbersome and stifling. Because the intent is not to revisit a decision which already has been made, a great deal of effort must be spent ensuring that the stakeholders understand and buy-in to the key deliverables out of each step. If that does not happen, extensive rework and poor customer satisfaction will likely be the result when the product is delivered.

When capturing the requirements, decide what level of detail is desirable. Some detailed requirements should not be captured until there is an understanding of what the design will look like. If the business analyst pushes for a decision about detailed requirements too soon, it will lead to the customer making up requirements or not thinking through what is really needed. This tends to mean that in a waterfall approach, some of the detailed requirements will not be captured until the design phase, which actually shows that even a waterfall approach will have elements of iteration in it. There is a more in-depth discussion about desired level of detail when gathering requirements in chapter 6.

When to Use
- Large projects.
- Well-understood product/requirements.
- Using proven technologies.
- Enterprise solutions.

Advantages
- Easy to plan and manage.
- Sign-off at each step.
- Sets customer expectations up front.
- Limits revisiting the same issues throughout the project.
- Can easily be integrated with other initiatives at a corporate level.

Disadvantages
- Tends to limit customer involvement.
- Focus is on retrieving requirements rather than discovering them.
- Misunderstandings are often not realized until the end of the process.
- Can cause extensive rework.

Tips to Make It Successful
- Stakeholder sign-off at the end of each major step.
- Use prototyping and modeling to ensure that each stakeholder understands the results of each step as it is completed.
- Focus on key requirements and don't go too deep too fast.
- Realize that even with this approach there will be an element of iteration to it.

5.5 Iterative

Although there have always been projects performed using iterations (sometimes even on purpose), it was Barry Boehm who formalized it in the iterative, and later the spiral, life cycle. For the purposes of the analysis phase, the spiral life cycle is considered to be just a specialized version of the iterative life cycle (which is a simplification, but an acceptable one). Figure 5.2 gives an idea of the two approaches.

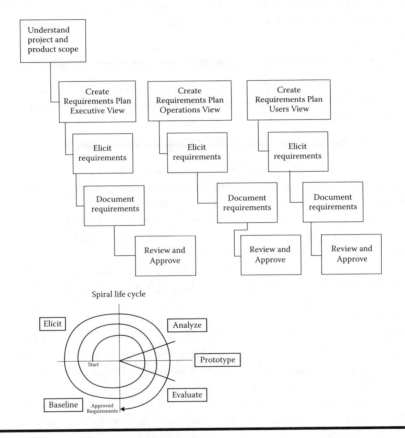

Figure 5.2 Iterative and spiral life cycle.

Instead of the nice, clean flow of the waterfall, each activity is now revisited multiple times, albeit with a different objective each time. Looking at the pictures it is easy to see that from a project management view; this may be a difficult process to manage. However, it is often a very natural approach to a business analyst. The gradual uncovering of requirements, gradually learning more about the customer needs and the resulting requirements tends to mirror the way most people will learn any activity. Start simple and expand.

The first step is to understand the product and the project, identifying the goals and the objectives. This will often be at a high level for an iterative approach, but it is necessary to ensure that there is an understanding of the final destination. Without overall product vision and goals, each one of the iterations will eventually move in uncontrollable directions. This first step is the same start as in the waterfall model. Do not underestimate the importance of this activity; it is maybe the most critical one to the success of the iterative approach. There must be a framework established that shows what it is that the future iterations will accomplish. Not only should this show what the end product will (though at a high level), it should also show the unique goals and objectives of each of the iterations.

> Without overall product vision and goals, each one of the iterations will eventually move in uncontrollable directions.

Next, the first iteration is initiated — in this example; the executives' view. The iteration goes through the four-step approach of planning, elicitation, documentation, and review and approval, often accomplished in the form of a prototype. At the end of the iteration, the decisions and documents created should be baselined. It does not mean that changes are not expected, because they are, but any changes to a previous iteration should be formally documented and be approved by the stakeholders from that iteration. In the book example of C.V. Green and the Prescription Interaction Project, this first iteration would focus on the executives of C.V. Green, possibly including directors of marketing, sales, regional centers, and corporate quality functions.

The process is then continued into the next iteration and the next level of stakeholders — the operations' view. Here the store managers, the pharmacy managers, and other first-level managers would get involved. The steps above are repeated, within the context that was established during the first iteration.

Then finally, the effort goes to the users' view. This could be the pharmacist or the clerk in the pharmacy. At this level the key functionality should already have been established and the focus is on how the user interfaces and detailed requirements will look. There is no theoretical limit on the number of iterations. For the example above there could be an integration iteration, looking at integration with accounting, distribution, and purchasing. There could also be a support iteration, and possibly others added as well. However, because iterations tend to lend themselves to scope changes, it is good to minimize the numbers.

Basically, the product is gradually built and the customer verifies each level of requirements as they are being captured. This step-by-step approach ensures buy-in throughout the process, and it also lets customers gradually refine requirements based on what they learn as they go through the process. The focus of each one of the iterations can vary from project to project, but it must be predetermined. Starting an iteration without clear goals and objectives is likely to result in chaos in the end.

When to Use
- – Medium-to-large projects.
- – Unclear requirements.
- – Research and development.
- – New technologies.

Advantages
- – Learn from previous iteration.
- – Customer sees the product evolve.
- – Customer and business analyst will follow a logical path to create new ideas.

Disadvantages
- – Each iteration may rework the previous.
- – Difficult to contain scope.
- – Hard to know when to stop iterating (like the old Energizer bunny commercial, it just keeps going and going…).

Tips to Make It Successful
- – Establish change control early in the process.
- – Baseline the outcome of each iteration.
- – Treat each iteration as a mini project with objectives, tasks, and deliverables.

One of the most popular implementations of an iterative life cycle today is the Rational Unified Process (RUP®), owned by IBM. It is both a framework and an actual product. It is customizable and has a lot of helpful tools for developers. It is primarily for larger organizations and larger projects because the learning curve can be high and the cost of the product can be significant.

5.6   Agile

The hottest (or coolest depending on your vocabulary) concept in development methods today is agile development. It sounds neat, it sounds state of the art, and it sounds a bit dangerous. It can be all of those things. Agile approaches are great for many development projects, but like all other approaches that have come around in the last few decades, it is not the end-all solution to all software development problems. Keeping that basic premise in mind will make it much more likely that the agile approach will succeed.

So what is it? Agile is really a grouping of a number of approaches and techniques that appeared on the scene mostly in the 1990s, such as XP, Scrum, Dynamic Systems Development Method, and to some extent RUP. Rapid Application Development (RAD) which came onto the scene in the mid-1980s can in many ways be seen as a precursor to the agile approaches, and for the purposes of this book, it will be grouped with them. Developers were contrasting the long development cycles and the development rigors of waterfall, and even iterative development life cycles, by focusing on making software releases that were smaller and more manageable. It is often seen as a risk mitigation strategy, and rightfully so. Studies have shown that one of the largest drivers of failed projects is size. The larger the project, the more likely that it will fail. So, making the projects smaller and more manageable makes sense. Does that mean that agile is only for very small efforts? Not necessarily. Even a large project can often be broken down into smaller sub-components, especially if the approach is to do only a portion of the project using agile methods: maybe requirements gathering is agile, and the rest of the project is waterfall or vice versa.

> The larger the project, the more likely that it will fail. So, making the projects smaller and more manageable makes sense.

5.6.1 Rapid Applications Development

When RAD became a popular approach in the 1980s through books like James Martin's *Rapid Application Development,* it was really a grouping of a set of tools and techniques that could be combined to increase project success. Figure 5.3 shows the three cornerstones of RAD: process, tools, and people, with the premise that the only way to be successful was to focus on all three areas.

At that time, there was a tendency in the industry to believe that if there just was a better tool, all the development problems would go away. Development tools were getting more sophisticated, especially with the onslaught of a multitude of computer aided systems engineering (CASE) tools. Although some of the tools were very good, the danger with all of them was that they often focused too much on the tools part of the development, often forgetting about the development process and the skill sets of the people using the tools. The mantra became "If you just use this tool, all your problems will go away!"

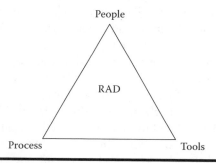

Figure 5.3 RAD comer stones.

RAD discouraged this "silver bullet" belief and promoted a more complete, three-pronged approach:

- People: It always starts with competent people. By having small, dedicated SWAT (skilled with advanced tools) teams, typically 5 to 7 people, who worked together on multiple projects, learning the processes and tools, and learning how to work together, productivity can be dramatically increased.
- Process: Having a well-defined process will make the competent people even more productive because they can take advantage of their lessons learned and spend less time trying to figure out how to get started on a new project. Part of the process relies on checklists and roles and responsibilities which have incorporated past lessons learned.
- Tools: With the right people and the right process, a good tool can now be utilized. The people will be trained on it and the tools will support the process that is being used. Instead of the tool driving the development effort, the tool is supporting it.

Although RAD was popular in many organizations, the reason was not always good. Often management in an organization would complain that development was too slow, too costly, and the quality too low. So, they called it RAD, cut the expected duration in half, and expected a miracle. The miracle rarely happened. RAD does work, but it has many components. It assumes a stable organization and process. It utilizes techniques such as time boxing (set a fixed time frame for development or requirements gathering, and limit the scope to what fits into that time frame), evolutionary prototypes, JAD sessions (discussed in Chapter 7), and CASE tools. If these techniques were implemented and supported, then the organization would see a dramatic productivity increase. However, productivity increased not on the first project, but rather on the second or third attempt, when the organization was up to speed on the tools and techniques and had learned what pitfalls to avoid. Like so many approaches, RAD needs patience.

5.6.2   Scrum™

One of the most endearing things about agile approaches is all the cool names that are used for the techniques. Scrum (named after a rugby term) has its roots in object-oriented (OO) development, even though most of the practices are usable in any environment. It focuses on short cycles, often 30 days or less, where a specific deliverable is created. These cycles are called sprints. From a business analysis view, the requirements are defined by the business owner in the beginning of the sprint and stored in a backlog of work to be done.

In general, Scrum assumes that requirements are typically not well understood early in the process and that they are likely to change during the development.

Also, the development process tends to be unpredictable with frequent surprises. To counter this, deliverables are smaller and more manageable. Each deliverable may be a piece of software, a model, or a prototype. Either way, it is small enough to be well understood by all the people involved.

There is also a strong focus on communication between the development team and the other stakeholders. For example, there is a daily status meeting, often called a "stand-up meeting," with a time limit of 15 minutes. These meetings are led by the ScrumMaster, the team facilitator, who must make sure that the meeting is focused and stays on topic.

There are three questions each team member must cover in each meeting:

1. What tasks have you worked on since the last meeting?
2. What are you planning to work on next?
3. Is anything blocking you?

The purpose of this meeting is not just status, but to make the work of each team member transparent to the team and to other stakeholders. It allows "bad news" to be raised quickly, identifies obstacles that other team members may be able to help with, and lets everyone know of any changes to deadlines or expected completions. Because agile development is less formal, these daily communications become critical for success.

Another key role of the ScrumMaster is to remove obstacles, shield the team from external noise, and in general provide a productive environment. Anyone exposed to a large corporate environment knows that there are many distractions for a project team. Most of them are not even related to the project, such as meetings, reorganizations, personnel changes, announcements, etc. The ScrumMaster's job is to minimize the team's involvement in those activities.

Most of the Scrum process is concentrated on the development rather than the requirements portion of the project, but it is important for the business analyst to understand the Scrum approach. Even though the requirements are defined up front, the assumption is that they will change so the business analyst will need to be involved throughout the process. In addition, the analyst will be a part of the sprint reviews to make sure that the right functionality was created.

5.6.3 Dynamic Systems Development Methodology

DSDM is an extension of RAD. It is taking RAD from the large system, using the Integrated CASE tools (I-CASE) approach, and making it fit for a more discovery-oriented approach. The concept centers on tight deadlines and budgets, and is utilizing some key principles such as empowered team and heavy user involvement, and includes frequent delivery of products which are "good enough" to be used. This "good enough" approach works when the user is involved and can see the effort moving from "good enough" to "perfect." This approach is also seen in the sequencing and management of project tasks. Tasks are overlapping and as soon as a task has enough information from a predecessor, it can be started. Testing is done throughout the process; every deliverable is tested as it is completed. Figure 5.4 shows the five stages of the DSDM project cycle.

Stage 1, "Feasibility Study," looks at the project's ability to meet the business need and also looks at whether DSDM is the right approach for the project. In workshops it evaluates the risks involved with the project and with using DSDM. In stage 2, "Business Study," the stakeholders are again meeting in workshops, defining the requirements of the product, and time boxing the development effort (setting a schedule for each product release with a scope for the release). Stage 3, "Functional Model Iteration," takes the requirements and builds a functional model or prototype which will eventually evolve into the product. The business analyst is heavily involved with these first three stages. Stage 4, "Design and Build," is the product development, and Stage 5, "Implementation," does just that.

When the requirements are identified in Stage 2, they are also prioritized (both functional and non-functional requirements). These prioritized requirements are then matched with a time slot or available schedule to create a prototype plan. The process relies on functional prototypes which are developed and tested before more detail is added. Most prototyping is usually meant to be thrown away, something that's a quick-and-dirty draft, but in this case the prototype is intended to eventually become the system, which was also the case with prototyping for the RAD approach The team's reward system is set up on being rewarded for product completion.

Another key component of DSDM is the risk log. Risks are continually being updated and evaluated. In any iterative approach, risk is an important consideration, but even more so when evolutionary prototyping is being used. Although a clear

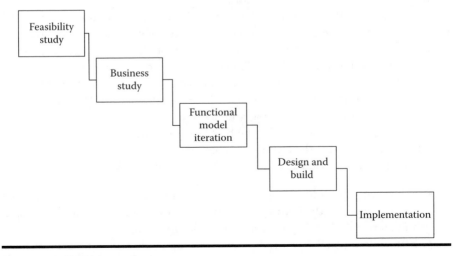

Figure 5.4 DSDM stages.

advantage of evolutionary prototyping is that all the work being done on it will actually be used in the final product, it is also a risk. Any issues, requirements, and conflicts which are not caught early in the process will be more expensive to find and correct later on. There is a danger with functional prototypes when needed changes are not made because too much work must be redone. Whenever these issues come up, a risk assessment should be done to determine what happens if the changes are done versus if they are not done.

> Evolutionary prototyping — any issues, requirements, and conflicts which are not caught early in the process will be more expensive to find and correct later on.

5.6.4   Just-In-Time (JIT) Requirements Gathering

Scott Ambler discusses a different approach called Just-In-Time (JIT) "model storming," and it can be used with any of these other processes. This approach is still based on capturing high-level requirements early in the process, but the detailed requirements are worked out when it is time to develop a specific piece of software. With the high-level requirements in mind, a sub-team involving both users and developers spends a relatively short time frame modeling what the functionality of this portion of the system should be. This allows the team to be much more focused on a well-defined piece of the product. There is less need for large requirements documents because the developer, the business analyst, and the customer work closely together and define, develop, and deliver the product or portion of the product in a very short time frame.

Looking at the Prescription Interaction Project, this approach would probably be difficult because there would be users all over the world, they would have local differences, and there would be a need to have a more formal requirements document which could be reviewed and signed off by everyone. However, the approach would lend itself better to a subset of the project, the development of the online entry of prescription drugs, for example. There would be few SME's, the requirements would be under their control, and it would have a relatively low impact on the rest of the corporation because the business function of entering prescriptions is still the same, it is just the technology changing.

Some of the advantages that are seen with this approach are:

- Minimizing unneeded requirements. Because the focus area is small and there is less of a theoretical "what could you ever possibly want" approach and more of "what do you need right now" approach.
- Better interaction with the stakeholders by limiting the scope of the discussions.

However, there are also some difficulties that may be discovered:

- There are often difficulties trying to get stakeholders together for short, small meetings when the business uses common systems across many functional or geographical areas. JIT works best when stakeholders are co-located.
- Dealing with conflicting requirements coming up in different JIT sessions can be cumbersome. Typically there are different people involved with each session so consideration must be made regarding undoing decisions already made.

With all that, there are many great applications of this and other agile approaches. As implied by the name, agile approaches are agile and, as such, are likely to keep evolving with new methods being added. All of them add value to the thought process of capturing and documenting requirements, none of them should become an obsession.

5.6.5   Agile Summary

This is really just scratching the surface on agile approaches. Many of the techniques used for agile can also be used very successfully with both waterfall and iterative. Other techniques falling in this area are:

- Prototyping: Creating quick versions of the system to reduce abstractness (more on prototypes in Chapter 6).
- XP (eXtreme Programming): Focus on short cycles with two people working together on all deliverables, increasing speed and quality.

In general, for all the agile approaches:

When to Use
- Small projects or projects that can be subdivided into small pieces.
- Projects where it is necessary to constantly adapt to what is learned during the development cycle.
- Small teams.
- Teams which are co-located per PMI.

Advantages
- Flexible.
- Limits documentation.
- Keeps the users involved.

Disadvantages
- Focuses on delivering small pieces of software, may not see the big picture.
- Sometimes used as an excuse not to do planning and analysis.
- Does require training.

Tips to Make It Successful
- – Frequent communication with all stakeholders.
- – Organizational commitment and prioritization.

5.7   Summary

Selecting a process or methodology for the analysis phase of a project is a key decision not so much because there is a "best" methodology, but rather that without any methodology or with one that has no stakeholder buy-in, the project is virtually guaranteed to fail.

As a business analyst, add techniques, tools, and processes to the toolkit and use each of them when and where appropriate. Also educate the organization on the approaches discussed. Customers cannot buy-in to a process unless they understand the purpose of it, the steps involved, and the potential risks in each specific approach.

5.8   Activity

Review the Swede-Mart case study in Chapter 11. Determine how the three main approaches discussed in this chapter can be used for the order systems development. Using the table below, identify risks with each of the three major approaches discussed and identify risk mitigation strategies for each. What approach will you recommend for Swede-Mart? (It may very well be a recommendation which contains elements of all three approaches.)

Approach	Risks	Mitigations
Waterfall		
Iterative		
Agile		

Chapter 6

Categorizing Requirements

How many legs does a dog have if you call the tail a leg? Four; calling a tail a leg doesn't make it a leg.

—Abraham Lincoln

Gathering and documenting requirements can be difficult. Knowing how to create a structure that enhances comprehension and makes it easier to divide and conquer the analysis phase can be useful and is actually critical for success on large and complex undertakings. There are many approaches to categorizing requirements and in this chapter some of the more common ones will be explored. The International Institute of Business Analysis® (IIBA) approach to classification will be reviewed, and there will be a review of other, equally good approaches. It is not the intent in this chapter to promote one specific classification system; rather it is my view that different projects and different business situations need different classification approaches, and the reasoning for this will be explained in this chapter as well.

6.1   Objectives

- Identify the need for categorizing requirements.
- Determine what level of detail a requirements gathering effort should go to.
- Review different categorization schemes.
- Review situations where each scheme of categorization may work.
- Determine roles and responsibilities involved with different categories.

6.2   Overview

Sometimes starting to capture and document requirements seems like a daunting task. It is hard to know where to begin, what level of detail to get into, and it is almost impossible to know when a complete set of requirements has been captured. A well-defined classification system, or taxonomy, can help with these issues. It is similar to going to an automotive dealer to buy a car. It helps to organize the discussion into categories. For buying a car those categories may be interior, exterior, and performance related. For a system it will be different categories, but the purpose is the same: to enhance communication.

> … it is almost impossible to know when a complete set of requirements has been captured. A well-defined classification system, or taxonomy, can help …

6.3   Requirements Taxonomy

What is taxonomy? According to *Webster's Dictionary,* it is an "orderly classification." The first famous taxonomy, developed in 1735 by the Swede, Carl Linne, classified plants and animals. Basically a good taxonomy focuses on finding common elements to create a structure which makes the comprehension of a knowledge area greater. It could be different attributes such as color or speed, or it could be related to different sources like governments or users.

The Software Engineering Institute® (SEI) has developed a risk taxonomy (TR06.93) for software development which is available from the SEI Website. It basically breaks the system down in classes, elements, and attributes for the purpose of evaluating risk, as seen in Figure 6.1.

There are three classes identified:

- Product engineering
- The development environment
- Program constraints

Each class is then further decomposed into a number of elements. One of the elements within product engineering is requirements, and this element is further decomposed into a number of attributes:

- Stability: Are the requirements changing throughout the process or are they well known, understood, and static in nature?
- Completeness: Are there still areas that have not been explored? Are external interfaces well understood? Does the customer have expectations which are not clearly recognizable in the requirements document?

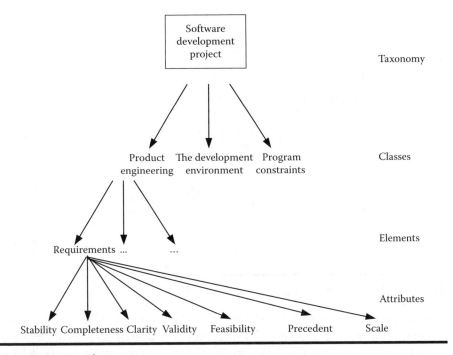

Figure 6.1 SEI risk taxonomy.

- Clarity: Are you able to understand the requirements as written? Will different stakeholders interpret them the same way?
- Validity: How are the requirements validated? Are there things in the product which the customer does not want?
- Feasibility: Are these requirements possible to implement? Have any feasibility studies been done?
- Precedent: Are these requirements that have been implemented in this organization before? Have they been implemented anywhere else?
- Scale: Is this project size similar to past projects? Does the organization have the capability to implement a project this size?

In this example the hierarchy is intended to evaluate the quality of the requirements gathered and the risk associated with them. The business analyst should use this type of checklist during the requirements checking, when the Business Requirements Document (BRD) is finalized and reviewed.

In its basic form a requirements taxonomy is little more than a checklist which helps the analyst to ask the right questions and ensure that all key areas of the business have been covered. Using the requirements element of the risk taxonomy above, the checklist would simply say:

- Are the requirements stable?
- Are the requirements complete?

and so on.

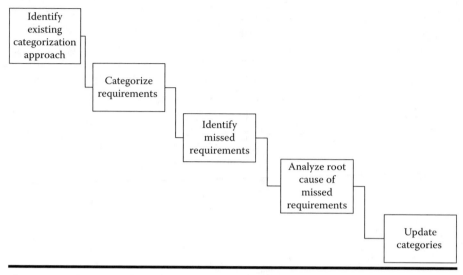

Figure 6.2 The building of a classification system.

In addition to covering different areas of the business, or the technology, it also encourages the business analyst to delve deeper into each part of the taxonomy. For example, a requirements category of "security" may list a requirement such as "The system must limit access to sensitive financial data." This should prompt the analyst to ask "What is the definition of sensitive financial data?" and "What other types of security requirements are needed?"

Building a classification system for an organization takes a formal process and a repository for lessons learned. Figure 6.2 shows a process for building and improving such a system.

Step 1 is to identify any existing ways of categorizing requirements based on the type of project being developed. Often there is no official standard for categorization within an organization; however, that does not mean that there is no categorization being used. If no formal document exists, such as a BRD template, then check with the people who have experience with projects in the organization. Ask what types of requirements are important here. Are there internal, corporate requirements? Are there any external requirements? What organizations will typically provide requirements? By asking these types of question, a rudimentary structure for a taxonomy (or classification system) will start to appear.

In Step 2 the actual requirements collected are put into their respective categories. Put any requirements not fitting into the categorization system into an "Other" bucket. At the end of the project these can be used to identify potential new categories for the future. Some requirements may fit into multiple categories. Decide on one and then make a note in the other category or categories referencing the selected category. Why? Often different categories will be assigned to different groups or individuals for analysis. Adding the reference without putting the requirement itself in multiple categories will help minimize duplication of effort, while still keeping the lines of communication open.

Step 3 is done during reviews of the BRD, during testing, and ideally in post-project reviews. It identifies missed requirements, which will be used for many types of process improvements; here they will be used to evaluate root causes related to requirements categorization.

In Step 4, the root cause analysis is then performed to try to identify why a requirement was missed. Was it due to poor elicitation techniques? Or, was it due to not asking about certain types of requirements? If so, these requirements will be taken to the next step.

Step 5 then updates the categories of requirements based on the input of the root cause analysis in the previous step as well as the content of the "Other" bucket mentioned in Step 2. This newly created list will act as a repository for lessons learned for future projects.

By the time this process has been used on multiple projects, the classification system will become more helpful and actually assist in standardizing the organization's approach to requirements gathering.

6.4   How Much Detail Do You Need?

When looking at requirements taxonomies, it is easy to get the impression that the more detail the better. That is not true. There should be as much detail as is needed, not a bit more. Naturally, the difficulty is to judge where that line is. With the standards and processes from PMI®, SEI, and IIBA in their back pockets, many organizations are now developing large, detailed, sophisticated, and utterly confusing requirements documents.

> There should be as much detail as is needed, not a bit more.

Karl Wiegers states in his book *More about Software Requirements*:

> The requirements may be vague, but the product will be specific.

Karl Wiegers uses the statement to emphasize the need for precision in requirements definition, which is of course needed, but there is also another thought being triggered by the statement. Who should determine the specifics of the product? Does it have to be the customer? What if the customer doesn't care? Or, what if the customer is clueless?

Development organizations often feel that if customers working with developers do not know what they want, or do not understand the business, then the developing organization must push to get different customers involved to ensure that all the requirements come from the customers. It is true that there must be safeguards against making assumptions about the customers' competency, but it is also true that many times customers do not know what they want, do not want to be involved with the development process, and should not have to be involved. The customer's expertise is not systems development or process improvements. The business analyst, together with the developers and the customers, must make an assessment up front on what requirements come from the customer and what requirements come from other sources. Compare it to buying a vehicle. Going to a car dealer, most people would not expect to have to tell the dealer that they want four wheels, a steering wheel, carpet in the trunk, seat belts, etc. Although it is true that the customer would notice (and complain) if those items were not there at the time of delivery, the customer has a right to assume that the product developers will do some thinking on their own. Some organizations struggle with taking on that responsibility. They create hundreds of pages of requirements, overwhelming the customers and forcing them to think about things that they should not have to think about.

> . . . many times customers do not know what they want, do not want to be involved with the development process, and should not have to be involved.

A good taxonomy can help with deciding what the customer should or should not be involved with from a requirements-gathering standpoint. If the customer just wants a good sales-reporting system, they should be able to tell the analyst what type of sales reports they want at a fairly high level (business requirements level), and then expect the analyst to work out the details. The analyst can research what packages are available, what other organizations do, and come back with some ideas that the customer can verify as being on the right track.

For the Prescription Interaction Project, the customer should be able to state that they need a system where they can enter all the prescription information, check inventory, look up customer information, but should not necessarily have to state every piece of data, how to interface with other areas, or what the look and feel of the system should be. That can be handled through organization standards and research by the business analyst and the developing organization. On the other hand, if the customer has strong feelings about what the system should look like, then they need to be involved in the detailed definitions of the user interface.

So when trying to define how detailed the requirements-gathering effort should be, keep the following rule in mind: the user has a responsibility to provide the requirements for the things they care about, but the developer has the responsibility to be able to create a good solution for the areas that the user does not care about.

In general, different approaches will require different levels of details. If the effort will result in buying a package, something available off the shelf, then the requirements should be defined at a higher level, with a focus on what should the system do, rather than what it should look like or how it should flow. Changing look and flow is normally not a good idea when getting a package. If the user is not willing to live with the basic look and feel and flow of the package, it would be better to go to custom development.

Customer development can be broken into two categories for the purpose of this discussion. If the system will be developed in-house with the analyst, developers, and the users co-located, then there is less need for a lot of detailed requirements. Unclear areas can be worked out as the effort progresses. However, if the development will be outsourced, the customer is dispersed globally, or the development team is in a different location, then the requirements document must be much more formal. This is especially true if the development team is offshored, involving time zone, language, and cultural differences. The key here is communication. How easy (and how likely) is communication between the parties? If ongoing communication is rare, then more rigors must be adopted in the development effort.

6.5 Stakeholder-Based Classification

One of the best ways to classify requirements is by stakeholders. By documenting whose requirements have been captured, it is easier to see if any stakeholders were overlooked. This helps with the prioritization of requirements, by identifying which stakeholder is the most important (as defined by the sponsor). It also helps with assigning responsibilities for sign-off.

There are two general categories of stakeholders:

- External: Government, customers, vendors
- Internal: Management, users, other departments

Within each high-level category, add the people and organizations whose requirements may be pertinent for the project. As an example for external, sub-categories may include:

- Local government for building codes
- IRS for tax laws
- FDA for drug laws
- Major customers who have requested services
- Vendors who will provide part of the product

For internal, it may look like:

- Project sponsor
- Product manager
- Purchasing Department
- Order entry clerks
- Pharmacist

Once the initial list of stakeholders has been captured, a review of that list should be done with the sponsor, project manager, and other key decision makers. There are three main goals to be accomplished by this review. First, look for completeness. Are there any other key stakeholders who should be added to the list? Second, evaluate the priority of the stakeholders. Not all stakeholders are of the same importance and when prioritization of requirements is needed, it helps to know whose requirements matter the most. The third reason for the review is to identify representatives from each stakeholder group. The earlier they are identified and notified about their participation in the requirements effort, the more likely it is that they will be available for the requirements gathering sessions. Because these representatives will actually be the people from whom the requirements will be gathered, the process of buy-in and commitment must start as early as possible.

6.6   Sequence-Oriented Classification

Sequence-based classification recognizes that different levels of the organization have different requirements of the product being developed. It also recognizes that these requirements should be captured in a certain sequence, from high level to detailed, and from the upper levels of the organizations to the end users. For top management, these may be captured as goals and objectives; for middle management, it may be operational improvements; and for the users, it may be what they need to get their job done. The following is a description of a possible sequenced-based structure, followed by an example of the corresponding organizations or people who will provide the different categories of requirements for the Prescription Interaction Project. The categories are:

- Regulations, Industry Standards, and Corporate Policies: These may be mandatory or they may be recommendations. They are often documented as constraints on the solution. IIBA does not currently list this one as a category. It is probably assumed that it is included in the Assumptions and Constraints category mentioned below. Examples: FDA for drug information, FCC for how data can be transferred, local government for reporting requirements.

- Business Requirements: This category identifies what management is expecting out of a project or product. When looking at business requirements, they are gathered at all different levels. It is a good idea to sub-categorize into:

  - Strategic: Where is the business heading? This may have been documented in the product vision or within business goals and objectives. Understanding the strategic requirements will tell a lot about executive expectations and can also drive the type of questions the analyst should ask. If the strategy is global expansion, it is likely to create a different set of interviews than if the goal is cost reduction.

  - Tactical: How will the strategic goals be reached? Often the project is part of a corporate initiative which should be tied back to the strategic vision of the organization. The analyst needs to understand what those initiatives are and how this project fits in with them. This is often focused within segments of the business in support of the strategic goals. So at this level the customer could be the director of marketing, the operations manager, or the person in charge of data entry. The focus for the business analyst is to find out what these people need to be able to support and operate within the strategic requirements. The requirements being given here must be traceable back to the strategic level.

  - Operational: How should the business operate on a daily basis? This will include requirements dealing with productivity, training, process performance, security, and other requirements important to the first-line manager in the organization who will be using the system. It will also include information about what reporting and outputs that manager is looking for. This is targeting the first-level manager, the supervisory level. It could be a supervisor over the group whose people will be using the system, or someone who needs to be informed about impacts on the business by the system.

- User Requirements: These are requirements needed by the person who will actually be using the system being developed, or who needs to perform some of the needed tasks manually if that is what the eventual solution calls for. For most users the system is a tool to help them perform their job. Different users are looking for different things. Some need higher productivity, some need more security, and others just need a repository of information. When capturing user requirements, do not be too narrow in the requirements elicitation. The focus should be on what the users need to do in their job, not what they need the system to do (that will be captured in the next bullet). This means that some of the user requirements that are captured will never be implemented within the system. Depending on the solution selected during the design phase, some of these requirements may be automated, some may be handled manually. For example, the requirement of "User must be able take an order" will likely be automated, and "User must verify customer's home phone number" will likely be a manual job requirement, dealt with outside the boundaries of the system.

- System Requirements: What will the system do to assist users in their job? It can be sub-categorized into:

    - Functional Requirements: This identifies the core reason for the system. These requirements concentrate on what the system does and tend to be what first comes to mind for the customer. Examples: "System must allow for entry of orders," "System must print out a receipt." Functional requirements are things that the business would need to do even if the system was not there and the process was manual.
    - Quality-of-Service Requirements: This is an IIBA term. In other standards this is often referred to as non-functional requirements or supplementary requirements. These requirements are really the characteristics of the system. They are sometimes hard for the customer to determine because the requirements relate to the system more so than the business problem that the customer is trying to solve. In general, if there were no system most of the quality-of-service requirements would not apply. Quality-of-service requirements come in all different flavors and can be sub-divided in many ways. Some common sub-categories include:

        - Environmental: Where will the system be located? Are there weather-related concerns? Are there concerns about infrastructure? Are there legal issues? This can deal with accessibility outdoors, or legal restrictions on where a certain piece of hardware can be placed.
        - Interface: Most systems today interface with other systems. What are those systems and what type of interface is needed? The interfaces may be internal or external, new or existing, depending on how the current effort will change business processes.
        - Operational: This can include number of operators, operational environment, and access issues. Does the system need to be accessible without using a keyboard? Does it need to have voice recognition?
        - Performance: At this level the requirements deal with system performance. Process performance is included under Business Requirements, but here the focus is on expected systems responses. How much time is acceptable for the system to look for potential drug interactions? This will potentially drive the design later on. If the requirement is for sub-second response time, then most of the information may need to be stored locally.
        - Privacy: Is there sensitive information which must be kept private? Who should have access to what information? How to prevent unauthorized use of the information? Are there legal issues with using the data in a way that may not be visualized by the customer?
        - Safety requirements: In what environment will the system be used and are there any safety concerns related to that? As an example, if

a navigational system is developed, how do you ensure that it is not impeding the safety of a driver using it?

- Security: Who should have access to the system? Who can see data? Who can update data? This may be overlapping with privacy requirements which bring up a point worth remembering. Quality-of-service categories are often overlapping. It is not terribly important to put a requirement in the right category; the focus should be on looking at a project from different angles to get a complete picture. Whether the requirement has been classified as a safety versus a security requirement is less interesting than the fact that it has been discovered.
- Training: What training is needed for users, support personnel, and other stakeholders? This includes formal training but also "train-the-trainer" approaches and in self directed learning.

   – Assumptions and Constraints: These are predetermined characteristics of the solution. Assumptions are educated guesses. The right answer is not known, but in order to make progress an assumption is made and work is done based on that. For requirements an assumption may be that "the current infrastructure will be able to handle the new workload." As the requirements gathering progresses this may prove to be false and, if so, this will lead to a change control item. All assumptions carry a risk, but it is impossible to make progress capturing requirements unless some are made. It is important to document them and get agreement from the key stakeholders. Constraints are limitations. A constraint it may be that "the new system must use the existing infrastructure." This is a requirement and it must be captured and communicated to the developers.

   – Implementation Requirements: This deals with the capabilities that the solution must have for the transition into the solution. How much downtime can the business afford? Is there a need to run two systems in parallel? Does data need to be converted? Example: "All historical data must be converted and available for the new system when it is installed," and "A system back-out plan must be developed that allows the business to revert to the old system with a maximum downtime of 15 minutes."

All of these requirements should be traceable to and from each other as seen in Figure 6.3. This is a key concept of scope control. If a requirement is found at the system level and cannot be traced to the levels above, there should be an evaluation of why the requirement exists. Is it scope creep? Did a higher level requirement get missed? Quality-of-service requirements are often traceable to regulations, industry standards, and corporate policy type requirements, and functional requirements tend to trace back to user and business requirements.

The following a review of an example of this traceability for the Prescription Interaction Project. For each requirement level it identifies who the requirements provider is and gives an example of a requirement that belongs at that level.

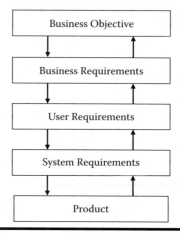

Figure 6.3 Traceability.

Regulations, Industry Standards, and Corporate Policies
Source: FDA

> Requirement: All prescriptions filled must be checked against the FDA recall database for any open recalls. Any prescriptions with a recall issued against them should result in a rejection of the prescription, a notification to the doctor, and a notification of the attempt to FDA.

Strategic
Source: Executive Steering Committee

> Requirement: The Prescription Interaction Project must reduce lawsuits based on known drug interactions by 75 percent. Currently C.V. Green is receiving 100 lawsuits per year and is paying $10,000,000 in compensatory damages. Both of these measurements must be reduced by 75 percent.

Tactical
Source: Sales and Marketing

> Requirement: The Prescription Interaction Project must integrate information from all C.V. Green's locations to discover potential prescription drug interactions with medications purchased at a different C.V. Green location.

Operational
Source: Pharmacy Manager

> Requirement: All attempted overrides of drug interaction warnings must be approved by a senior pharmacist. The senior pharmacist can, after consultation with the doctor or the FDA, override a potentially harmful interaction when a decision has been made that the risk of taking the drug is less than the risk of not taking the drug.

User
Source: Pharmacist
Requirement: Must be able to enter a customer prescription drugs purchased from other pharmacies in order to search for drug interactions.

System — Functional
Source: Pharmacist
Requirement: The system must be able to print out a complete set of drug interactions found for a specific prescription. This includes drugs available locally and for all applicable government agencies.

System — Quality of Service Requirement
Source: User and developer
Requirement: The pharmacist must be able to enter a prescription for one drug in less than 60 seconds. This assumes that there are no drug interaction warnings and that the customer is an existing customer, already in the system.

System — Assumptions and Constraints
Source: Organizational standards
Requirement: All data must be stored in the corporate Oracle™ database, accessible from all locations.

System — Implementation Requirement
Source: Customer
Requirement: Past prescriptions must be converted and available on the day of implementation. Prescriptions from the 24 hours prior to implementation can be converted and added to the system within four hours of implementation.

Similar to the stakeholder classification system discussed earlier, the sequence-oriented classification is likely to need different people involved with giving the requirements for each level. Start with regulations, industry standards, and corporate policies. Then move down through strategic, tactical, and operational requirements, and continue with the user, and finally the system. It is likely to be an iterative process though. While progressing down the list, it is likely that it will be necessary to back up and go through the process multiple times.

In this structure, the requirements should be traceable from top to bottom (and vice versa). All system requirements must come from somewhere. It could be based on a user requirement, or a business requirement, or maybe even an external requirement, but it cannot just appear at the system level. If it does, then there is scope creep or a missed requirement at a higher level. There are two ways of solving this issue. The customer can either decide that this is a valid business requirement, which means it should be added to that category, or it is not a valid requirement, which means that it should be eliminated as a system requirement.

6.7   Purpose-Based Classification

In this type of classification the project is classifying requirements based on the type of functionality desired. Is it behavior related? Does it relate to security? Does it define the features needed? Is special reporting needed?

Tying purpose-based categories back to what was reviewed earlier for functional requirements, one way to identify the purposed-based categories is to ask different stakeholders what they want to accomplish with the system. Another way is to think of it as functions that the business needs to perform, regardless of whether or not they are to be automated. Examples include:

- Enter order.
- Pay bill.
- Collect customer information.

From a non-functional requirements view, the purpose-based categories deal with the things that are needed because of the system. Categories such as training requirements, security requirements, and performance requirements fit in here. They are really the same as the quality-of-service requirement category mentioned above.

Purposed-based requirements are often tied in with specific job functions. What does the order clerk need? What does the Purchasing Department want? Does finance have any requirements related to this project? The advantage of this approach is that it is easy to set up an interview with the representative for that job function and document the result in its own category. However, there are often conflicts between different job functions about what they would like to have the system do, and those conflicts can be difficult to find in this type of approach.

Another purpose-based approach is to focus on key modules of the product. What are the reporting requirements? What are the data entry requirements? What are the query requirements? This is a common and effective approach when the system being developed is large and complex and contains natural modules.

6.8   Combining Structures

The business analyst must always keep in mind the purpose of using a taxonomy. It is used as a communication tool to help identify a complete set of requirements and to group related requirements. It organizes the thoughts of the analyst and of the customer. Identify as many structures as possible and review them to find applicability to the current business. There is probably more than one classification approach that will work well within the business area, but do not assume that any classification system will work. The classification system selected should reflect the customers' view of their business in a manner which is easy for them to follow.

Customers can be frustrated if they are forced to fit a requirement into a category with which they do not agree. Don't argue with the customer; just add a category and customize the classification system for the project. Then, as a part of lessons learned for the project, evaluate if it is a value-added category that should be kept, or if it is just a one-time event. Look at the taxonomy as any other tool that must be customized for each project and realize that the main drive behind having a strong taxonomy is to improve communication.

> There is probably more than one classification approach that will work well within the business area, but do not assume that any classification system will work.

6.9 Summary

The best approach for classification is to start with a simple base, maybe a combination of stakeholder and purpose-based classification. Then evaluate and add on to the structures for each project the organization completes. This eventually builds a taxonomy that the organization is comfortable with and that reflects the uniqueness of the organization's business. When discussing it with the customer, review the taxonomy and also have examples available for each category.

6.10 Activity

Review the case study in Chapter 11. Document a requirement for each of the following categories:

- External
- Business — Strategic
- Business — Tactical
- Business — Operational
- User
- Quality of service
- Assumption
- Constraint
- Implementation

When documenting these requirements, focus on making them specific, unambiguous, and verifiable. There will be a further discussion of how to write good requirements in Chapter 8. Write the requirements so that they will be meaningful to someone reading them three months from now without having been involved with the development effort. If you do that, many misunderstandings will be avoided in the future.

Chapter 7

Ways to Gather Requirements

Seek first to understand, then to be understood.

—Stephen Covey

This chapter will primarily cover what the International Institute of Business Analysis (IIBA) refers to as requirements elicitation. While much of the business analyst's work is structured and well defined, and really is centered on discipline, this portion of the job is more of an art than a science. A business analyst needs very good communications skills, a strong ability to deal with different personalities, and good facilitation skills. This section, the capturing of the requirements, is where those skills are put to the test. The first part of the chapter will discuss some of the drivers behind the process of selecting the appropriate elicitation techniques for a project. After that there will be a summary review of all the techniques covered, followed by a detailed exploration of each technique.

7.1   Objectives

- Identify the drivers behind selecting an appropriate elicitation technique.
- Determine best requirements gathering technique based on customer situation.
- Identify different techniques for gathering requirements.

- Describe best practices for each technique.
- Evaluate pros and cons with each technique.

7.2 Overview

As stated earlier, the goal of the business analyst is to be a communications link between the customer and the developer. To do that, the right elicitation technique must be found. When using the word "elicit" we mean capture, discover, uncover, or simply just write down the requirements. It does not mean invent, create, or guess. Sometimes it may be as easy as sitting down to interview a customer, other times it may take a facilitated session attended by people from all over the world, maybe even with a touch of videoconferencing. Each situation is unique, so part of the upfront work is to identify which technique (or techniques) best suits a specific project. Is this a survey project? How about job shadowing? Will this customer work well in a facilitated session? Is there political tension in the organization which will make one approach more desirable? Each of them have pros and cons and are useful at times.

> Each situation is unique, so part of the upfront work is to identify which technique (or techniques) best suits a specific project.

The elicitation techniques presented in this chapter are from IIBA-defined approaches, industry best practices, and other approaches that I have come across over the years. Although there may be some techniques that are not covered here, those techniques are likely to be a close approximation to something that is covered. It is by no means intended that the business analyst choose only one of these techniques. View these techniques and approaches as tools for the business analyst toolbox. There is enough material here to assist with creating a customized plan for any project by combining and customizing techniques.

Figure 7.1 shows an overview of the techniques covered in this section and some of their main uses within the analysis phase. Notice there are many overlaps in the uses of the techniques. Use the guidelines from Section 7.3 to identify which techniques may work best. In this chapter the techniques will be explored to determine when to use them, and to identify some best practices for them.

Technique	When Used	Comment
Customer Interviews	All situations	Often a subset of other techniques
Observation/Job Shadowing	User requirements Business analyst new to environment User not experienced with systems	Requires time commitment from both business analyst and user
Studying existing systems	Understand As-Is Pre work to customer interview Technology change with old business processes	Can be time consuming Documentation must be available
Studying interfaces	Understand big picture Understand project impact	May involve people outside of the project team
Surveys	Wanting to reach a large population Geographically disbursed population Wanting consistency in interviewing	Realistic expectations on return rates

Figure 7.1 Requirements gathering techniques.

Discovery/JAD/Facilitated Sessions	Multi stakeholder environment Consensus building is needed	Large undertaking, requires formal planning
Focus Groups	Gather a lot of ideas without committing to implementation Early phase of project	Set realistic expectations
Market research	Early research Evaluate what is available on the market	May limit creativity
Evaluate best practices	Early research Evaluate what the competition is doing	Information may be hard to find
Prototyping	Reduce abstractness Bridge language gaps Do throughout requirements process	Use with other techniques from this list
Story Boarding	Speak customers language Reduce abstractness Do throughout requirements process	Subset of prototype but no functionality
Idea generating techniques (Brainstorming)	Early stages Gather large number of ideas	Must keep focus

Figure 7.1 (*Continued*)

7.3 How to Select the Right Technique for Gathering Requirements

What drives a project toward one technique versus another? Although it is often just a matter of what the analyst is comfortable with, it actually should be driven by a situational analysis. The three main drivers explored in this section:

- Customer
- Category
- Geography

There are others as well though. Existing skill sets, past experiences, preference of decision makers, and just plain intuition are also factors to be considered. The selection of the best technique is an important decision. If the project manager decides to do customer interviews and then finds that the customer is a diverse group with diverging opinions about what the requirements are, the whole project may fail because of it.

For example, to look at the Prescription Interaction Project again, the pharmacist will have requirements about the system which will deal with usability, the customers (of the pharmacy) are likely to have privacy concerns, and management will focus on productivity and minimizing legal liabilities. If all of these stakeholders are interviewed separately, these conflicting requirements are not likely to be raised and resolved. However, if there is a facilitated session with all three parties represented, the discussion will likely bring up these differences and they can be dealt with right in the session as they are identified.

7.3.1 Different Ways for Different Customers

The biggest driver of selecting an elicitation technique is the customer. There is a set of start-up questions that must be analyzed in regard to the customer:

- Is this a single or multi-stakeholder environment? A multi-stakeholder environment is the hardest one to manage, especially where there is some level of controversy or disagreement expected in regard to the requirements. When stakeholders from different organizations have conflicting, and maybe valid, opinions about what a product should do, the role of the business analyst becomes much more difficult. It is not the analyst's job to make the decisions or to decide the "right" requirement. However, it is the analyst's job to create an environment where stakeholder prioritization will lead to a consensus on how to go about decision making in this scenario. It will take strong facilitation, extensive communication, and a lot of flexibility to be successful. In the end, it must be the customer who makes the decision.

- Are all the customers located together, or are they spread out geographically? If they are spread out over all of North America, or over the globe, it will take more creativity to get to the requirements. Travel cost, limits of technology, and priority of stakeholders all must be used to evaluate the best technique. Although a face-to-face interview may often be the preferred approach, in reality phone conferences and e-mails may be more practical.
- Is this a well understood business environment, or is this brand new to the customer? If it is well understood, there will be less need for discovering the requirements and more for just documenting them.

7.3.2   Different Ways for Different Categories

When working with executives on business requirements, there is typically a need to be more conservative with the time they need to spend with the project as well as a need to be flexible with scheduling. When working at the user requirements level, there may be a bigger need to actually spend time with the customer while they are performing their work, or to show them different potential scenarios in a prototype. When exploring regulatory requirements, the focus tends to be on reviewing existing documents and talking to subject matter experts (SMEs). The requirements gathering approach for each category should be reviewed independently and evaluated for the best approach. Even though interviewing may be the best approach for the executives of the organization, that approach may not work at all for the end users. Looking at the Prescription Interaction Project, there may be a need for interviewing executives, surveying doctors, and job shadowing of pharmacists.

7.3.3   Impact of Globalization

In recent years, globalization has had more and more of an impact on requirements gathering, at multiple levels. First there is the obvious one, with users and business organizations located in different countries, speaking different languages. Then there is the development aspect. When the intention is for the system to be developed in a different part of the world than where the customer is located, there must be special attention to not only getting the right requirements in the right fashion, but also making sure that those requirements are documented in a clear, concise, and understandable manner. That may increase the need to use prototypes and review sessions including both customers and developers.

There are three obvious concerns with a global team:

1. Language: Although this can be a sensitive topic, it must be thought through. If some of the customers or developers don't speak (or read or write) English (or whatever the primary project language is) very well, this must be addressed early on in the project. It may involve translators, selecting different team members, or just selecting a different approach to communicating.

To avoid the misunderstandings of verbal communication, there should be a stronger focus on models, prototypes, and written communication. Language difficulties, where they exist, should be documented in the risk list, and plans for how to deal with them must be developed. It is a risk that is tempting to understate because it is often emotional to bring it up. It should be remembered that no one benefits from communication issues: not the project, not the customer, and most definitely not the person with the communication problem. Is this a risk that should be handled by the project manager or the business analyst? It could actually be done by either. The project manager looks at potential risks to the overall project and may very well identify this risk. However, because the business analysts are responsible for creating the Business Requirements Document (BRD), they may identify this as an analysis phase risk. Either way, the project manager and the business analyst must share this type of information with each other.

2. Culture: Much has been said about different cultures around the world and the impact they have on communication styles. Steamrolling Americans, team-focused Europeans, and non-argumentative Asians are stereotypes that may be true in some cases, but it is much more important to focus on the people involved and their personalities rather than a whole culture. That said, when gathering requirements from a group of people, it is important to understand the customary way of communicating in their environment. In a discovery session in Asia, there may be a tendency for people to appear like they agree with the stakeholder, while in reality all that is shown is that they are hearing and understanding the discussion. In those cases there may need to be one-on-one sessions to further explore and get buy-in. Remember though that individual differences are often great and that a specific customer in the United States may very well have a more Asian or European approach to communication. So ... be aware of differences, learn about cultures, but don't assume that every person in a culture acts the same.

3. Time zone differences: This is sometimes the most obvious issue when dealing with overseas projects, but it is also often overlooked. It is very difficult to get people together and fully focused in the middle of the night. Some of this can be overcome by doing more written communication and by having each organization alternate who attends the meetings as well as varying the timing of the meetings. Remember that just because the contact person located on the other side of the globe is attending the phone conference at 2 a.m. local time and seems to be on the same wavelength as the rest of the meeting participants, it does not mean that the rest of the team on the other side of the globe will get the same message. What often happens is that there is another layer of communication added where the contact person acts as a go-between who must then bring that team up to speed. If there are further questions or if the contact person missed an important detail, the team may be heading down the wrong path. One good "best practice" is to follow-up with a detailed,

written account of what was discussed in the meeting. Toward the end of this chapter there will be a discussion about some of the tools that can help with communications to virtual teams.

One good "best practice" is to follow-up with a detailed, written account of what was discussed in the meeting.

7.4   Customer Interviews

Although customer interviews can be a stand-alone technique for gathering requirements it should be noted that most of the other techniques covered in this chapter also contain interviews in some form. So much of what is covered during the interview discussion is also applicable for job shadowing, surveys, and discovery sessions.

The basic, traditional interviewing approach is to identify key stakeholders, interview each of them, and then analyze the results from all the interviews. This technique works well when there are only a few customers and a limited amount of disagreement expected between them. It is also a necessary approach when there is a geographically dispersed team, meaning it is difficult to pull the whole team together, or when dealing with stakeholders who have very little time to set aside. When the main approach is one-on-one interviewing it is important to make sure that the requirements are shared with all stakeholders after the interviews are conducted. This will assist in obtaining buy-in and will allow potential disagreement and differences in assumptions to come to the surface. When customers give their requirements in an interview, they will typically state what they think are the most important things for the product, from their viewpoint. There will be a lot of items that they will not state not because of not wanting to do a good job, but rather because they assume that the analyst already knows the information. Different customers will make different assumptions, and by verifying and comparing different customers' requirements, there can be an identification of conflicting assumptions as well as conflicting requirements. Start this verification process by compiling all the requirements in one document and send it out to the whole population that provided input. If there is a concern in regard to them actually reading this document, consider meeting again with them one-on-one or conduct a formal walk-through of the document.

Different customers will make different assumptions, and by verifying and comparing different customers' requirements, there can be an identification of conflicting assumptions as well as conflicting requirements.

There are two main types of interviews. First, there's the open-ended interview, where the interviewer starts with a list of key questions, and then expands on them based on the answers from the interviewee. This is the most common approach and it works well, especially when there are few stakeholders and the interviewer is experienced. If there are many stakeholders or if the interviewer is less experienced, the second approach, a survey interview, often works better. In this scenario the interviewer predefines all the questions and goes through the same list of questions with each stakeholder. It is very similar to the written survey, which will be discussed later in this chapter, with the main difference being that it is a live session so there is a chance to probe into areas which may not be clear.

Interviews, even though common, are sometimes the most difficult requirements gathering technique to perform properly. There is a tendency to view the interview as an informal approach and, as a result, not do enough preparation or not capture the result from the session in a formal enough manner. This is especially true when the customer is someone that the analyst has worked with in the past and with whom there have been many meetings before. When using interviewing as a requirements gathering technique, it is better to use a formal and repeatable process. That will increase the customer's understanding that this is more than just small talk and it will ensure (or at least improve the odds of) a productive session. The following steps are a good approach to interview preparation:

1. Determine the high-level need for an interview. This should come out of the stakeholder analysis discussed in Chapter 4. Because there may be many people to interview and there is often a need to select who to include in the interviews, this initial selection must be done as early as possible. Make sure to review this with the sponsor and the project manager; they may provide insight on key stakeholders who should be included. The analyst tends to select interviewees based on the quality of the information they can provide. The project manager and the sponsor can often point out people who need to be included for political reasons, which may be just as important. In most organizations there are different types of power. The person who has the power on the organization chart is not necessarily the person who will bless the requirements. There are often subject matter experts within the organization, the person or persons to whom the official decision maker will go in order to review the requirements. Always try to identify these "key users" or "super users" within each organization. These are the users who know the most about the current environment. If they don't buy into the requirements and the final solution does not meet with their approval, the whole effort is likely to fail. They can be very rooted in the current environment and may not be willing to accept significant change. Typically, they have been successful in the current environment and may feel threatened by any drastic change. The business analyst should strive for

inclusion of both these experts as well as people with less experience in the current environment. After all, the goal is to capture good requirements for the future, rather than documenting a future that is a personal agenda of one customer.

2. Schedule the interview with the customer. At this time all the details about the interview are yet to be worked out, but there is at least a slot reserved on the customer's calendar. Let the customer know that more information regarding the interview will be forthcoming, but that the purpose of this notice is to give as much lead time as possible. Always show the customers that the analyst realizes that they have a regular job to do, which is important, and that there is a high level of respect for their time commitments.

3. Do the homework. Research the customers' area of knowledge and determine what the boundaries of their involvement should be. Review existing documentation (if any), both for the business area and any current systems. If this customer is not known to the interviewer, also spend some time finding out more about the interviewee: talk to other analysts, the project manager, or the sponsor. It is good to understand the personality of the person being interviewed as well as any personal or professional biases. It is the job of the analyst to distill requirements and to try to remove personal preferences. Sometimes this homework will actually lead to a change in the requirements gathering approach. Based on understanding the personalities involved, there may be a better technique to gather the requirements (such as job shadowing, which will be covered a little bit later in this chapter).

4. Draft an initial list of questions. It always leaves a good impression when the interviewer can show that time has been spent preparing for the interview. It also provides a safety net if the conversation runs dry. Most importantly, it ensures that the right questions are being asked. It is easy to get distracted and forget what the intentions were going into the interview. A sample question list has been included in Figure 7.2.

   Review this list of questions and then augment it with questions specific to the current project. Some examples to add for the Prescription Interaction Project are:

   - Who can enter a prescription?
   - How long does it take to fill a prescription?
   - What are the customers' responsibilities in this process?

5. Update the customer on the details of the interview and provide the list of questions ahead of time. Even if the customer may not read them, it sends the message that this is something that the analyst is preparing for and that it should be taken seriously.

- What do you expect this project to accomplish for you?
- What other projects are helping you achieve these goals?
- What organizations within your company will be affected by this?
- Have you attempted this, or a similar, project in the past?
- Do you have a clear image of what the end product should look like?
- What should the system do?
- What business areas must the system interface with?
- What are your schedule and cost requirements?
- Is schedule or cost most important for you (or are they equal)?
- Have you seen a product like this that you liked?
- How do you accomplish these goals today?
- How will you evaluate the end product?
- What are your criteria for success for this product?
- Does this project have the support of your management?
- What are your competitors doing for these types of functions?
- Are there any government regulations we should be aware of?
- Is there a Union impact?
- Are there interface requirements to other parts of the business?
- Are any other projects dependent on this project?
- Are there any other projects which we are dependent upon?
- Who else should we talk to?
- Who is the most knowledgeable person on this topic?
- Are there any security issues?
- Are there technical standards that we have to meet?
- Are there any training needs?
- Are there penalties for being late, rewards for being early?
- Are there industry standards concerning this product?
- Who is the primary user?
- Who else will use the system?
- Do you have specific performance requirements?
- How will change requests be managed?
- Are there any potential liability issues?

Figure 7.2 Sample interview questions.

When planning for the session, there is a natural flow of questions that should be followed. There are four main types of questions that the interviewer will use:

1. Open-ended ("Tell me about …"): This allows customers to open up and be descriptive about what they do in their environment. It also allows them to introduce topics that the interviewer may not have been aware of. Some customers can become overly verbose here and lose focus; others may not have

much to say at all. If either of these situations is the case, it may be better to use closed-ended questions, which will be discussed next. Examples for the Prescription Interaction Project:

- What do you do with a prescription when the customer gives it to you?
- What are some of the difficulties with the current process?
- What would an ideal system look like to you?

2. Closed-ended ("Do you enter orders into a system today?"): These questions require short answers, sometimes yes or no, and are intended to keep customers focused and to let them know what type of information is needed. Some of the closed-ended questions can be prepared ahead of time, but many of them will come from responses that were received earlier in the interview. Identifying these additional questions throughout the interview takes both experience and active listening on the part of the interviewer. Examples:

- How many customers in a day will fill a prescription?
- Of those customers, how many have drug interaction problems?
- What are the peak hours at the pharmacy?

3. Probing ("What do you mean by 'zero defects'?"): These types of questions are used when there is a need to clarify what the interviewee means by a statement. There will always be some assumptions involved with any documentation, but there should be an effort to minimize them. For example, the customer may state that the system must be available during regular working hours. Some examples of good probing questions:

- Are your peak hours consistent throughout the year?
- Do all pharmacies have the same open hours?
- What does the customer do to fill a prescription when you are closed?
- Do you plan to expand into overseas markets?

4. Validating ("Here are the requirements that have been captured so far. Are they correct?"): An interview can be a lengthy process, and the discussion may have taken many turns along the way. Stop at times and make sure that there is agreement of what has been said so far. Because each step builds on the previous responses, any invalid information captured will be with you for the rest of the process. If the documentation states "All print-outs will be in English," when the customer really meant that "All internal print-outs will be in English, all external customer print-outs must be customizable," then that difference can result in drastic changes to the overall project. Examples of validating questions:

- Does this flowchart accurately reflect your prescription fulfillment process?
- I heard you say that the customers often use relatives' prescriptions, which is a problem. Is that correct?

In general, the flow through these questions would be in the sequence shown: starting with open-ended questions, narrowing down answers with closed-ended questions, clarifying with probing questions, and getting commitment with validating questions.

The interviewer should follow a standard, repeatable process for the interview itself. Although a good business analyst must have strong communication skills, those skills should not be confused with a good ability for small talk. Naturally the more personable the interviewer is, the more relaxed the interviewee tends to get. This is good, but make sure that there is an agenda for the meeting and that the goals and objectives for the interview are known to both parties. Figure 7.3 shows a sample agenda for a customer interview that can be customized to fit the situation.

> …make sure that there is an agenda for the meeting and that the goals and objectives for the interview are known to both parties.

Interview agenda: Prescription Tracking Project

Stakeholder: Diane Walgreen

Interviewer: Bonnie Smith

Date: January 4, 2007

- Introductions
- Establishing boundaries
- Current situation – defining problem
- Identify problem cause
- Envisioning the solution
- Requirements of the solution
- Recap and validation
- Next steps

Figure 7.3 Sample interview agenda.

Start the meeting by ensuring that the interviewee knows what is going on. If the parties are not familiar with each other, then start the session with introductions and backgrounds. It is important to be conscious of the interviewee's time commitment and not to go into a lengthy life history, but the rest of the session will go much smoother if good rapport is established up front. If possible and the interviewees are responsive to it, then get the questions to them ahead of time. That allows both for them to consider the questions before the interview and also to check with other people in their departments.

Also spend some time learning about the interviewee's background and level of expertise. This is important for multiple reasons. First, it shows an interest in the person and that the expertise that they bring to the session is valued; second, it will bring out useful information needed to ask the right questions and determine the right way to document and model the results of the session. If the interviewee has little experience and knowledge in the systems development area, there must be a much stronger focus on validation of the requirements, and the models used to document the requirements would mostly be simplistic and intuitive in nature, such as a workflow diagram. However, if interviewees have been through this process many times before, they are more likely to know what type of information is needed, and they are often more familiar with more advanced modeling techniques, such as data models or use cases. There is a more in-depth review of modeling techniques in Chapter 8.

Have two analysts attend each interview. This will allow one to focus on scribing and one to focus on questioning. They can take turns and tag team, which will be less stressful. It also allows for two views on what the customer actually said, and avoids potential misinterpretations.

After introductions it is time to start building the interview step-by-step on the concept of starting with what is known and then gradually moving into the unknown. There are five main steps for the analyst to follow:

1. Understand the boundaries. The analyst should already have a good understanding of the boundaries of the project at this point in time. The interviewee needs to be brought up to the same level of understanding. In addition it needs to be clear what the boundaries of this specific interview are. Although the project may be focused on prescription tracking, this interview may only be dealing with drug interactions. Figure 7.4 shows an example of using a Functional Decomposition Diagram (FDD) to show the boundaries of an interview. In this example the interview is focusing on process 1.3.1 Enter Insurance Companies and 1.3.2 Enter Covered Drugs. By clearly establishing this up front, the analyst and the stakeholder can stay on track and avoid lengthy discussion on topics outside the objectives of the session. The FDD itself and how it is constructed will be further explained in Chapter 8.

2. Define the problem. Projects are typically done in response to a problem. It can be a regulatory problem or a business-driven problem, but either way the problem must be defined so that the stakeholders can see why it needs to be fixed. If the problem is stated as "Pharmacist cannot see prescriptions filled at other pharmacies," then it may be viewed as a problem, but not necessarily a critical one. On the other hand, if it is stated as "Pharmacy is being sued over drug interaction problems," then that is a more urgent-sounding problem. State the problem in terms of the real impact. The project problem should have been stated up front; here the focus is on stating what the problem is from this stakeholder's perspective.

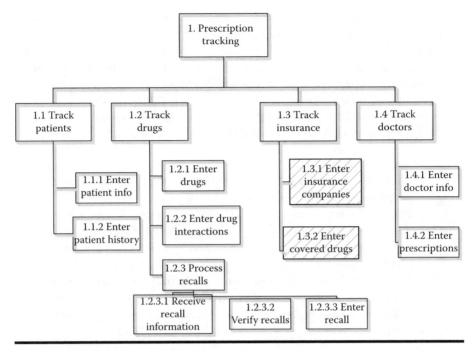

Figure 7.4 Establishing interview boundaries through the FDD.

3. Identify the root cause. There are often multiple causes for a problem. The main root cause may not be within the domains of this stakeholder, but there should be a review of what the stakeholder views as the root cause. There should also be documentation of root causes which have been discovered but not addressed by this project. The problem statement "Pharmacy is being sued over drug interaction problems" can be caused by:

a. Poor tracking of prescription drugs within our pharmacy
b. No information sharing with other pharmacies
c. Patient buying drugs overseas
d. Patient getting drugs from relatives

This project may deal with a and b, but not with c and d. Because that means that the whole problem will not be solved, just a portion of it, this should be documented and communicated.

4. Envision the future. As an analyst there is a tendency to get into the details of a potential solution too quickly. Because the deliverable will be a BRD that must be detailed enough for the systems developers, there is a rush to move from the fluffy to the precise. Instead, spend some time exploring what the stakeholders would envision their job and environment being like after the problem has been solved. Envisioning the future provides context and reality to the actual requirements. It helps transition the conversation from

the AS-IS situation (the problem and root causes) into a TO-BE discussion (vision and requirements of the solution).

5. Determine requirements of the solution. The focus here is on what this stakeholder needs to make the vision a reality. Not "how" it will be done, but rather "what" must be done. This is true whether this is an interview with a core end user or if this is defining an interface with a different system. In either case the focus is on capturing the information that the interviewed party or organization needs to be successful in the new "envisioned" environment.

Advantages of Interviews
   – They are easy to schedule because there are normally only two or three people involved with the session.
   – They can be more informal, which may work best with some stakeholders.
   – They are flexible, meaning they can be rescheduled if conflicts arise, and they can go off into unplanned directions, allowing for more exploration of different issues.
   – They allow for probing into more details than some other techniques. If an answer is not clear or if you find inconsistency in the answers, it is easier to question and explore that when there's only one customer in the room.

Disadvantages of Interviews
   – The customer often feels less committed to an interview. If a conflict arises, the customer often cancels the interview or cuts it short.
   – It is more difficult to control interruptions in an interview than in a group setting. Customers often will accept phone calls or even allow interruptions by other people in the middle of the interview. Try to get their dedicated time and meet in an area other than their office.
   – Interviews tend to be time consuming (especially in a multi-user environment). There is a lot of information that needs to be revisited with each person being interviewed and there is often a need to go back to someone who has already been interviewed, based on information discovered in later interviews.

Best Practices
   – Go into the interview prepared. Have a list of questions and share it with the interviewee ahead of time.
   – Have two analysts in each interview.

7.5   Observation/Job Shadowing

Observation/job shadowing can be done actively (interacting with the user) or passively (using video recordings or one-way mirrors). This technique is primarily used with the end users of the system being developed, most likely the pharmacist in the example used here. It can be a very effective technique when trying to understand what the user is doing on a daily basis, because it is often difficult for a user to spend a lot of time explaining the business and the system needs to the analyst. This approach can be effective because just talking about business needs and requirements without a solid frame of reference can be too abstract. Often users do things without thinking about the details of what they do. Job shadowing allows the business analyst to see the work actually being done, rather than hearing what the users think they are doing (or what they are able to explain to the analyst). A much more productive result can be achieved when the analyst can work alongside the pharmacist and ask questions. However, being observed might also alter the pharmacist's behavior, so that must be taken into consideration.

There needs to be careful consideration of the method of observation used as well as the subjects of the observation. Most people are a bit uncomfortable with the thought of being observed while they are working, and there is often a concern regarding what the observation results will be used for (sometimes rightfully so). The main methods of observation are:

- Job shadowing: This is one-on-one interaction between the analyst and the user. The analyst sits (or walks) together with the user, watches what they are doing, and asks questions (either in real-time, if the situation allows, or at the end of the day, if that is more suitable).
- Video tape: In this situation the user is recorded while performing tasks. The tapes are then edited to get a variety of situations and users to analyze. This can compress the time frame needed to analyze data and may work better in some customer environments.
- One-way mirror-type set-ups: Here the analyst observes the user real-time, but the user does not see the analyst (however, the users normally know that they are being observed). This can allow for observing multiple users at the same time.

Regardless of which way of observing is done, there must be a strong emphasis on building trust with the person being observed. There needs to be a clear understanding of what is observed, why it is being observed, and what the data will be used for. When gathering information for systems development, the data gathered must not be used for evaluation of individual job performance. If it is used for that purpose, then the results will inevitably be skewed and unreliable.

While observation is a great technique to increase the analysts' understanding of what the users actually do in their work, it is also a technique that can be very time consuming and difficult to limit to what is important for a specific project. Because the purpose is to observe what the user currently is doing, it is primarily an AS-IS situation obtained by using this technique. If the intent is to drastically change the way the customer does business, then there may be limited value in the results achieved. Another natural limitation of the technique is that users are observed doing their whole job. Normally what the analyst is interested in is only a subset of a user's job, so too much time may be spent on areas outside the scope of the project. It is also likely that most of the effort will be spent observing the normal behavior (the way that business is normally done), while there are probably many exception scenarios that the analyst would never see during the time that the observation takes place.

So, with all this said, should observation be avoided? No, for many stakeholders it is a great way of capturing their requirements, but be aware of the drawbacks and compensate for them. Supplement the observation results with closed-ended, probing, and validating questions. The observation will give a good base of what the user needs. The interviews and discovery sessions will bring it to the next level.

When planning for observations, the Hawthorne effect must be considered. The Hawthorne effect was named after a plant in Cicero, Illinois, where Western Electric conducted a productivity study in the 1920s. They changed the lighting in the plant and then studied the impact on productivity. For some people they increased the lighting, for some they kept it the same, and for some they decreased the lighting. The surprising result was that for all three situations productivity increased. The productivity increase had less to do with the lighting than the fact that people were walking around in the plant observing and writing down what people actually did. Most people focus more on the task, take shorter breaks, and waste less time by the water cooler when they are being observed. So be aware that the observation of the users will actually change the way they do their job.

Advantages of Observation
- Allows analysts to see what users actually do, not what they think they do (or would like the analysts to think they do).
- Multiple users can be observed at the same time to see what the differences in individual practices are.
- Removes the need to take the user away from the work environment.
- Less abstract than interviewing because the actual work being done is observed.

Disadvantages of Observation
- Sometimes hard to discern reasons for behavior. The analyst can see what the user does but may not know why.
- People act differently when observed.
- A lot of time may be wasted watching the users do activities outside of the project boundaries.
- Recording and documentation may be difficult.

Best Practices
- Make sure all participants know why they are being observed, what is being observed, and what the observation data will be used for.
- Complement observation with interviews and discovery sessions.

7.6   Studying Existing Systems

If the analyst goes straight to the customer and starts asking for requirements without first evaluating the existing systems, then it is likely that the customer will get frustrated. The customer will expect that the analyst has done some homework and has an understanding of the AS-IS environment, especially from a systems viewpoint. Another reason to study existing systems is when the main purpose of the project is to introduce new technology. In other words, the project is driven by a technology change, not by a business change. Customers may not feel the need to meet and discuss requirements because, from their viewpoint, they just want things to work in the future the same as they work today. Although it is a good starting point to review existing system documentation to know what currently exists, it is also important to realize that the systems in use today may no longer be used as originally intended and documented, and the users may have many workarounds for things not functioning well. If those areas are not identified up front it is likely that the customer will get a new and pretty system with the same problems as the old system. This is sometimes a valid approach, especially when investing in a new platform, but it should be a conscious decision, and the customer should have the right expectations going into to the project.

Examples of artifacts to review to get an understanding of the current situation:

- System documentation
- Enhancement requests
- Problem logs
- User manuals
- Training manuals
- Product literature (both for the existing product and for competing products)

Because this can be a very time-consuming effort the analyst needs to make some judgments as to which documents are valuable, which ones are outdated, and how much time and effort is worth spending on this activity.

Advantages of Studying Existing Systems
- Limits customer involvement.
- Might give project a jumpstart with a lot of existing documentation.
- There may be valid requirements built into today's systems that the users would not think of mentioning.

Disadvantages of Studying Existing Systems
- May not have updated documentation.
- May not reflect the way business is done.
- May be time consuming for little return on investment.

Best Practices
- – Determine how relevant current system is to the future functionality.
- – Determine accuracy of documentation.

7.7   Studying Interfaces

IIBA groups user interfaces together with other interfaces when discussing interface analysis, but in this section the reference means system interfaces. User interfaces are discussed in other sections of this chapter such as prototyping, storyboarding, and in Chapter 8 when modeling is covered.

Most systems being developed and used today will need to interface with other systems. Even though it is possible that a system is self contained with a user entering, analyzing, and reporting on data in the system, that scenario is uncommon. Instead, systems are typically dependent on other systems for data and processing of information, and other systems may be dependent on data and functionality from the system being developed.

Identifying the needed interfaces can be a complicated process. Many of the interfaces can be identified by reviewing existing systems, analyzing where their data is coming from and what triggers them as well as identifying where information is being sent to other areas. If there is a current system in place and if the business process is not intended to greatly change, then most interfaces can be discovered this way.

However, if the business process is changing or if more of the business process is being automated, then identifying the needed interfaces becomes more important as well as more difficult. This analysis needs a well-performed enterprise analysis (as discussed in Chapter 3) to be able to see how this system fits in with the rest of the organization. It is typically not enough to just ask the immediate customer. Although customers probably can explain what other areas and systems they are dependent on, they may not realize who in the organization is dependent on them.

> … if the business process is changing or if more of the business process is being automated, then identifying the needed interfaces becomes more important as well as more difficult.

In addition, system interfaces may be beyond the knowledge or even the interest of the immediate customer. A system interface may consist of two different systems sharing a customer database. Each customer may view it as their own database, but from an organizational view, it is preferable to standardize on one common set of data. Processes can have similar interfaces. If the system needs to perform a credit check, and there is another system already doing that, it would make sense to use the same common functionality, which is really a form of an interface. Again, while valuable in the long term, the customer may not see the connection when discussing the project, so the developers and the business analyst must identify these types of interfaces.

Often in projects, the interface analysis is more of an afterthought. It is on the task list, but is relegated to the end of the requirements phase. This is a mistake! System interfaces are really constraints for the product being developed, and constraints must be identified as early as possible. If the product being developed must use the corporate customer database, then that should be considered when conducting JAD® (Joint Application Development) sessions and developing prototypes. If not, the customer may either develop the wrong set of expectations, or may be spending time defining functionality which has already been defined.

Another reason to identify the interfaces early on is because they may need to change. If the efforts of the current project require new or updated interfaces to other products, someone will need to make those modifications. Often those modifications are beyond the estimates done for the project, meaning there is also an additional financial consideration for that effort. Even if that can be resolved, the resources needed to make the changes are possibly from a different organization, with different priorities, which may require getting the sponsor involved to help negotiate for priorities. In an ideal world this was all part of the initial development of the project charter and scope statement, but many interface requirements will be discovered later in the process. When that happens they should trigger a change control request, and an impact analysis should be performed.

Advantages of Studying Interfaces
- Understand system dependencies.
- Fully estimate cost and impact of the project.

Disadvantages of Studying Interfaces
- None; at some level this must be done for the project to be successful.

Best Practices
- Get existing interfaces from developers.
- Review business process changes to identify new interfaces.
- Look for common data and processing across business areas.

7.8   Surveys

In situations where there are a large number of customers or users, or where logistics make it difficult to get together in person, a survey is a common technique to capture requirements. Surveys are good at reaching large numbers of people in a short time frame and also help the customer stay focused on the topic of discussion. However, surveys also have some clear disadvantages. It is sometimes hard to understand how to interpret an answer without the ability to ask follow-up questions. There might also be some difficulties getting responses back from busy customers.

Designing a survey is not an easy task. Most of us at some point have seen a survey that was poorly designed, too complicated, too lengthy, or it just seemed useless. Part of the problem is that when the survey is designed it is tempting to try to capture as much information in as many areas as possible: since the customer will do the survey anyway, and you have the customer's attention, you want to get as much out of the survey as possible. That's the wrong premise to start with when designing a survey. Instead of asking "What are all the things the project needs to know about?" ask "How much can I realistically get this customer base to give me?" If the survey has 100 questions and they are all complicated and hard to read, then customers either will not return the survey, will answer without thinking, or will selectively answer the questions that they are interested in. A much better approach is to pick five to ten key questions and ask them in simple language. With that approach the survey results may actually be returned and the information provided useful.

Make sure to write the questions in a neutral way. Sometimes it is easy to see the preference of the analyst come through in the phrasing of the question. A good question should be clear and non-leading. Also avoid the use of negatives as they tend to confuse the reader.

The following decisions need to be made before the survey questions are actually written:

- Who will be the survey participants? If there is a large population to choose from, a random selection can be used. If the population is smaller and there is a need to get a representative level of participation from different customer types, a targeted survey group would be more appropriate. The level of response may also be higher if a targeted group is selected.
- What is the reading level of the survey participants? Part of the user profiling done earlier in the analysis phase (and discussed in Chapter 4 of this book) should review what level of education most users have as well as their computer literacy. There is no point sending out a brilliant survey only to find that most survey takers either misunderstood the survey questions or just gave up on the whole survey because of the language being too complicated.
- Are there any language concerns? Is the survey population comfortable with English? Should the survey be translated to multiple languages?
- What type of questions will be used (open-ended, rated on a scale, or multiple choice)? Open-ended questions give the survey taker more of a chance to expand on a topic. However, if there is a large population, the evaluation of the survey results will become very time consuming. There is also a tendency for most people to be very brief when answering written questions (or not to answer them at all). The most common survey approach is to have statements with a rating scale indicating how the survey takers agree or disagree with

a statement or question. An example: How important is it that the system supports multi-lingual input? The survey taker can then mark any value on the scale. Most scales have between 5 and 10 options. Some people recommend an even number of options because that makes it impossible to select the neutral, middle choice. Make sure that the survey states which value is good. Some surveys use 1 as the best value, some use 1 as the worst value. It does not really matter which way, but because there seems to be a dominance toward the higher number being better, that may be the best way to go to avoid confusion. The final type of question is multiple choice. This is a good way to present some optional solutions and get the users view on their preferences. This is also a great way of ranking requirements to find out which ones are more important to a large user population.

- How will the survey be returned and who will compile the results? Hidden in this question is one of the most asked questions about surveys. Should they be anonymous? If the survey is not anonymous it is less likely that the answers will be totally honest. However if it is anonymous, there is no opportunity to ask follow-up questions and probe for more details. Review how controversial the survey may be viewed and make a decision based on that. If it is anonymous, there is also a need to set up a process where the survey is returned without anyone being able to trace who turned it in. One way to do that is to have the participants send it to an independent person in the organization who collects the surveys, collates the results, and forwards it to the analyst. If it is not anonymous, it can just be sent to the analyst.

Because there is always a concern that the survey won't be returned in a timely manner or at all, try to involve management in the distribution of the survey. It does help when management shows support of the process and asks the survey takers to make it a priority to fill out and return the survey.

There are survey tools available to help. One that was used to get feedback for this book was surveymonkey.com. It can help with the administration, set-up, and evaluation of the surveys. Currently the Website offers a free basic version and, for a fee, there is a more full-featured version.

Advantages of Surveys
- Can reach a large population.
- Can focus the users on specific topics.
- Can be used to prioritize requirements.

Disadvantages of Surveys
- Difficult to probe into negative responses.
- May be difficult to get the surveys returned.

Best Practices
- KISS (Keep It Simple Stupid). Few questions, easy to read.
- Encourage participation (through management support).

7.9 Discovery/JAD/Facilitated Sessions

This section covers facilitated sessions, discovery sessions, or JAD® (Joint Application Development) sessions which are all different terms for basically the same thing. Simply put, it is a session where the stakeholders are brought together to reach consensus on what the system requirements should be.

7.9.1 *History*

JAD, which was originally called Joint Application Design, was pioneered by IBM in the late 1970s and developed into a formal development tool in the early 1980s. It was a part of the concepts of Rapid Application Development (RAD) as described by James Martin in the book with the same name, and it was also integrated with a lot of the CASE (Computer Aided Systems Engineering) tools that were popular at that time.

Originally there was Joint Requirements Planning (JRP) as well as the Joint Application Design(JAD), but over time they have merged under the umbrella of Joint Application Development. It has also moved from being fairly specialized and integrated with design tools to a method that can be used in any situation where there are multiple stakeholders and where there is a need to reach consensus between them.

7.9.2 *Characteristics of a JAD Project*

Not every project is suitable for JAD. It only makes sense if there is a multi-stakeholder environment where there are some potential disagreements expected. It also requires that there is stakeholder buy-in to the process. JAD sessions can be high risk because they are based on confronting different opinions and creating a consensus solution. Emotions often run high and if the participants have not bought into being at the session, it can be very difficult to keep it on track.

> JAD sessions can be high risk because they are based on confronting different opinions and creating a consensus solution.

There must also be a willingness by the sponsor to delegate authority to the JAD team. If the solution has already been decided or if the JAD team's recommendations are likely to be overturned, then a JAD session may not be the way to go. JAD sessions are very time consuming, and if the results are ignored it will be even more difficult to hold other JAD sessions in the future.

Finally, there need to be realistic expectations of the commitment needed for a successful JAD session. It takes significant planning, training, and dedication of resources to do a successful JAD. If there is not enough time to do the JAD right, it is better not to do it at all.

7.9.3   What Is Created in a JAD Session?

The main goal of any requirements gathering session should be capturing, documenting, and modeling requirements. JAD is a technique used to do that in a multi stakeholder environment. While JAD in itself is a technique, it is also a combination of many other approaches, techniques, and tools. There is no one approach or tool that is better or more suitable for a JAD session. The documentation tools may be activity diagrams, use cases, or data models, as discussed in Chapter 8. There could be elements of idea generation (or brainstorming) as well as prototyping within the JAD session (both techniques are discussed later in this chapter). Like all of the techniques discussed throughout this book, view JAD as a tool for the analyst's toolbox, a tool that can be to used in combination with other tools. Each situation will be unique and any approach to requirements gathering should be customizable.

7.9.4   The JAD Participants

Because JAD is based on group dynamics and consensus building, it is easy to see that the people participating will be critical to the success of the session. There are many potential participants. Below is a review of the most common ones; however, try to keep the numbers down in the session. An ideal number may be 5 to 10 participants. Sometimes the session may have 15 to 20 people, but any more than that and it becomes questionable if it is really still a JAD session where everyone is heard, or if it's more of a meeting.

7.9.4.1   The Facilitator

While the customer is the most important person when gathering requirements, the most important person to the success of the JAD session is the facilitator. A good facilitator can sense how well the team is functioning, can guide the team when the team is struggling, and can ensure participation by all the team members. A poor facilitator will create chaos in the session and quickly lose control. It is one of those many thankless jobs where a good facilitator is not noticed, but a bad facilitator becomes the center of attention for the session.

While the customer is the most important person when gathering requirements, the most important person to the success of the JAD session is the facilitator.

The facilitator should be neutral to the outcome of the project. In other words, the facilitator should have no interest in the result, only in the successful completion of the JAD session. If the facilitator is viewed as being partial to one customer group over another or favors the development organization, the facilitator's job will be made much more difficult. Facilitators can be brought in from a consulting organization and, for large, high visibility projects, that is a recommended approach. But for smaller projects, outside consultants are often cost prohibitive. An alternative often used is to get a person with good facilitation skills from a different project within the organization. As a last resort, use one of the project team members (or even the project manager), but make sure that the person chosen is aware that they are now playing a different role on the project. Instead of focusing on what the impact of the JAD session will be on his or her workload, the focus should be on getting the best possible outcome.

Following are some of the key roles the facilitator will play in the session:

- Timekeeper: The JAD session may last multiple days and normally there are many agenda items to get through. The facilitator must be able to stick to the agenda, determine when it is time to move on, and decide which discussions need to be set aside for a later time. Consider having someone on the team, maybe the scribe or the business analyst, help with this by letting the facilitator know when the time is up for a topic.
- Mediator: Although conflict is a normal and healthy part of the JAD session, there is always a risk that it will move from healthy to unhealthy. It is the facilitator's role to sense when it is time to step in and mediate a dispute.
- Coordinator: There are many groups involved with the JAD session, and the facilitator needs to spend a significant amount of time scheduling participants, facilities, and other resources. It is more and more common that some participants may be attending through conference calls, videoconferencing, or over the Internet. This adds another level of risk which must be carefully coordinated. If at all possible, it is recommended that all the participants attend in person.
- Counselor: This may be the most difficult part of the facilitator's job. When putting a group of people together in a room, some participants may be uncomfortable with the process, with the outcome, or with the other participants.

The facilitator, being in charge of creating a good environment for the session, may need to work with some participants on how to state their opinions and help them become part of the team dynamic.

- Salesperson (for the process): There will likely be naysayers and unwilling participants in a JAD session. The facilitator must be able to get buy-in and commitment to the process and to the techniques used in the session. If there is upfront agreement among the whole JAD team, it becomes the team's session and the team's deliverables rather than the developer's or the business analyst's.
- Clarifier: Not every participant will be a master communicator. Part of the role of the facilitator is to probe and to restate and bounce statements against other participants to ensure clarity in all requirements.
- Summarizer: After a lengthy discussion and before moving on to the next point, there should be some time set aside to recap and summarize what was discussed and what was agreed upon. That will minimize confusion down the road.
- Diplomat: The JAD session will include likeable people and probably some less likeable. The facilitator needs to be the rock that is stable in the middle of emotions and disagreements. The only way to be an effective diplomat is to be neutral in regard to the outcome. The focus must be on the parties agreeing, not on the facilitator steering or driving toward a certain result.
- Team builder: The facilitator must create an atmosphere which is professional and objective, but also where creativity can thrive and the team can work well together.

It sounds like finding a good facilitator can be a very difficult task, and that is true. That is why it is recommended, whenever possible, to use a professional facilitator. Some characteristics to look for when trying to find an internal facilitator:

- Strong listening skills
- Good speaker
- Able to read people (both speech and body language)
- Approachable
- Quick on their feet
- Calm demeanor

When finding that person, train and hold onto him or her. They will be invaluable for the organization.

7.9.4.2 The Business Analyst

The role of the business analyst has already been discussed in general terms, but in the context of the JAD session, the role will be to ask the right questions, ensure that the right stakeholders are in attendance, and provide input in the analyst's areas of expertise. The business analyst should work closely with the facilitator. It is actually common that the business analyst is the facilitator, but it is not recommended. The business analyst would not truly be neutral in regard to the result of the JAD session because that result is likely to have an impact on the analyst's future deliverables.

Going into the session the business analyst needs to explain to the facilitator what the goals of the session are and agree on the best approach to reach those goals. It is typically the business analyst who prepares the questions for the session and decides what modeling and documentation will be used. During the session the business analyst may advise the facilitator in regard to participants who need to provide more information and areas that may need more attention.

7.9.4.3 The Scribe

If the facilitator is the key to a successful JAD session, the scribe is the key to making sure that everything of value from the session is accurately documented. If at the end of a three-day JAD session there is a blank piece of paper for meeting minutes (or a very short document), it probably means that there is a reliance on memory which, even in the best of cases, is unreliable. It is recommended that there are two scribes in most JAD sessions. One of them should focus on the decision-making process and the conversation, the other should document the work being done on the flip charts and white boards. They can also tag team on those tasks, which makes it easier to pay attention.

It takes a special person to scribe well. The scribe needs to understand the topics discussed and to sort out what is important and what is not. It is not a speaking role in the JAD session, but the scribe can and should ask for clarifications when needed. Take time during the session, at natural transition points, to review the notes taken so far. It is best to get consensus on what has been decided upon while the areas of discussion are still fresh in everyone's mind. If possible, bring the notes up on a screen that everyone can see and review point by point.

When selecting the scribe, look for the following traits:

- Good note taker
- Good business understanding
- Good understanding of modeling techniques used
- Ability to stay focused

7.9.4.4 The User (Customer)

With all the discussion about who is the most important person in the JAD session. suffice it to say, without the user the need for the session goes away. Too often the session gets stacked with the people that are available rather than the people who are the most knowledgeable. Getting the right user into the session is not only important for the session itself, it also ensures that the result of the session will be accepted in the end. If the user who attended the session does not have the respect of the people in the organization, those people are not likely to accept the outcome.

> **Getting the right user into the session is not only important for the session itself, it also ensures that the result of the session will be accepted in the end.**

Negotiate for the right user. There is a tendency to just accept the person selected by management, and it may be true that there is no option. But start by identifying the characteristics that would make the ideal participants, including criteria such as subject matter knowledge, experience in the organization, reputation, and ability to work in a group environment. If those criteria have been communicated ahead of time it will also be easier to come back and ask for a replacement candidate if the first one does not work out.

It is also important to have a cross-section of users. The experienced user can provide big-picture views and will know what is important to the organization. However, the novice user may be better at explaining what the difficulties are in today's environment. The things the novice struggles with on a daily basis may never come up when you talk to the experienced user who has learned how to work around those areas.

The user must be trained on all the techniques used in the JAD session, and must understand the JAD process itself as well as have a clear understanding of how to read and use any of the modeling techniques used in the session.

7.9.4.5   The Subject Matter Experts

Sometimes there will be a need to bring in SMEs to a JAD session. They may bring expertise on a topic of discussion, the capabilities of a new technology, or information about government regulations. SMEs are in the session to provide information, not to be decision makers. They would typically only stay for a portion of the session.

When involving SMEs, make sure that they are acceptable to all parties in the session. If SMEs are brought in by one user to support their viewpoint it must be ensured that the SMEs are objective and their only role is to explain facts.

7.9.4.6 The Developer

It is important for the developers to be at the JAD session to gain an understanding of the customer's thought process and to understand what will be asked of them. The developers, though, should not play a major role in the early JAD sessions. They must be given clear instructions on what to discuss and what to stay out of. In the early JAD sessions the purpose is to understand what the requirements are, not how they will be implemented. Naturally, the developers' minds will be thinking about how this will be implemented, but that topic is for a different time, quite possibly a later JAD session.

In the early JAD sessions the purpose is to understand what the requirements are, not how they will be implemented.

Part of a requirements JAD session is often to discuss potential solutions to make the systems discussion less abstract. There may be a prototype or a similar product being used to frame the discussion around requirements. The developers will play a key role in developing and presenting those, but always keep in mind that the focus should be on "what" before "how."

Also be aware of the ratio between developers and customers. Some JAD sessions will have two or three customers and eight to ten developers. That is not a good ratio as the customers are likely to feel that it is a developer session rather than a customer session.

7.9.4.7 The Sponsor

The role of the sponsor varies from organization to organization. Here sponsor is defined as the champion of the project within the customer organization. This may in fact be the paying customer, but it does not have to be. The sponsor is an escalation point for the project, meaning the person who removes obstacles on the customer side.

There are strong disagreements in regard to the sponsor attending the JAD session. Some organizations prefer to have the sponsor in for the kick-off and then have them leave; in other organizations the sponsor stays the whole time. There are pluses and minuses either way. On the plus side, with the sponsor there, you have a quick escalation process, and it shows the commitment of the organization. On the minus side, if the sponsor will intimidate other participants and stifle a free exchange of ideas, it is probably better to keep him or her out of there.

Regardless of whether or not the sponsor attends the session, they are key to the JAD preparation process. It is much easier to get organizational commitment to attend JAD sessions and to send the best representative when the sponsor is asking for the resources. This is especially true if the sponsor is well respected within the organization. The sponsor should also be the one setting the stage in the kick-off meeting, laying out the goals and objectives and showing the organizational commitment to the effort.

7.9.4.8   Observers

Observers are not really participants of the session, but are typically there to either learn about the project or to learn about how to conduct a JAD session. They can be future facilitators, business analysts, or scribes who are being trained in the details of how to conduct a JAD session. It is also possible to treat the developers as observers, especially in the early session.

The rules for the observers are simple: stay quiet and don't interfere with the session. The facilitator may ask for feedback during breaks, but during the session it will just add confusion if the observers are interacting with the participants.

7.9.5   The JAD Process

Although there are many JAD processes defined in different books, a simple four-step approach as seen in Figure 7.5 will be used as an example.

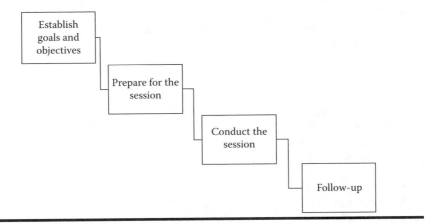

Figure 7.5 JAD process.

7.9.5.1   Establish Goals and Objectives

The JAD session is a sub-project within the analysis phase and needs to be treated as such. There can be one or many JAD sessions conducted to capture requirements. If there are multiple sessions, there should be goals and objectives established both for the overall effort as well as for each individual session. Don't just state the goal as "gather requirements" for multiple sessions. Rather, each session should have a unique objective and a unique deliverable. Otherwise, there will be a tendency by the users not to get real serious until the last session.

7.9.5.2   Prepare for the Session

The JAD checklist in Figure 7.6 is a tool that can be used as a starting point for planning and executing a JAD session to help ensure nothing is forgotten. Because

---

Initial
- Define who the sponsor is
- Determine the goals and objectives
- Establish participating organization
- Determine what process to use
- Determine who the Project leader is

Research
- Become familiar with business environment
- Research similar products
- Select participants

Workshop Plan
- Hold kick-off meeting
- Create Agenda
- Prepare materials
- Prepare room
- Create Straw man (initial thoughts to kick off session)
- Train participants
- Script the session
- Dry run of session (practice)

The Session
- Opening speech
- Review agenda
- Review Objectives
- Establish ground rules
- Get buy-in to process
- Conduct the session
- Document issues

Follow-Up
- Complete Documentation
- Present result to Sponsor
- Evaluate the process
- Follow up on issues
- Feedback of end result to participants

Figure 7.6 JAD checklist.

every JAD session will be unique, make sure to customize the process to fit the specific environment of the current project.

Select a location where interruptions can be minimized. It should be away from the customer work environment. There should be enough room to comfortably facilitate the session and it is a plus if refreshments can be provided. Well-fed people tend to be more open for consensus building. A sample room layout is shown in Figure 7.7.

Figure 7.7 JAD room.

Notice the U-shape layout of the tables. This serves three purposes. First, it allows everyone to see everyone else. Second, there's no head of the table so everyone is equal (at least from a seating standpoint). Third, it gives the facilitator great access to all participants, especially if there are any problem participants. If there are two people having a side conversation, it is easy for the facilitator to walk into the U-shape and stand right next to the people talking while continuing the facilitation. Most people (but not all) will take the hint and quiet down.

Decide and communicate what the format of the deliverable from the session will be. Will it be a text document? Is there a template being used? What modeling techniques will be in the session? The participants must know this going into the session and in some cases they may need training to become familiar with some of those deliverables and modeling techniques.

Create an agenda for the session and send it out to the participants ahead of time. Make sure to include some contingency time in the agenda. Have some extra time added to the end of the day's activities, or try to place some activities on the agenda that can be skipped if there is a need for it. Don't make the agenda fluffy, because then the participants will not take it seriously. Plan for surprises. Allowing the participants a chance to review the agenda ahead of time gives them a chance to voice any concerns in regard to why they should attend the sessions, and maybe even suggest some other people who should be attending. Those are concerns that are better addressed prior to the session rather than during it.

7.9.5.3 Conduct the Session

The session can be started with a kick-off meeting, if that has not already taken place. It is recommended that the kick-off is made a separate event, but that is not always possible due to time restrictions or sometimes due to people traveling in for the JAD session. There should be some form of ice-breaker in the beginning of the session. Sometimes this is viewed as too juvenile and is skipped, but there is a real need to mark this as the beginning of a new endeavor for the team and as an occasion to establish a team identity.

Also make sure to establish ground rules up front. There are some obvious ones such as:

- Turn off (or silence) cell phones.
- No personal attacks.
- Return on time after breaks.

But there are also some ground rules that will vary from session to session. In some sessions the team may limit discussion on any one item to ten minutes, in others the team may decide to go until consensus has been reached. Also in some sessions the team may vote on a decision, in others there may have to be full agreement by the whole team. When establishing the ground rules, they should be suggested and approved by the team itself. The facilitator may suggest one or two to get the team started, but the real decision and buy-in must come from the team. That way the rules belong to the team and are more likely to be enforced by the team, making the facilitator's job much easier.

When conducting a JAD session or any team activity, it is good to be aware of what the state of the team is. Are the members working well together? Are they fighting? Are they even talking? A good model for the stages that a team goes through is shown in Figure 7.8. The figure 7.8 shows the steps a team goes through from the first time the members meet each other until they are a fully functioning, productive team. In the forming stage, the team members are hesitant, there is limited interaction, and no one wants to speak up for fear of looking stupid. The facilitator needs to do more controlling in this stage. There should be specific activities, ice-breakers, and team assignments to force the team members to open up and start interacting. Once they do, they move into the storming stage. This stage can be uncomfortable for the team, but it is critical. Here the team members start testing the knowledge and resolve of other team members. Arguments are frequent and tempers often flare. The role of

Stage	Group Functions	Leadership style
Forming	Poorly	Autocratic
Storming	Poor-Ok	Guiding
Norming	Ok	Democratic
Performing	Well	Hands-off

Figure 7.8 Forming/storming/norming/performing.

the facilitator is to minimize bloodshed, but also to step back and let the team sort it out. As the issues are sorted out, the team moves into the norming stage. It is during this stage that each member of the team starts falling into their natural role and responsibilities and utilizing the strengths of the team. Once that is complete, you have a performing team. At this point the facilitator's job becomes easier and the team pretty much manages itself with the facilitator just guiding. Be aware that as soon as the topics of discussion change or the team members are changed, the process starts over again. Good facilitators learn to observe the team and determine what stage it is in and then adjust their facilitation style based on that.

Once the session is underway, the facilitator's job is to assess whether the goals and objectives of the session are being met. Those goals and objectives should be posted in the JAD room and used to determine if a discussion pertains to meeting those objectives. There will be many topics that are near and dear to the participants, they may even be important for the project itself. But at this point, if they are not relevant to the objectives of this session, then they should be set aside. A tool that is useful for these situations is the parking lot. The parking lot should be on a white board or flip chart, visible to all in the session. Whenever a topic is brought out that is not part of the scope of this session or a topic has been going on for too long and it needs escalation, then it is put on the parking lot for later action. Although it is true that in many cases there is a plan to come back and look at the items in the parking lot, quite often it is just a techniques for the facilitator to get the group to move on and accomplish the actual objectives of the session. It is sometimes easier to diffuse an issue and move off a topic by telling a strong-minded stakeholder: "Yes, that's a valid point, but outside of the scope of this session. Let's put it in the parking lot and assign someone to look into it after the session."

Time keeping is another focus area for the facilitator during the session itself. It often works well to delegate this to someone on the team who will track the agenda and the clock and point out when it is time to wrap up a topic. So, what to do when it is time to end a discussion and the team wants to keep going? This is actually a common problem and there are different options to consider depending on the circumstances. Some of the more popular are:

- Assign a sub-team of the JAD group to take the discussion offline and come back with a recommendation. This is often a great way to solve the issue unless the rest of the topics in the JAD session depend on a resolution of this issue.
- Review the agenda for other items that can be deferred while the current discussion is extended. There should be some contingency set aside on the agenda by the facilitator for this type of occasion. There may also be a topic later on the agenda that can be shortened or deferred to a sub-team.
- End the discussion and vote on a decision. Although this is not usually the best way to go, sometimes enough is enough and it is time to make a decision and move on. The decision itself should not be the facilitator's; however, a strong facilitator can drive the team to make a decision on the issue being discussed.

One of the main purposes of a JAD session is to build consensus. Having consensus obviously makes the rest of the project much easier and improves the odds of having strong buy-in to the final solution. But how is this actually achieved? First of all there must be a clear definition of what is meant by consensus. Does it mean that everyone on the team will love it and agree that it is the ultimate way to go? Or does it mean that the participants agree not to agree and vote on the outcome? Or is it that even though it may not be what each participant would have preferred, they all agree to support and live with the decision outside of the JAD room? Although it is up to the team to decide, and voting is a common option to make a decision, the recommendation for a real consensus is that each person is willing to support the decision outside of the room.

In my past experience working with Saturn Corporation, I saw a great example of having a corporate focus on operating through consensus. In their JAD sessions they would often use a Red/Yellow/Green approach to reach agreement. It is an approach fairly common in the industry. The basic premise is that when a decision is needed, each team member has to state where they stand and why. The three options are:

1. Red: Against the decision, and not willing to support it. However, it is not enough to just show red. It is also the responsibility of the person showing red to let the team know what it would take to get him or her to yellow.
2. Yellow: Not in favor of the decision, but willing to support it. Again, this person needs to state what it will take for him or her to get to green.
3. Green: In favor of the decision.

It takes patience and trust to build consensus. It is likely that in the first few JAD sessions, there will be hesitation and some game playing by the team members to try to get it their way. There is a tendency in most organizations to have a win–lose attitude, meaning that for one party to win, the other party must lose. For the consensus process to work, that attitude must change to one of win–win.

There is a need to listen, open mindedly, to the opposing views and to find a way to tweak the decision, or to augment it, to find an option that both parties view as a good option.

There is a tendency in most organizations to have a win–lose attitude, meaning that for one party to win, the other party must lose. For the consensus process to work, that attitude must change to one of win–win.

An example: On the Prescription Tracking Project, Ray, the pharmacy manager wants to be able to track how long it takes for each pharmacist to fill a prescription. Meanwhile, Diane, the pharmacist representative, is uncomfortable with that; she feels that it will encourage the managers to view it as a way to measure individual performance and fears that it may lead to the pharmacist sacrificing customer satisfaction to rush the fulfillment of the prescription. After further discussion it is found that Ray really doesn't care about evaluating an individual's performance, but rather to evaluate the overall efficiency of the pharmacy. Diane doesn't mind the measurement, but doesn't want it attached to a certain individual. After further discussion it is decided to attach the time measurement to the prescription drug rather than to the pharmacist. That satisfies both parties' goals. Although it is not realistic to always find a solution that satisfies everyone, it is possible more often than not. It takes a willingness to listen and to be flexible with expectations.

One final point on conducting the JAD session: because they are often lengthy there will be a need for breaks and maybe for lunch as well. Sometimes it is difficult to get the team back to the room again after breaks. Make sure that one of the ground rules deals with breaks and sets the expectation to return from them on time. If there is a need for the JAD team members to check back in with the office during breaks, it may be smarter to have less frequent but longer breaks, allowing for checking e-mails and voice mails.

7.9.5.4 Follow-Up

There will be a lot of documentation coming out of a JAD session, especially a session that may have gone on for three days or more. Don't try to send out a play-by-play review of the session, rather focus on the decisions made and the rationale for the decisions. If the scribe did a good job, and if there were frequent reviews of the documentation during the session, this final deliverable should be ready to go very shortly after the JAD session. Sometimes there is a desire to wordsmith the documentation to make it perfect. Although it certainly should look professional, time is of the essence and a normal JAD deliverable should be ready to go out to the team within a day of the session. This excludes any prototype development needed if that was a part of the deliverables. The first round of the follow-up should go to the JAD team members only, with a request for a quick review and approval. Once that has been accomplished, the document can go out to a wider distribution. Then if there are disagreements, the JAD team is formally behind the document. Some of the outputs from the JAD session, such as models, prototypes, and decisions made, should also be added into the BRD.

7.9.6   Facilitation

The importance of strong facilitation for a successful JAD session has already been stated. Although it is recommended that a professional facilitator is used, most projects will need to find and train an internal resource. In my JAD workshops there is an activity on facilitation fears and another one on problem participants. Over the years those activities have generated a wealth of information that demonstrates that most people have some fears about being a facilitator, and also that most of us have been exposed to problem participants many times in both JAD sessions and regular meetings.

The most common facilitation fears are:

- Fear of public speaking
- Fear of losing control of the session
- Fear of not knowing the topic
- Fear of silence
- Fear of not meeting objectives

What can be done to deal with these fears? The simplest answer is to prepare. Because JAD sessions are high risk and high pressure, the facilitator must set aside sufficient time to prepare for the session. A facilitator must practice facilitation to be successful. The first time a facilitator is doing a JAD session with a customer should not be the first time they are facilitating. Practice by facilitating meetings and doing dry runs (practice runs) of the actual JAD session with the internal project team. This will give practice both for facilitation techniques as well as the modeling and documentation approach that is planned for the session. Another way is to join public speaking organizations where the facilitator can get used to talking in front of a group.

Meet with all participants ahead of time. If the fear is losing control or a silent team, knowing the participants and having met with them ahead of time will help minimize this. It is important for the facilitator to have a good understanding of the topic of the session. It is not good if the facilitator looks lost during the session. However, the facilitator is not intended to be the expert, but must have enough knowledge to be able assess how well the session is going. Beyond that, the good facilitator will use the knowledge of the team.

Make sure that each of the JAD participants are clear on what the objectives are. It is also worth remembering that not all objectives are reachable. The purpose of the session may be to gain consensus on requirements, but there may be mutually exclusive interests from the participants, in which case there may be a need to escalate to the sponsor.

The term problem participant is probably better to stay away from, even though that is what it often feels like when the JAD team appears out of control in the middle of the session. It is better to focus on problem behavior. One reason is that behavior is easier to change (sometimes) than the actual participants. What are some common behavior issues and what can the facilitator do to deal with them?

- The Talker: Some people talk more than others. It is never the intention to have equal participation in a JAD session, but it is the intention to have equal opportunity for participation. If someone monopolizes the discussion, the facilitator must address it. Within the session the facilitator can steer the conversation to other participants by asking them to comment on what has been said. Outside of the session, on a break, talk to the Talker on the side and tell them that although you appreciate their ideas and enthusiasm, there is also a need for some of the less outgoing people to be comfortable in voicing their comments. If done correctly, the Talker can become an ally of the facilitator.
- The Quiet One: This is a case where it helps if the facilitator has actually met with the person ahead of time and gotten to know their personality. Some people are quiet because they are uncomfortable speaking up and some are quiet because they don't have anything to say (a rare but desirable quality). Be careful about putting too much spotlight on the person as that may just cause them to withdraw even more. Try to find a topic where the pre-session conversations showed that this person had an interest, and then draw the person into the conversation. A good ice-breaker in the beginning of the JAD session can also help with this.
- The Disagreer: This is not a real word, but maybe it should be. Whatever term is used, the Disagreer is easy to find in a meeting. While there could be many causes for disagreement, the one that is discussed here is the opponent of the project. The Disagreer doesn't like the project, doesn't agree with the objectives, and would be very happy if the project was cancelled. Start by doing some root-cause analysis. What is the reason for the disagreement? Does the person feel there is a better way, or that they should have been involved earlier? Or is this a project which will, if successful, have some negative impact upon their working condition?
- The One Nobody Understands: Some people have difficulties articulating their ideas. This is probably the most sensitive situation to deal with. It takes a lot of patience from the facilitator and some hard work. Try restating what

the person said and ask for confirmation. Prototyping and using live examples may also help narrow down the discussion. The goal is to understand the point the person is making without making them feel uncomfortable.

- Side Bars: A JAD session can quickly deteriorate if there are multiple conversations going on at the same time. That said, it is normal in a creative environment to have some one-on-one interaction between the team members. The facilitator must find the balance between too much control and too much chaos.
- The Attacker: This is the person responding to someone else in the session with "That was the stupidest thing I heard you say since last time you opened your mouth." For this scenario the facilitator must step in. It is easy for a session like this to deteriorate into name calling, and this person would definitely move it in that direction. First of all, there should be a ground rule dealing with personal attacks; if there is not, it is OK to add it at any point. It is also recommended that the facilitator raises the issue with the person during a break. If it is a serious attack, it may be worth taking the break right then to make sure that the session does not get off track. Although it is OK to address it in the session itself, be careful with that because it may just make the person defensive. One-on-one communication tends to work better for negative conversations.

7.9.7   JAD Summary

Few people are successful with their first JAD session. But after finding a toolset that the participants are comfortable with and the organization gets more comfortable with the concepts, it can be a major improvement to an organization's requirements gathering. It does take a large investment in training and in time, so JAD should not be something that is introduced to an organization unless there is a strong commitment to it.

Advantages of JAD
- User involvement and ownership.
- All players hear the same message.
- Disagreements are solved at the session.

Disadvantages of JAD
- Can generate conflict.
- Hard to facilitate.
- Takes high level of organizational commitment.

Best Practices
- Select a top-notch facilitator.
- Use multiple scribes.
- Hold session offsite.
- Have clear goals and objectives for each session.

7.10 Focus Groups

Focus groups are similar to JAD sessions, but the group in the session is advising, not decision making. They are typically used when developing a product for a large user base to find out what features most users are interested in. There can be more people in a focus group because there tends to be less controversy. The outcome is not a consensus decision, but rather some ideas for the team to consider. The sessions tend to be shorter and they can be with people from one area of the population (all Accounts Payable clerks or all executives), called a homogenous focus group, or they can be with a cross-section of people, called a heterogeneous focus group.

Like JAD sessions, the focus groups need to be well facilitated, but it is a different form of facilitation. Because the purpose is to gather opinions and ideas, it is important to create a positive atmosphere in the room. There is not as much concern about participation, and if someone wants to mentally check out, that's not a disaster either. With focus groups it is more common to look for volunteers, trying to find the people that are interested in enhancing the product on which they are working. Some of the ideas coming out of a focus group can be used as input into later decision-making JAD sessions. The players in focus groups are pretty much the same as in the JAD session except there is a larger group of users.

When using homogenous focus groups, the session typically deals with the details of a process or work function. A detail flowchart or process model may be a good modeling technique to use in this type of session to stay on track. For a heterogeneous focus group, a workflow or swim-lane diagram may work best because the main interest here is on communication or interfaces between functions and organizations. These techniques will be explored in Chapter 8.

Advantages of Focus Groups
  - Generate a lot of ideas in a short time frame.
  - Can get input from a large number of existing users.

Disadvantages of Focus Groups
  - Can deteriorate because they are not decision makers.
  - Difficult to keep on track.

Best Practices
  - Set realistic expectations up front. The participants must realize that their recommendations may not make it into the product.
  - Keep short in time frame (two to four hours).

7.11 Market Research

It is common that organizations will take the BRD and use it to help evaluate if they want to build a system in-house, outsource the development, or buy a package. It is often overlooked though that those same packages can be used to extract requirements. Especially in the early stages of the requirements gathering, it can be very productive to review the features and functions that exist in commercial off-the-shelf software (COTS). It can serve as an initial prototype to make the systems discussion less abstract.

Before selecting one or more packages to evaluate there are some important recommendations to keep in mind:

- Set the customer's expectations. This is not intended as a preview of what the customer will get. For a large company, the package may be too simplistic and the customers must understand that this is just to kick off the requirements gathering. For a small company it can also be an issue, sometimes a more serious one. If the customer is shown functionality that would be too expensive and complex to implement, the eventual final product may be poorly received, because the customer has already seen something nicer. Imagine walking into an automotive dealership looking for a car and the salesperson brings out a Corvette for the test drive. By the time the actual deal is signed on the four-door mid-size, there is probably some disappointment with the process.
- It can be very time consuming to locate a package and to bring in a demo version (or a trial product). If this is a small project with a tight timeline, this may not be a realistic option. There also must be some subject matter expertise on the product, often provided by a consultant; but again, there is a cost associated with that. If there is a package that may fit and that will be considered, then there is an option to try to get the vendor involved with the evaluation. However, remember that the vendor's objectives and the project's are usually different.
- It can limit the creativity. By looking at an existing product, the customer will get some preconceived notion of what the product should look like. It may limit the thought process, it being easier to just go with what the package has versus determining what would be the best solution for this organization.

Advantages of Market Research
- – Sample of a working solution.
- – Can be used as initial prototype.
- – Find "Best Practices."

Disadvantages of Market Research
- – Limits creativity.
- – Time consuming.
- – Additional cost.

Best Practices
- – Level set the customer's expectations.
- – Select a package with a target market matching the customer's organization.
- – Be aware of vendor help.

7.12 Evaluate "Best Practices"

Best practices can involve market research such as discussed previously, but it can also involve reviewing what the competition is doing. If the project is an Accounts Payable system, there is probably not much difference between organizations, but if the project is market analysis or data warehousing, then it may pay off to look at what the lead companies in the market are doing. How is it determined what a "Best Practice" is? Look for the industry leaders in the same industry as the customer. Traditionally in automotive Toyota has been studied for best practices. This can be a chance to look outside of the immediate industry as well. If the project is to develop a new ordering system, maybe Amazon.com should be studied. If it is logistics, then maybe FedEx or Wal-Mart would be worth looking into. Make sure that the customer agrees with the evaluation of what the "Best Practice" organizations are.

Sometimes a wealth of information can be gotten from trade journals and trade shows. Keeping up to date on those areas is discussed in Chapter 3. A business analyst with broad industry exposure is key in this area. If that person doesn't currently exist, there may be a need to bring in a consultant.

Advantages of Evaluating "Best Practices"
- Not re-inventing the wheel.
- Making significant improvements in a short time frame rather than gradual enhancements based on current environment.

Disadvantages of Evaluating "Best Practices"
- Information may not be readily available.
- Information may be skewed depending on the source.

Best Practices
- Use trade shows and trade journals.
- Use consultants.
- Create business analysts within the organization with a broad industry knowledge.
- Ask the customer "who's the best?"

7.13 Prototyping

Prototyping is one of the most popular tools used for systems development and requirements gathering. A stumbling block often encountered when discussing requirements with the stakeholders is the abstract nature of systems. If the customer is buying a car, they can go for a test ride and decide what features they like and which ones they want to avoid. If the project is the construction of a house the customer can meet the builder in a model home to visualize and decide on features.

However, with a system this is a difficult process. Prototyping can help with the visualization.

Prototyping can help with the visualization.

James Martin defines prototyping in his book *Rapid Application Development* as "a technique for building a quick and rough version of a desired system or parts of that system ..." which "serves as a communication vehicle." This is an important definition, because the main purpose of prototyping is to enhance communication. The impact of those statements is often forgotten and the prototype becomes the product in itself. It is constantly refined and perfected with so much time spent on it that it becomes difficult to abandon, or even to criticize it. A question I always ask my students when discussing prototypes is "What is the worst thing that can happen when customers see the prototype?" Typically the answers are "They hate it," "They want to change it," or "They think it is too basic." None of these are the answer I'm looking for. Actually, the worst thing that can happen is that they love it, they will take it as is, just implement it tomorrow and the project will be finished! This is an indication that the analyst has done a poor job managing the customer's expectations. The customer must be told ahead of time that this is just a shell, held together by sticks and chewing gum, and that there is no way that this will be implemented for quite a while. It is possible it may never be implemented, because it is a communications vehicle and may even contain features that are not technically feasible, or at least not in sync with the technical architecture of the organization.

It is worth noting that in some projects the prototype will become the product. Some methodologies from Chapter 5, including RAD and Dynamic Systems Development Methodology (DSDM), are based on evolutionary prototyping where eventually the prototype evolves into the product. The prototype may be "good enough" or at least close to it. That approach is OK, but that possibility of implementing the prototype should be decided on up front. If developers know that the prototype may end up in production, they can prepare for that by following standards and incorporating required interfaces, at least at a conceptual level. In many cases, implementing a prototype may lead to problems down the road, but it can work, especially if the prototype was developed with that in mind. Make sure to do a risk assessment when moving in that direction.

Start the prototyping effort by establishing realistic objectives. Determine what is expected as a result of the prototype. Is this to determine requirements for the user interface? Is the customer's workflow being evaluated and analyzed? Is it trying to decide which high level features should be included? Based on the answers to those questions, the prototype may go in very different directions.

In the early days of prototyping there where two main types of prototypes:

- Evolutionary: Where the prototype gradually gets refined and eventually becomes the final product. This type requires more effort in creating the prototype, because the system being developed may eventually become the production system. However, it does have the advantage of not having to start over.
- Throwaway: Where the prototype is not intended to be used for anything other than communications. The advantage being that it is very fast to develop. It can be done using just paper and pen or a white board, and allows requirements to be captured at a quick pace.

A different way of classifying prototypes is by looking at the scope. Is it a broad scope or a narrow scope? This can lead to the following two types of prototypes:

- Horizontal: Shallow but broad. The purpose here is to make sure that all business functions are included, but there is typically not much working detail below the surface.
- Vertical: Here the prototype is focusing on a small portion of the system, but going down into a lower level of detail. This may be done to try to understand how a function would flow at a detailed level, or it could be part of a feasibility study to figure out if a certain technology will work.

Although there are some sophisticated tools for prototyping, with more of them coming into play all the time, many prototypes developed today are using screen prints, frames, or PowerPoint®, which is really more of a storyboard approach (covered in the next section). It is fast and simple and, for the most part, it is obvious to the customer that this is not the real system.

Advantages of Prototyping
- Good tool for communication with customer and developer.
- Involves the customer.
- Reduces abstractness.
- Can help determine feasibility of a solution.

Disadvantages of Prototyping
- Can result in unrealistic expectations.
- Can take a significant amount of time to develop, especially if they are evolutionary prototypes.
- Different look and feel than final product.
- May need additional resources from the development team, which may slow down progress or increase cost.
- Easy to focus on "how" rather than "why."

Best Practices
- Set realistic customer expectations.
- Define the purpose of the prototype up front.
- Don't overengineer the prototype.

7.14 Storyboarding

Some analyst's would view storyboards as a form of prototyping, and technically it is. The line between a storyboard and a prototype is vague. For the purposes of this discussion, a prototype uses a tool, has some level of functionality, and has a higher degree of sophistication than a storyboard. The primary purpose of a storyboard is to show what the user will do with the system. It can be using a tool like Visio® or it can be done with white boards or Post-It™ notes.

Early on in the requirements gathering process it is often better not to use a computer-based tool with screen prints and flows. In the early stages the solution is still up in the air, and there is actually a good chance that some of the things being discussed may not even be automated. Using a sophisticated tool will often put customers in the frame of mind of "what they see is what they will get." For the initial set of storyboards, use the following process:

1. Identify main scenarios within the scope of the project. These scenarios should outline the key functions that someone will use the system for. If use cases have been developed, then they can often be used for the initial scenario identification (Use cases are covered in Chapter 8).

2. Determine which scenarios need to have a storyboard developed. Just because it is something that a user needs to do, does not mean that it should be storyboarded. Many scenarios are obvious and a storyboard does not add value. A storyboard should be specific: its purpose is to allow the requirements-gathering process to focus on something that is key for the project. For the Prescription Interaction Project, some scenarios worth exploring may be:

    a. Existing customer wants to fill a prescription for a medicine which has a number of potentially harmful interactions, but none with any of the drugs from the patient's history.

    b. Same as a, but for a brand new customer.

    c. Same as a, but the drug is potentially interacting with a different prescription which has been used by this customer.

3. Meet with the stakeholders who will provide the requirements and outline the steps in the storyboard. Reach consensus on the high level of the flow.

4. Develop more detail on each part of the storyboard. Use a template to cover the main information that should be captured. Include elements such as:
    - Storyboard identification
    - Description
    - User(s)
    - Trigger of the process
    - Inputs
    - Outputs
    - Issues

5. Validate with users and developers. Regardless of who was involved with defining and documenting the scenario, it must be reviewed with all key stakeholders. This includes the developer and the user, but also representatives from other functional areas which may be impacted by the scenario.

When developing storyboards, it is easy to get bogged down in details, exceptions, and error conditions. Sometimes this will take an intuitive and user-friendly approach and turn it into an exercise in frustration. When working on the storyboards, always focus on the "happy path" initially. The "happy path" tells what will happen most of the time when the process is successfully executed. It ensures that there is a correct understanding of what the process should do before the focus becomes "what could go wrong." It is OK to take some of the more complicated and involved alternative paths and errors and storyboard them as well, but it is good to be restrictive about when to do that. The customers and the developers often love a little bit of storyboarding, but as with most things, it can easily get overdone. Some signs of this are:

- Customer loses focus and participates less.
- The storyboard appears to have a lot of duplication.
- The storyboard becomes the requirements document.

For the last bullet it is important to remember that the storyboard is a tool to help with capturing requirements; it is a communication tool, often a very good one. But the storyboards are not the requirements. They do not necessarily even need to be a part of the BRD (even though it may help). In many cases the storyboard may be used again when the test cases are developed.

Advantages of Storyboarding
- Can be used early on to reduce abstractness.
- Intuitive for the customer.
- Can be done without tools.

Disadvantages of Storyboarding
- Different look and feel than final product.
- Easy to focus on "how" rather than "why."

Best Practices
- Keep it simple, especially in the early iterations.
- Keep customers involved.

7.15   Idea-Generating Techniques (Brainstorming)

Like prototyping, brainstorming and other idea-generating techniques can be used with virtually any requirements-gathering techniques. They are often used in JAD sessions and focus groups as well as in traditional interviews. In this section brainstorming and some of its common variations are explored. The variations to be covered here are:

- Basic brainstorming
- Anonymous brainstorming
- Affinity diagramming
- Brainstorming in a non-group environment
- Brainstorming for a virtual team

7.15.1 Basic Brainstorming

This starts with a group of people in a room working with a specific problem, trying to generate solutions for it. The purpose of brainstorming is to use group synergy to generate a lot of ideas and then have the team build on those ideas to generate even better ideas. Sometimes it is said that there are no bad ideas. That is obviously not true; there are a lot of really bad ideas out there. But by allowing them to be raised and captured in the brainstorming session, it allows other participants to tweak them and to build on them to generate a better idea. The process to be followed is:

1. Clearly state the problem. One of the difficulties with brainstorming is to keep focused and to stay within the boundaries of the problem that is trying to be solved. Make sure that the problem statement is clear and that all the participants agree with it.
2. Define the ground rules for the session. The ground rules should typically include "no disagreements allowed", "all ideas are captured and visible", and "allow everyone to participate."
3. Start the brainstorming. The facilitator's role is to make sure that each idea is captured and is stated in a way that is agreed to by the person stating the idea, and that is understood by everyone. Be careful about the difference between clarifying an idea, which is valid, and questioning an idea, which is not allowed at this stage.
4. Run the session for a pre-determined amount of time, or until the team is running dry on ideas.
5. Go through the list of ideas and combine any duplicates. Also evaluate and see if there are any ideas that everyone agrees should be removed. It could be because they are outside if the scope of the brainstorming session, or that they are better stated in a different idea, or that after further thought, they were not very intelligent. Make sure though that everyone agrees that the idea should be eliminated.
6. Identify conflicting ideas and make a decision. When doing the brainstorming it is likely that there will be two, or more, different ideas which are conflicting. Go through the consensus building approach discussed under JAD sessions and make a decision on which way to go. If this is not the team that is

empowered to make the decision, then document the ideas as conflicting and pass that information on to the decision makers.

7. Organize the ideas into a format that is easy to read. If there are only a small number of ideas, this may be very quick, but if there are hundreds of ideas this organization needs its own process. One approach is the Affinity diagram, which will be covered later in this section.

The purpose of brainstorming is to use group synergy to generate a lot of ideas and then have the team build on those ideas to generate even better ideas.

When brainstorming, facilitation is important, both for what the facilitator does (stay focused, encourage participation) as well as for what they don't do (question ideas, laugh at ignorance). During the session the facilitator must watch out for "Group Think." In most groups there are some people that want to take control and there are some that sit back and wait. When the session is hijacked by a few participants, they tend to take the whole group with them in a certain direction. This can stifle creativity and a lot of potentially great ideas may be overlooked. One way to address this problem is through anonymous brainstorming.

7.15.2   *Anonymous Brainstorming*

One rule of brainstorming is for everyone to leave their ego at the door. Although this is a good intention, it is not always easy to achieve. Anonymous brainstorming is a way to get the ideas captured without knowing who actually stated the idea. An idea submitted by the inexperienced intern may be ridiculed and ignored, while an idea by the sponsor is likely to be considered (regardless of its stupidity). There are different ways to make brainstorming anonymous. This section will present a low-cost and a high-cost alternative. By using some creativity there are many ways in-between.

The low-cost approach is to use the analyst's favorite tool, the yellow Post-It™ note. In the beginning of the session give everyone a set of Post-It notes and start the session by having everyone write down five ideas. Each idea should be on its own note. Then collect the notes and shuffle them before writing them down on the white board (or flip chart). Once all the ideas are displayed, give the participants a few minutes to review them and then ask them for two more ideas. Go through the same process again and keep going until the ideas run dry. Some guidelines to ensure anonymity are:

- When someone does not have any more ideas, ask them to write down "no idea" on the note and still collect them. That way there will be notes from all participants.
- Do not ask for clarification of ideas. Rather if an idea is not understood, ask the participants to rephrase it for the next round.

The high-cost approach is to use what is known as a "creativity lab." There are a number of them around the country, run by different organizations; IBM has three or four of them. These are facilities that can be rented for the duration of the session. They come fully equipped with facilitators experienced in brainstorming and a room set-up where each participant gets their own computer. The ideas are then typed into the computer and are displayed on a screen at the front of the room, seen by everyone. This allows more of a regular brainstorming environment where, when an idea is shown, the rest of the room can react to it and build on it right away. However, there are some disadvantages as well. If one person is continuously typing and the rest of the team is not, it may reveal whose idea it is. Typing errors can also be revealing here. One good compromise is to send the ideas through a moderator who checks spelling and displays the ideas at even intervals.

7.15.3   Affinity Diagramming

The purpose of the affinity diagram is to group ideas together into categories. Affinity diagrams can be created bottom-up or top-down. For the bottom-up approach start with all the ideas displayed to the team, then let the team start moving the ideas around, putting those that have similar topics next to each other. Some people recommend doing this is silence, to minimize the more verbal people from taking control, but in most situations it works well for the team to be talking while doing this. It is likely that some ideas will be moved back and forth because they may relate to multiple other ideas. When that happens, review the idea and see if it is really a composite idea that can be split. If it is not a composite idea, then pick one group and put the idea there. Do not put the same idea up on the board twice, as that will potentially lead to duplication of effort down the road. Once the team is satisfied with the groupings, create a category name for each group. The result is an affinity diagram, as seen in Figure 7.9.

The top-down approach starts with identifying key categories. Those categories could be based on organizational units (purchasing, marketing, and manufacturing) or on product deliverables (performance, features, training, and support). The advantage with the top-down approach is that it is possible to reuse a structure that has been successfully used in the past, and it is easier to define categories that can be assigned to different teams for further evaluation. The disadvantage is that because it is a predefined set of categories it may limit creativity and the team might assume that all ideas must fit within these categories. If top-down is used, also create a category called "other" to help track the ideas that were outside of the expected.

The affinity diagram will help with categorization of requirements as well as prioritizing requirements. When prioritizing it is often better to prioritize requirements in groups rather than prioritizing each individual requirement. For example, there may be hundreds of usability requirements and dozens of performance-related requirements. Prioritizing each requirement would be tedious and time consuming. It is often sufficient to prioritize the groups of requirements.

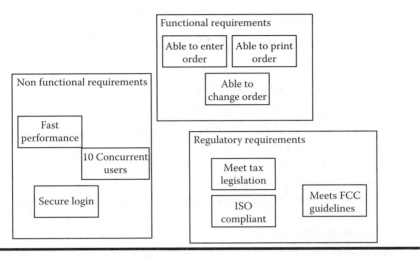

Figure 7.9 Affinity diagram.

7.15.4 *Brainstorming in a Non-Group Environment*

Because brainstorming is based on group synergy, performing it with an individual sounds like a contradiction. However, it is possible to simulate some of the benefits of brainstorming by asking the person being interviewed the same question multiple times. Document each answer on a board or flip chart, and repeat the question again. The thought here is that by digging deeper and having the thought process triggered by earlier ideas, it will make the interviewee come up with more creative ideas and be more likely to think "outside the box." Eventually the ideas will start being silly, and that may be a good time to stop.

7.15.5 *Brainstorming for a Virtual Team*

Brainstorming does not have to be done in real-time. For a virtual team it can be done by using online collaboration tools, but it is also a good option to do brainstorming using bulletin boards and online postings. This is especially true when the team is spread over multiple time zones across the globe. There still must be a facilitator and the topic of the brainstorming must be clearly stated (this may be even more important in a virtual environment). A simple non-interactive brainstorming approach for a virtual team is:

1. Send out the brainstorming statement and get agreement from the team.
2. Ask everyone to post their initial ideas on a bulletin board. Set a deadline.
3. Close the bulletin board and allow for review time.
4. Open the board for add-on ideas.
5. Repeat steps 3 and 4 again (this can be done multiple times, but it is good to set a limit for time consideration).

6. Review for duplication and see if there's consensus to remove any ideas.
7. Categorize (possibly using a top-down affinity diagram) and document.

7.15.6   Brainstorming Summary

Advantages of Brainstorming
- Large number of ideas in short time frame.
- Encourages creativity.
- Allows for group synergy.

Disadvantages of Brainstorming
- May lose control to strong personalities ("Group Think").
- Hard to get team to stay inside of boundaries.
- Can generate conflict.

Best Practices
- Create environment of acceptance.
- Everyone's input is valued.
- Group ideas into categories.

7.16   Tools for Virtual Environments

Each one of the requirements gathering techniques just reviewed may need to be done in some form of virtual environment. That environment may range from something as simple as a phone interview with the customer in the next building to something as complex as a JAD session with participants from three continents through videoconferencing and involving translators. Maybe the most important trick to be successful in a virtual environment is to realize that there will be problems and there needs to be a well thought-out plan on how to deal with them.

Some of the tools that may be used in the virtual environment are old existing tools, some are new and advanced. The drivers behind what to use are:

- Cost: Videoconferencing and such tools can be very expensive, especially if the participants are spread across the globe. They do give the advantage of seeing the other people in the session, being able to read body language, and build a sense of team. It is a good idea to try to do the first meeting in person because that can make future videoconferencing sessions more productive.
- E-mail: Using e-mail, although common and accessible for most organizations, also can cause some difficulties. Response is slowed down. Often there is a tendency to overcommunication, where the e-mail goes out to too many people. Limit the distribution lists and stay focused in the e-mails.
- File sharing, collaboration tools, project rooms on the Web: This area is evolving fast, and there are a number of places that can be used to set up

virtual groups where members of the group can share information, have discussions, post questions, etc. There are also tools like Wiki and blogs, which are again often free, easy to set up, and easy to use for sharing information and performing collaborative tasks. Be aware, though, of the level of technology maturity among the stakeholders. For many people using blogs and spending time online is second nature, but for many it is not. Seriously consider if the organization is ready for these tools.

7.17 Requirements Prioritization Techniques

Once the requirements have been captured there is often a need to prioritize them. It could be because the budget and timeline don't allow for all requirements to be incorporated, or it could be to help evaluate alternative solutions. To make these decisions it is important to know which features the customer needs the most. Quite often a product is planned to be released in multiple stages and prioritization can help determine what features and functionality will be included in each of the releases.

> Quite often a product is planned to be released in multiple stages and prioritization can help determine what features and functionality will be included in each of the releases.

The easiest way to prioritize is to walk up to the customer and ask "What is most important?" However, when doing that the standard answer is "Everything is important!" So over the years various techniques have evolved to get the customer to participate in the prioritization process and to make it as objective as possible. There are four distinct prioritization techniques which will be described here:

- The dollar approach
- Forced pair
- Density dotting
- Analytical Hierarchy Process (AHP)

Each one of them has advantages and disadvantages; the first three are relatively simple, the last more complex. It is recommended that you pick one approach and use that approach on all projects. Prioritization techniques can get very confusing and they really work best after the customer has used them a few times.

7.17.1 The Dollar Approach

This approach is easy in concept, but sometimes hard to put into reality. It is based on putting a price tag on each of the key features of the product. Stakeholders then get an amount of money to spend and can each go on a shopping spree. They can distribute the money any way they see fit, but they cannot overspend. Figure 7.10 shows how this may look in an environment with three stakeholders

The total cost for the features in the table is $650. Each department is given a budget of $450 and is told to spend that money any way they want. Based on their responses, feature 1 got 3 votes and features 3, 5, 6, and 7 each got 2 votes. The method can be tweaked for each situation, but the basic premise is that the customer votes with their wallet.

There are some key considerations that must be looked at with this technique:

- Is there enough information to estimate the cost? This is typically done in the early stages of the project, and because there has been no real evaluation of solutions any estimate will be crude at best.
- Consider using relative rather than real numbers. Use $100, $200, $500. The customer knows it is not the real number. The intention is to show that some of the features are much more complex than others.
- Not all stakeholders have the same priority. If one stakeholder has a higher priority than the others, then this techniques doesn't work well.

Feature	Cost	Marketing	Operation	Service	Total
1. Cross store synchronize	$100	X	X	X	3
2. FDA link	$200		X		1
3. Manufacturing link	$100	X	X		2
4. Patient analysis	$50			X	1
5. Drug Analysis	$50		X	X	2
6. Wireless access	$100	X		X	2
7. Web access	$150	X		X	2
	$650	$450	$450	$450	

Figure 7.10 Dollar prioritization.

7.17.2 Forced Pair

Forced pair is probably the simplest and most common ranking technique. All requirements or features are compared against all other requirements in a pair, and the most important one is selected. It works very well in a multi-stakeholder environment where all stakeholders have the same priority. The first step in forced pair ranking is to build the ranking matrix (which takes some training), as shown in Figure 7.11.

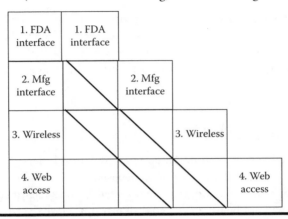

Figure 7.11 Forced pair.

With this structure in front of the group, each requirement is compared against all the other requirements. The group is asked "Which is most important: FDA interface or manufacturer interface?" In our sample team of five people there were three votes for manufacturer and two for FDA. Note that everyone must vote. Place the number 3 (the votes for the manufacturer) below the diagonal line in the box that intersects manufacturer interface and FDA interface. Place the number 2 above the line, closest to FDA. Go through the same process for all the other requirements. At the end the diagram should look like Figure 7.12.

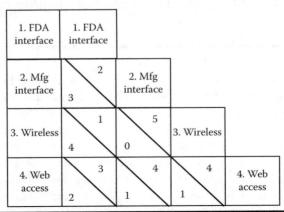

Figure 7.12 Forced pair filled in.

Next add up the numbers for each requirement. It should be:

- FDA interface = 2 + 1 + 3 = 6
- Manufacturer interface = 3 + 5 + 4 = 12
- Wireless = 4 + 0 + 4 = 8
- Web access = 2 + 1 + 1 = 4

Based on this we can see that manufacturer interface is the most important requirement, three times as important as Web access. This technique does take some time to get used to and most people struggle a little with finding the right numbers to add, so make sure to practice this before doing it with the customer.

7.17.3   Density Dotting

Another approach to prioritization, sometimes used in agile development, is density dotting. It is less formal than other approaches and can be used for a number of scenarios. In a facilitated session, there may be ten features identified and it may be clear that there will not be time to discuss all features. Have the participants grab a marker, go up to the flip chart, and put a dot next to the top three things that they wish to discuss and explore in more detail (or that they view as the top priorities). Density dotting will, often in less than 60 seconds, produce a visual representation of what the group wants to discuss, and in extension, where the most important features and requirements will be explored. The top three (or five, or whatever number there is time for) will then be the focus for a more detailed discussion.

> Density dotting will, often in less than 60 seconds, produce a visual representation of what the group wants to discuss.

This type of approach removes a lot of the tension from the prioritization and decision process. It is simple, equitable, and fast. However, it does assume that everyone on the team has the same power when it comes to deciding what to focus on, which may not be true. For instance, if on the Prescription Interaction Project the team decided that the top three topics to discuss were (1) entering customer information; (2) identifying previous prescription, which may cause a bad interaction with the current one; and (3) overriding drug warnings. This could mean that other topics, such as "Checking against family members' prescriptions" could be overlooked, because the only ones who wanted to talk about it were the sponsor and the lawyer. So before doing density dotting (or any prioritization effort), make sure that there is a buy-in to it from all stakeholders.

7.17.4   Analytical Hierarchy Process

The Analytical Hierarchy Process (AHP) is very similar to the forced pair method, but it adds the question when doing a forced pair comparison "How much more important is requirement A versus B?" In the forced pair the question simply asks which is most important. The AHP approach takes more time because the customer may have to do some analysis to know how much more important one feature is versus another. Part of this thought process should be the relative expense of the feature. Because this prioritization is typically done very early in the process it is likely that the benefit as well as the cost estimate will be at a high level. That's OK. The customer does need to know if this is a $1,000 requirement or a $10,000 one.

7.17.5   Prioritization Techniques Summary

Advantages of Prioritization
  – Allows for implementing most important areas first.
  – Gives information for trade-off between requirements.
  – Can be used to evaluate change requests.

Disadvantages of Prioritization
  – Can be very cumbersome and still be fairly subjective.

Best Practices
  – The customers must set the priorities.
  – If using to evaluate different solutions, only look at requirements which will vary based on the solution. If a requirement is met by all possible solutions, then there is no need to prioritize it. However, if the prioritization is to determine what to build and what not to build, then all the requirements should be prioritized.

7.18 Summary

The selection of the best requirements elicitation techniques is difficult and is key to the success of the analysis phase. Do not only consider the skills and personalities of the users, managers, and other key stakeholders, but also review the skills of the business analysts. It may be that a facilitated session would be the best way to capture requirements from a customer, but if there is no experience or skill, it may be better to select a different review process. The approach that is selected must be validated with the sponsor and other key stakeholders. Their time will be impacted, so their commitment is needed. Also evaluate stakeholder priorities, especially as requirements prioritization is taking place.

7.19 Activity

Take another look at the case study in Chapter 11. Identify all the stakeholders from whom requirements will be elicited. Some of these stakeholders may have been identified in the activity for Chapter 4. Include those but also add any others that come to mind.

1. Identify the best requirements elicitation technique for each stakeholder on the list and document what actions the analyst should take to make the effort more successful with each stakeholder. This includes actions to take before requirements are gathered, during the gathering, and follow-up actions.
2. Select one area where a discovery session would work well. Identify which stakeholders would be invited to the session and create an agenda for what to cover in that discovery session.

Chapter 8

Requirements Modeling and Documentation

To succeed in business it is necessary to make others see things as you see them.

—John H. Patterson

This chapter reviews the best, or at least the most commonly used, practices for modeling and documenting requirements. Each one of these techniques warrants its own book(s). However, the purpose of this book is to present them at an introductory level, giving the business analyst enough exposure to the techniques to be able to participate in a requirements gathering or review session where these techniques might be used. It is also intended to help in selecting which techniques to use. The analyst leading these activities should further develop the skills for techniques used for the project. Although modeling can be of great value when gathering requirements, if the business analyst struggles with it, the customer will soon lose interest as well.

8.1   Objectives

- Realize the value of modeling as a part of documenting system requirements.
- Recognize and read each model type.
- Gain an understanding of which area of the system each technique is modeling.
- Understand the strengths and weaknesses of each technique.

- See the applicability of each technique to the project being worked on.
- Practice modeling.

8.2 Overview

Although the main purpose of this book is to discuss requirements gathering techniques, to do that without looking at how to best document those requirements would be to miss a critical component of the requirements process. Requirements models and text documents are not only used as a repository for information, but are also key components of the communication process. Combining the use of models and text to reach a total understanding of the customer's needs is a great best practice in the field of business analysis. Text without pictures tends to be hard to read and hard to organize. Models without text can be fluffy and not contain enough information to understand the detailed requirements of what is being developed. Best practice is to do both. Set the context, the overview of the business and system, with models and pictures showing the overall scope and flow of what is being worked on, and then use the model as a communication tool to capture the detailed information in accompanying text documents.

Figure 8.1 shows models and text working together. This technique is especially effective when working with the customer in a requirements session. The customer stays focused by exploring one piece of the model at a time, and delving into the details of what the business requirements are for that part of the business. Without the model to keep both the customer and the business analyst focused, there is a

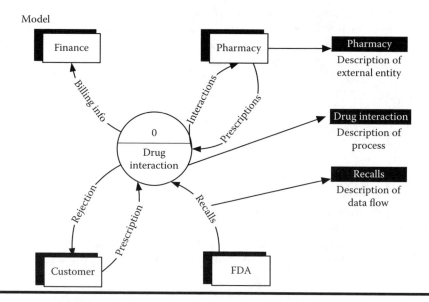

Figure 8.1 Models and text.

tendency to randomly move from one area of the system to the next and then back again without having a logical direction.

Without the model to keep both the customer and the business analyst focused, there is a tendency to randomly move from one area of the system to the next and then back again without having a logical direction.

The two topics, models and text documentation, have been combined into one chapter, because the outcome will be used together to understand the business. However, the skill set needed for each of these is somewhat different. Good modelers must have a mind suited for abstractions, pictures, and simplification. They must also understand what level of detail is appropriate for a user versus a developer. Their style of communication must be facilitative, with the ability to develop and review the models with a group of people.

The technical writers need a different skill set. They must be very detail oriented, thorough, and precise to make sure that a sufficient clarity has been accomplished. It is often difficult to find a single person who can successfully perform both tasks. In many cases it is best to team up a couple of people to perform this with the big-picture person focusing on the models and the detail person making sure that the models have real information behind them in the form of text documents.

Although there are many modeling techniques, and many ways of grouping them, for the purposes of this chapter there will be two major groups:

1. Traditional models
2. UML (or object oriented models)

Traditional models are rooted in structured analysis and design, and UML models in object-oriented concepts. Some modeling techniques can be used in both environments, such as use cases and activity diagrams. In this book the activity diagrams are covered as a part of UML; however, there are other notation techniques for the activity diagrams. Those notations would be used in a traditional development environment. The concept of activity diagrams are the same in both cases. There is no attempt in this book to make a case for a specific technique. Rather by looking at different approaches, the recommendation is for each organization to evaluate which ones best fit the developers, customers, and type of development efforts that are being managed. For example, research and development needs different techniques than legacy systems, upgrades, etc. A project to enhance an organization's existing Accounts Payable system, developed 20 years ago on a mainframe platform and integrated with other legacy systems, should normally use structured analysis and traditional modeling techniques. Since those were more than likely the techniques used originally when the system was developed, those techniques will likely fit the best into the existing architecture. In addition, there may be existing models and documentation from the original development which may be reused, saving both time and effort. On the other side, if this project is an organization's first venture into E-commerce and Web development, then it would make much more sense to look at object-oriented approaches because the tools that will eventually be used to develop the system more than likely have that orientation. Because most projects probably fall somewhere in between those two extremes, the decision may not always be clear, but the goal should be to look at the development environment for the system.

Although it is often acceptable, and sometimes even desirable, to mix and match between the approaches, the awareness that some techniques within one family of diagrams overlap with techniques from the other area is essential. Keep in mind also that, as with most efforts, there should be an attempt to minimize the duplication of effort when modeling. The concept of "one fact in one place" is a good goal to have. In the end, the most frequent determinants of which technique to use is a combination of the experience of the people involved and the tools that the organization has already invested in. If the organization has invested hundreds of thousands of dollars in a tool suite, it should be used. These tool suites, regardless if they are Oracle™, Rational™ (IBM), or a mix of vendor products, are intended to help with a significant portion of the development cycle. The training, the tool itself, and the experience built up with a tool are invaluable for an organization, and there must be a very strong and substantial reason not to use those tools for any projects within the organization.

> In the end, the most frequent determinants of which technique to use is a combination of the experience of the people involved and the tools that the organization has already invested in.

8.3 The Traditional Techniques

When sophisticated business computer systems became more prevalent, the need for an organized approach to develop those systems also became a higher priority. Some people referred to it as "Structured Design"; another popular phrase was "Information Engineering." The basic concepts of this approach was to model data and processes separately, often in a functional decomposition diagram (FDD) and an entity relationship diagram (ERD), and then model the interaction between data and process in a data flow diagram (DFD). These modeling techniques are still used today, sometimes combined with use cases or other approaches to show process requirements. Figure 8.2 shows the structured analysis techniques discussed in this section along with the purpose of each as well as possible alternative techniques which would provide a similar view and purpose.

Analysis technique	Main usage	Alternative techniques
Functional Decomposition Diagram	Describe business processes and functions from an internal view	Use Case IDEF0 Workflow diagram
Entity Relationship Diagram	Describes information needed for the business and the business rules regarding that information	Class diagram
Data Flow Diagram	Shows the flow of information in and out of business processes and how the customer views and groups the data	IPO models (Input-Process-Output) State diagrams

Figure 8.2 Structured analysis techniques.

8.3.1   Process Models

Functional decomposition is one of the most common techniques of documenting requirements. The diagram starts at a high level (business area) and then gradually decomposes into key functional areas and processes within those areas. This is a good way to pinpoint scope for a project, as well as identify which stakeholders will be able to provide further information and requirements. It also tends to view the business the way the customer views it, making it a fairly customer-friendly tool.

As shown in Figure 8.3, the diagram shows the business area on top, which could be a whole enterprise or something as small as a single process ("Enter Patient Information"). That is the starting point for a decomposition of the process into a higher degree of detail. How far down into the details should the decomposition go? The lowest level, referred to as the basic business process, should identify what the business needs to do without specifying how it is being done. If the lowest level becomes a how-to instruction or if it contains physical implementations, then there is too much detail, although it is often difficult to draw that exact line, and there is usually

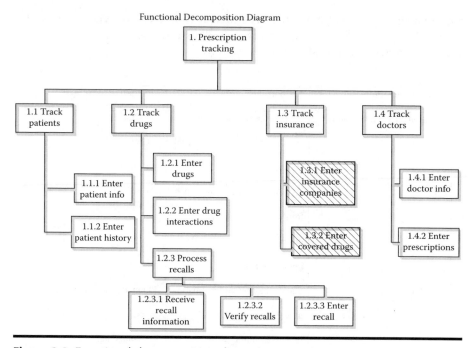

Figure 8.3 Functional decomposition diagram.

a certain amount of gut feel involved with that decision. The lowest level should be a detail of the "what" without going into the "how."

Looking back at Figure 8.3, a step-by-step approach to creating the FDD is:

1. Identify the focus area; in this case it is "Prescription Tracking." That is the scope of our project. Naturally, different people will look at those two words and read something different into them. So for every box in the FDD there must also be in a supporting document, a description that clarifies what is meant by the text in the box, in this case "Prescription Tracking." In some cases that has already been documented in the project scope statement, and if so, just reference that document. In other cases, the analyst may have to create a description and make sure that the customer agrees with it. Modeling can be of great value, but only if the analyst and the customer are modeling the same things.

2. Ask the customers what the main business functions or processes are within the area of "Prescription Tracking." In this case the customer came up with "Track Patients," "Track Drugs," "Track Insurance," and "Track Doctors." In a FDD there is no concern for sequence, so the processes (on the same level) can be shown in any order. Complete each level of the decomposition before moving on to the next level. Ask the customer if there is anything else that needs to be done within "Prescription Tracking" that is not covered by the

four high-level processes already identified. One of the rules of the FDD is that the sum of all the lower-level processes must have the same scope as the level just above it, only with more detail added. All activities from the "parent" level must be reflected somewhere on the "child" level.

3. Now review each one of the four processes from Step 2 to determine what the detail processes are below them. For the process "Track Drugs," the customer identifies "Enter Drugs," "Enter Interactions," and "Process Recalls." Again, there must be a balancing at the borders, so that the process of "Track Drugs" is fully described by the three detailed processes below it and that all of the detailed processes are necessary to describe that process.

4. Next review all the detailed processes and see if any of them need further decomposition. In the example, the process "Process Recalls" can be decomposed into "Receive Recall Information," "Verify Recalls," and "Enter Recalls." None of the other processes need further decomposition. There is no need to have all processes broken down into the same number of levels. Rather, let the business decide how many levels each process should have. In some cases the customer may want to go into too much detail. As an example, look at the process "Enter Patient Info." That could be broken down into "Bring up patient screen," "Enter name and address," "Enter phone number," "Enter preferred pharmacy." This is too much detail and should be avoided by applying the following tests:

   a. Is the process describing the use of a tool, such as "Bring up patient screen"? If so, it does not belong here. Remember, the process should describe what the business does, not how.

   b. The processes are mostly step-by-step instructions on how to do the higher-level process. "Enter name and address," "Enter phone number," and "Enter preferred pharmacy" fall into this category.

   There is no absolute test to see if there is enough detail. It is good to remember the purpose of the diagram: it is a tool to help communication. If the customer insists on more detail, then give more detail. But if the diagram gets too cumbersome to read, then consider staying at a higher level.

5. Determine if any of the boxes are outside the scope of the project. In the example, the processes of "Enter Insurance Companies" and "Enter Covered Drugs" are determined to be out of scope, covered by some other project, so they are marked with a shaded background. This is one of the great advantages of FDDs: they provide opportunities to graphically depict what is inside of the scope and what is outside.

6. Each process in the FDD must then be documented using a standard template, such as the one shown in Figure 8.4.

   It is in this template that most of the real information needed by the developers is captured. Both functional and nonfunctional requirements can be documented here. The role of the diagram is mainly to give structure and

Process Description	
Process Name: **1.2.3.1 Receive recall information**	**Documented by:** Jane Analyst
Documentation date: January 10, 2007	**Process Owner:** John Customer
Process Description: This process receives drug recall information from the drug manufacturers or from government agencies and starts a formal tracking of each recall request.	

Process steps:
   1. Receive recall physically, electronically, or through phone call
   2. Capture all relevant information
   3. Enter information into tracking system	

Business rules: All information must be entered into tracking system within 12 hours Any emergency requests must be escalated to management within 1 hour	
Is triggered by (other process or event) Government recall Manufacturer recall	
Is trigger for (other process of event): 1.2.3.2 Verify recall Emergency escalation process	
Comments High visibility process	

Figure 8.4 FDD process description.

context, while the template gives the detailed information. In the initial stages of documentation this template can be high level and focus on the business requirements, but as the requirements gathering effort progresses, this document should eventually show systems requirements as well.

Strengths of Functional Decomposition Diagrams
- Intuitive for the customer: Looks at the business the way customers do.
- Gives traceability between detailed business process and the business functions where they are performed.
- Helps discovery of duplicate and overlapping activities.

Weaknesses of Functional Decomposition Diagrams
- Takes an internal view of the business/system (what the organization is doing, not what the external customer wants to do).
- It is difficult to decide how much detail to get into.

Best Practices
- When working with executives, take a top-down approach, which tends to mirror the way they view the business.
- When working with end users, do a bottom-up approach, which will describe the level they work at, and build the structure afterward.

8.3.2   Data Models

The FDD shows the business processes within an organization. Because for the most part the business analyst is defining what an information system will do for a customer, there is also a need to define what information (or data) that system will actually need. This is not intended to be a definition of what the computer needs, but rather what data is important to the customer and what the business rules are guiding the use of that data.

The most widely used technique to show data needs within a business is the ERD. One of the pioneers in the development and standardization of the ERD was Dr. Peter Chen in the 1970s. It should be noted that creating ERDs is a large and complicated topic, which is only intended to be covered at a high level in this book. There are different ways to document them; many of the toolmakers use their own drawing standards, but they are all very similar. The basic components of an ERD are shown in Figure 8.5, with some alternative notations shown in Figure 8.7 toward the end of this section.

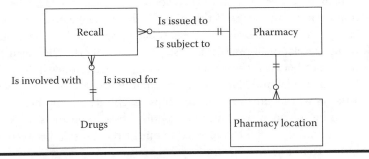

Figure 8.5 Sample ERD.

The key information captured in an ERD:

- Entities: Things, people, or organizations that the business needs information about. Typical examples are customer, order, employees, etc.
- Attributes: The information needed to be kept for each of the entities. Examples are name, address, description, quantity.
- Relationships: The business rules that govern the relationships between entities. Examples include "Each customer may place orders," "Each order must be placed by one customer."

Similar to the FDD example above, there is a step-by-step approach to create and verify an ERD:

1. Identifying Entities: Start by identifying the main concepts that are important to the customer's business. Listen to the customer's description of the business and then select the concepts that sound like items that the business may need to keep information about. Key nouns are often candidates for entities. The customer description of the business is, "Within prescription tracking we keep track of what <u>patients</u> have been sold what <u>drugs</u> and what <u>doctor</u> prescribed them. That information must be transferable to all

pharmacies within our network. We are also responsible to track recalls and drug interactions, which may be initiated by the manufacturers or the government." When evaluating that statement the analyst initially found the eight underlined concepts as potential entities. Each one of them should be evaluated against the following criteria:

a. Is the potential entity part of our scope?
b. Do we need to keep any information about the potential entity?

If both of those answers are positive, then add it to the list of entities.

2. Identify Attributes: Next determine what information the business needs to track about each entity. For the patient, the customer tracks name, address, and phone number. Those are the attributes of the patient entity. It is worth remembering here that the only attributes identified should be the ones that are important for the scope of this project. There may be other attributes for this entity that are used by other projects, but those should not be included here.

3. Identify Relationships: The third step is to identify the relationships and business rules between the entities. This helps answer questions such as "Who issues a recall?" and "How many manufacturers can there be of a drug?" The answers will identify the relationships. Each relationship between two entities is bidirectional and must be described by two business rules, one in each direction. Figure 8.6 has zoomed in on the relationship between Recalls and Drugs from Figure 8.5.

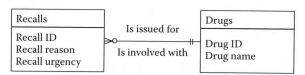

Figure 8.6 Recall/drug relationship.

4. Determine Cardinality: There are two symbols at the end of each line that describe what is called "cardinality." The one furthest away from the entity identifies whether the relationship is mandatory or optional (marked with a straight line across the relationship for mandatory and a circle for optional). This is called the "minimum cardinality." The other symbol, the one closest to the entity, describes the maximum number of occurrences of this entity that can be related to an occurrence of the other entity in the relationship (a maximum of one is marked with a cross line, and a maximum of many is marked with a crowfoot symbol). This is called "maximum cardinality." Sounds complicated? It can be, and it does take some time to get used to reading data models.

Review Figure 8.6 again, starting on the left side. The first business rule reads "Each Recall is issued for a minimum of 1 Drug and for a maximum of 1 Drug." Always start the statement with "Each." A business rule is always read clockwise so the statement for this rule is on top of the line (is issued for). Just to the left of the Drug entity are the two cardinality symbols, in this case two cross lines. The first cross line indicates that this is a mandatory relationship and the second cross line indicates that there can only be a maximum of one drug for a recall. Read the second business rule: "Each Drug is involved with a minimum of zero recalls and a maximum of many Recalls." Again the statement starts with "Each." Because the reading direction is clockwise, the relationship words are under the line "is involved with." The cardinality symbols are to the right of the recall entity. The first one is a circle, indicating that this is an optional relationship (not all drugs will be subject to recalls). The second one is a crowfoot, indicating that each drug may be subject to many recalls.

Some alternative notations for cardinality are shown in Figure 8.7. If a tool is used to create the ERD, it is best to use the same technique used by the tool. Stay consistent! ERDs can be confusing enough for the people reviewing them, without changing conventions.

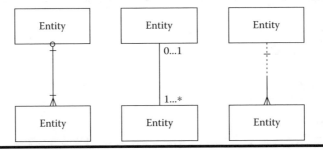

Figure 8.7 Alternative notations for cardinality.

5. Document: The final step is to create the documentation for each entity, attribute, and relationship. An example of entity documentation can be seen in Figure 8.8. Sometimes it is easier to review this text documentation with the customers and leave the actual ERD on the sideline. ERDs, although critical for a successful software project, are not always easy for the customers to understand.

Over the years, data models have evolved into three main categories:

- Conceptual data models: Primarily focused on communicating with the customer. Often only show key entities, attributes, and relationships. Data models can get confusing, and the conceptual data model attempts to stay at a level where the customer is comfortable.
- Logical data models: Focus on giving the developers the information necessary for development. Need to be fully defined and normalized. Normalization is a data modeling concept that can get complex, but for this book, it means ensuring that one fact is in only one place.

Entity: Customer	
Owned by: Sales department	Documented by: Jane Analyst
Date: June 1, 2007	Reviewed by: Joe BusOwner
Entity description: A customer is defined as anyone who has purchased a product or placed a prescription with the pharmacy in the past three years.	
Attributes: Name Address Phone Number	
Relationships: Each customer may have many prescriptions Each customer may have many bills	
Comments/Issues: Common entity used by many systems. Any changes must be coordinated through the sales department.	

Figure 8.8 Entity documentation.

- Physical data models: Looks at the technology and how the data will be used by the customer to determine the actual physical implementation.

Both the conceptual and the logical data models fall in the domain of the business analyst. Often the organization will have data architects that assist with this, but the overall responsibility is the business analyst's. The physical data model is for the developers. It should be noted that the conceptual data model and the logical data model can be the same. If your customer can go to the same level of detail and documentation that the developers need, it is OK to use the logical data model as the conceptual model.

Along with the data model is the data dictionary. Each attribute (or data element) must be defined. Some of the key parts of that definition include:

- Name
- Aliases: It is very common, especially in large businesses, that different parts of the business have different names for the same data. One business unit may call it "vendor" while it is called "supplier" by a different unit.
- Description/definition

- Format: This can be a number of formats such as numeric, text, date.
- Values: What are the valid values? Or the range of values?

Although it is difficult to standardize data definitions across an enterprise, it is important to standardize the definitions as much as possible across each business unit. Inconsistent definition will lead to miscommunication and poor requirements definitions. Many organizations leave the data definitions and much of the data dictionary to the system analyst, rather than the business analyst, which can cause problems. The system analysts will often make decisions based on what they have seen in the past, which may not reflect how this specific customer is running and defining the business.

Strengths of Entity Relationship Diagrams
   - Provide one place for all data needs for a system.
   - Serve as repository for future reuse.
   - Easy for developers to use.
   - Ensure integrity of information.

Weaknesses of Entity Relationship Diagrams
   - Hard for the customer to comprehend.
   - Hard to administer for large functions.
   - Different parts of the business have different definitions of data.

Best Practices
   - Review existing business descriptions and models to identify potential entities.
   - Review forms and screens to find potential attributes and relationships.
   - Use the customer's language to describe all components.

8.3.3 Data Flow Diagrams

In the traditional approach, the process model shows what the business does, and the data model identifies what information the business needs. The purpose of the DFD is to tie these two things together. The DFD ties the processes identified in the FDD with the information which is used and created by those processes. DFDs are done in levels, with each level tying into a level of the FDD, as shown in Figure 8.9.

The top level of the DFD, often called "level 0" or the "context level," is primarily a scope definition tool. It shows the boundaries between the project and the outside world. An example of a context-level diagram was shown in Figure 3.5, where the scope of the project and its ties to the rest of the enterprise were explored. Although often owned and developed by the project manager, the context diagram is a key document for the business analyst as the requirements gathering process starts.

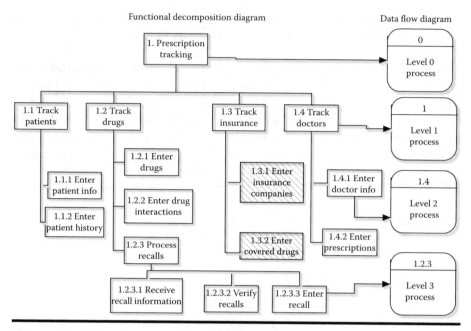

Figure 8.9 FDD and corresponding DFD levels.

The levels below the context diagram become increasingly focused on the internal dealings of the business system as the processes and functions are decomposed, mirroring the decomposition of the FDD. Figure 8.10 shows an example of a level 1 DFD.

The key components of the DFD are:

- Process: Activity or function done by the business
- External Entity: People, systems, organizations outside of this business area that will provide and/or receive data from the processes
- Data Flow: The data flowing in-between the processes and the external agents
- Data Store: Data that needs to be kept by the business for some time until some other process needs it

Three processes shown in Figure 8.10, "Track Patients," "Track Drugs," and "Track Doctors," are the same three processes shown at level 1 of the FDD in Figure 8.3. This is how the two models interact: each level of the FDD corresponds to another level in the DFD. In the example shown, there are four external entities, "Patient," "Doctor," "FDA/MFR," and "Physician tracking system." Those are the people, organizations, or other systems which are outside of the control of the Prescription Tracking System, but there is a need to interface with them. Any data flows going between those external entities and the processes being evaluated must be documented. A data flow is a concept that is real in the customer

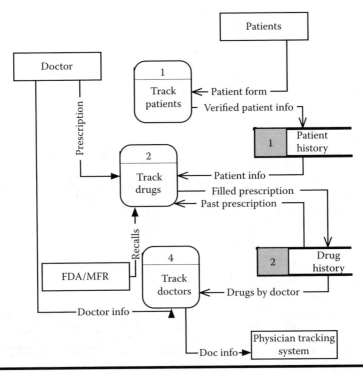

Figure 8.10 DFD level 1.

world. It does not always translate neatly to the data model, but rather it tends to be a combination of data from many entities. Typical examples of data flows are "Invoice," "Bill," and "Registration." Later in the project mapping between the data flows and the data model will be done to determine where the information will be stored. The last component is the data store. A data store recognizes that the business may need to keep information internally for different purposes and different time frames. Again, it is not a piece of the data model, but more a view of the data the business works with. It does not actually have to be stored in a physical database; it can be just a stack of papers. Look at the example of a telephone bill. It can be unpaid and it can be paid. If the process being defined used the unpaid bill as an input and the paid bill as an output, then the model would show those as two different data stores. In Figure 8.10 the model shows "Patient history" and "Drug history" as the two data stores of importance.

A data store recognizes that the business may need to keep information internally for different purposes and different time frames.

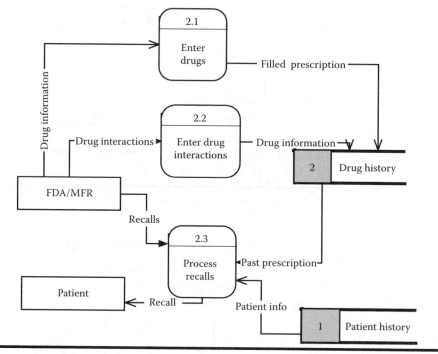

Figure 8.11 DFD level 2.

To create the level 2 data flow diagram, each process on the level 1 data flow diagram could, if needed, be decomposed to its detail processes. In this case that would result in three level 2 data flow diagrams, one per process. In Figure 8.11 the process of "Track Drugs" has been decomposed to the next level.

Again the processes at the next level should be taken from the next level of the FDD. That will ensure those two models remaining synchronized. One important concept of DFDs is that every level of the model must have the same borders as the process above it. This means that any input/output to one level of the model must correspond with the process above it. Compare Figure 8.11 with the process "Track drugs" in Figure 8.10. Are there any differences at the borders? Figure 8.11 shows "Recall Information" going to the patient and "Drug Information" coming from FDA/MFR. Those data flows are not shown at the parent level in Figure 8.10. That's an error and it must be corrected. If an advanced tool was used to create the DFD, it would prevent this from happening. But if these diagrams were drawn with simpler (and cheaper) drawing tools, these borders must be controlled manually. Figure 8.12 shows a corrected level 1 DFD. The problem can be in either (or both) of the level 1 or level 2 diagrams. The analyst must get the correct information from the customer.

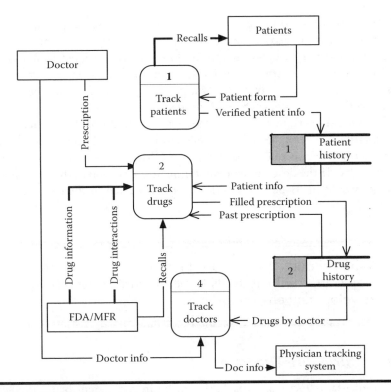

Figure 8.12 DFD level 1 corrected.

8.4 The Unified Modeling Language Family

UML is defined by the Object Management Group (OMG) and is a nonproprietary language for object modeling, even though many organizations today use it beyond the boundaries of object-oriented (OO) development. In the context of this book it is viewed as a software modeling approach, but it can be used to model business and systems engineering. UML contains a lot of modeling diagrams and there are many ways to organize them. The method selected here helps to look at the modeling in a hierarchical view and uses three major concepts:

1. Structure: Models like class diagrams and object diagrams fall in this category.
2. Behavior: Activity diagrams, state diagrams, and use cases are examples of this.
3. Interaction: Examples include collaboration diagrams and sequence diagrams.

The Unified Modeling Language evolved in the early 1990s with inputs from many sources, culminating in the efforts by James Rumbaugh, Grady Booch, and Ivar Jacobson, commonly known in the industry as "the three amigos." Their UML 1.0 draft was submitted in 1997. It has gone through many revisions, and UML 2.0 is the current version (with 2.1 underway).

UML is a set of recommendations and guidelines. Most everything is optional and needs to be customized by the organization developing the system. It does tend to be used in a way that makes it appear closer to the developer (system-centric) than to the customer (business-centric), so organizations sometimes struggle with the use of it in the very early stages of a project when it may not yet have been decided whether or not a new system is needed.

When should UML be used rather than a more traditional approach? It tends to be primarily driven by the development environment. If the organization's development methodology is object oriented, then UML would normally be the technique of choice. If the development environment is traditional, then the modeling techniques would likely be the traditional ones reviewed in the early part of this chapter.

> **When should UML be used rather than a more traditional approach? It tends to be primarily driven by the development environment.**

8.4.1 Structure Diagrams

Structure diagrams focus on what needs to be in the system being modeled. It includes models for data, hardware, program modules, files, etc. One of the more common diagrams that a business analyst may be exposed to is the class diagram.

8.4.1.1 Class Diagrams

Classes basically define components within a system, such as customers, orders, parts, and other key components. Classes can also be used to define hardware- and system-related items, but in general the business analyst must be careful in deciding what level of detail to take these diagrams. At their simplest form they can be very usable, and they can look a lot like a data model, but they also include processes, called methods. So a class, such as customer, can have attributes such as customer name and customer address, and it can also have methods, such as add new customer, change customer address, remove customer. It is a different way to view and discuss these concepts with the customer. Class diagrams look at data and process together. Figure 8.13 shows a common representation of a class with the class name, its attributes, and the methods.

Classes are also related to other classes. A customer can place orders, an order can have parts. These relationships are shown in Figure 8.14.

As seen, this looks very similar to the ERD shown earlier, and in reality, much of what is described in a class diagram is the same information as the ERD.

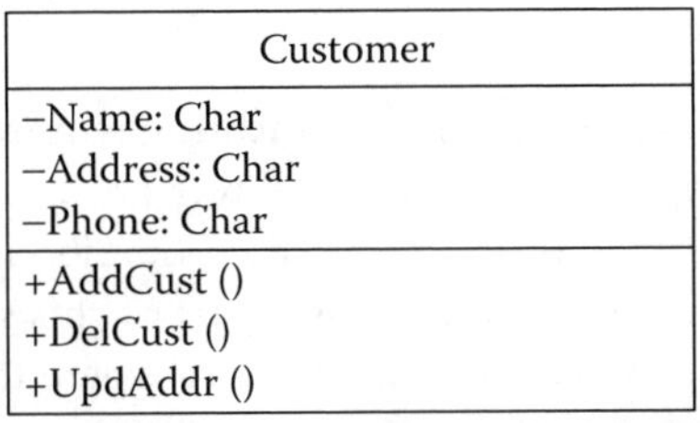

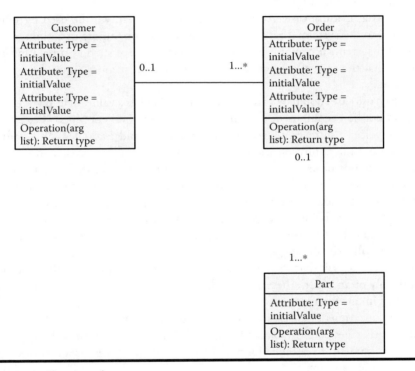

Figure 8.13 Class diagram.

Figure 8.14 Class interfaces.

However, the addition of methods is significant, as are some of the rules on how classes work together.

8.4.2 Behavior Diagrams

Typical models here include activity diagrams, state diagrams, and use cases. These models are perhaps the ones where the business analyst is most involved. The expected behavior of a system must be defined by the customer. Other areas, such as data and nonfunctional requirements may be defined by standards or regulations, but behavior requires customer involvement.

8.4.2.1 Use Cases

Probably the most popular method of documenting requirements today is with use cases. Use cases were originally developed by Ivar Jacobson at Erikson. They were originally linked primarily with object-oriented development, and although they predated UML as a standard, they are now a part of this standard. Use cases have expanded outside of just the OO environment to where today many corporations use them as the standard way of documenting all types of systems requirements. Although there are business use cases as well as systems use cases, this section will only deal with the latter.

So what is a use case? A use shows how the system will be used by someone external to the system. That someone may be a person, an organization, or even a different system. It can also be a more abstract concept such as time. One guideline is that the system cannot start its own use case, it must always be externally initiated.

Each use case should be a standalone action that has a value on its own. Use cases should not be decomposed; they are relatively high-level concepts. "Place Order," "Pay Invoice," "Hire Employee" are typical real-world examples. This definition can cause some confusion leading to projects defining hundreds and sometimes even thousands of use cases. It is important to try to avoid this because it causes a lot of duplication of functionality between use cases. To start the identification of use case candidates, ask the stakeholders (including other systems) who will be using the system being developed. Then ask what those "users" will want to do. It is likely that there will be a fairly comprehensive list of potential use cases. Some of them will probably be detailed processes of the same use case. For example, customers may say that they want to place an order, change an order, and print a hard copy of an order. These are all related to "Place Order," and can probably be handled in one use case.

Organizations often create too many use cases early on and then consolidate them as they get comfortable with the modeling approach. One technique, shared by a past student, to evaluate for potential consolidation use cases is to ask the following three questions:

1. Are the use cases typically done by the same user? This does not mean that there cannot be two actors performing the same use case. That happens frequently; for example, both a customer and an order entry person can place an order, but it does mean that the actor who starts the use case will normally finish it.
2. Are they typically done in the same timing interval? If the use cases are "Place Order" and "Pay For Order," determine if they happen at approximately the same time. Can you place five orders and then pay? If the actions are not on the same interval (and frequency), it may be good to split them apart (but it is not a necessity).

3. Do they both need to be implemented at the same time? In other words, if one use case is part of the project scope, must the other use case be included as well or can it be handled manually? With the previous example of placing an order and paying for it, it may be conceivable for the customer to implement one of those functions, but not the other (due to some type of constraints). If so, it may make sense to have two use cases.

If the answer to all three questions is yes, then there is a good chance that this is one use case. Although this is not an official, foolproof technique, it does help the analyst to get an understanding of what requirements belong together.

A use case has two components, the diagram and the template. Although most people may recognize the diagram, the real information and the value are in the template. Actually, a student from one of the large U.S. auto companies mentioned that they are no longer using the diagram, just the template. The diagram gives the big picture, the scope, which can sometimes be seen in other diagrams such as context diagrams (discussed in Chapter 3). The template portion is where the details of the requirements are captured, at a user level, a system level, and sometimes at a business level. Both the diagram and the template will be detailed over the next few pages.

Figure 8.15 has an example of a use case diagram and some of its key components.

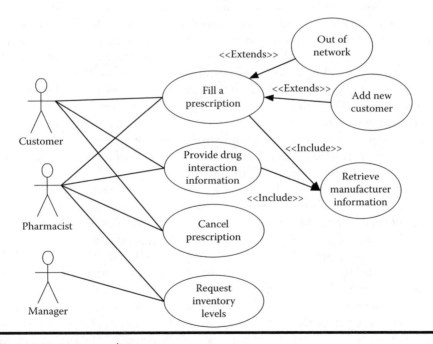

Figure 8.15 Use case diagram.

- Actor: Initiates the use case. It is noteworthy that all use cases must be externally initiated. The system cannot initiate any use cases. There can be secondary actors who are part of the response to the use case, but the primary actors will be the ones initiating the use case.
- Relationship: Simply shows what actor is executing which use case. Each actor can have a relationship with many use cases and each use case may be initiated by many actors.
- Use Case: The actual action that the actor is trying to accomplish. The guideline again is to have an action that accomplishes a business value for the user.
- Includes and Extends: They are special-needs concepts that can be used to add flexibility to the use cases.

The <<includes>> is basically a way of calling a different use case from within the one being defined. This may be done if there is a piece of common functionality between two or more use cases. The <<includes>> would allow the documentation of that duplicate functionality once. A good example is the two use cases "Fill a prescription" and "Provide drug interaction information." Both of these use cases will need to "Retrieve manufacturer drug information." Instead of defining this process twice, once per use case, an <<includes>> use case is identified, reducing duplication of effort.

The <<extends>> allows for identification of exception criteria. These exceptions may be error conditions or just unusual circumstances. In the use case "Fill a prescription," the normal use case may be that an existing customer is a part of this pharmacy's network. An <<extends>> could be added for "Out of network" processing or for adding a new customer. This would be something that is valid functionality, but not needed all the time. Some experts are strongly discouraging the use of <<includes>> and <<extends>>, expressing the opinion that it is really a form of decomposition. There may be valid reasons to use them on occasions, but it may also be wise to evaluate if these constructs are really needed. The <<includes>> seems to be the most value-added of the two, because it reduces the duplication of information, and that is always recommended.

Each use case is really a placeholder for the use case template. Although there are many examples of use case templates, such as the one shown in Figure 8.16, these templates should be viewed as starting points that should be evaluated for applicability to the standard processes within each organization.

The use case template is not officially part of UML, but it is the part of the use case modeling technique that most organizations are concentrating on. Some large organizations have gone as far as no longer using the diagrams, but rather only documenting the requirements in the use case template. Technically then, this is not really part of the UML family, but it is a good example of how it is more important to customize a concept making it work better within an organization rather than strictly enforcing an external standard. It should be noted though that if the organization is using an advanced tool such as the Rational Unified Process®

(RUP), then deviating from the standard process will cause the organization to lose some of the features within the tool. An example of the use case template is shown in Figure 8.16.

Some of the most common fields on the template are:

- Use Case ID: Each use case should have a unique identifier.
- Use Case Description: Overview of what the use case is supposed to do. This should be written in terms of the actor. What is the actor looking to accomplish when this use case is initiated?

GENERAL CHARACTERISTICS	
Use Case ID	Unique identifier
Description	What is the use case intended to do
Pre-condition	What has happened prior to the use case being started
Post-Condition	What will happen after the use case is completed
Success Criteria	How will successful completion be judged
Main Scenario	What will the flow be most of the time (see below, this is sometimes called Happy Path)
Alternative scenarios	Variations on the main flow
Exceptions	Errors
Includes	Common subroutines
Applicable business rules	What business rules applies to this use case
Frequency	How often will the use case be executed
Primary Actor	Who will initiate the use case
Secondary Actor	Who is involved with the completion of the use case
Security	Special security considerations for the system
Back-up and recovery	What happens if the system is not available

Figure 8.16 Use case template.

Assumptions and Constraints	What environment is assumed
	What are the system constraints
Version control	What version of the use case is this
Author	Who wrote this document

Main scenario (Happy Path)	
Step	**Action**
S	Starting point of use case
1	Actor initiates use case
2	System responds
3	Actor continues the use case
4	System responds
5	Completion

Figure 8.16 (*Continued*).

- Pre-condition: Describes what the starting condition is. Is the user logged into the system? Have security checks been done? It helps to identify what the actor and the system must have done prior to entering this use case. Sometimes the activities described in the pre-conditions are outside of the scope of the project. If so, they don't need any further documentation. If they are within the scope of this project, they can be documented in other use cases or in a different type of requirements document (sometimes referred to as supplemental requirements).
- Post-condition: Describes what happens after the process is finished; "Print receipt," "Update balance." Again this may refer to something out of scope, a different use case, or a requirement documented in a different document. Together with the pre-condition, the post-condition helps define the boundaries of the use case. This is a critical definition because it helps focus the customer on what the starting and ending point should be for the discussion.
- Success criteria: How will the actor define a successful completion of the use case? When talking about requirements there tends to be a lot of focus on error conditions and alternative paths. This section is where the desired outcome of a use case is documented. In other words, what does a successful end result look like? What will the actor accomplish when everything goes right?

- Main scenario: This is the normal scenario. It describes what is expected to happen under normal circumstance. Note that it doesn't mean 50 percent or more of the time. Rather it means that when the customer thinks about this process and how to reach the success criteria identified above, this is what would be described as the normal path. It also should be one of the main test cases. The example in Figure 8.16 shows the interaction between the actor and the system. Because the use case must always be externally initiated, the first action must be taken by the actor. There can also be secondary actors shown, people or systems involved with the completion of the use case. However, because this is discussing a systems use case, what is shown is interaction between actors and the system, not interaction between two actors. The interaction can also be documented using an activity diagram or a flow chart. The scenario can have loops and decisions in it to repeat certain steps in the process or to skip other steps based on a predefined criterion.
- Alternative scenarios: Although there is only one main scenario, there could be many (hundreds) of alternative scenarios. Alternatives deal with valid conditions that happen less frequently than the main scenario. For the use case of "Fill a prescription," alternative scenarios may be "New customer," "Prescription not available," or "Customer has no insurance coverage." These are valid conditions, the requirements for the processes must be documented, but it is not the norm. The alternative scenarios may be documented as complete scenarios, looking similar to the main scenario, or they may be partial scenarios, where the alternative actions starts at a certain step in the main flow and ends at a different step.
- Exceptions: Similar in form to the alternative scenarios, but deals with error conditions. What happens when a customer orders an invalid product? What is the result if the customer does not pass the credit check? Again, like with the alternative scenarios, it is likely that there will be a substantial number of these conditions.
- Includes: Documenting what other use cases are called from within this use case. Typically used when there is identical processing done between two or more use cases.
- Applicable business rules: Although business rules do not have to be enforced by the use case (even though it is desirable), it must allow for the business rules to be enforced. An example of this is the business rule, "Only pharmacy manager can see confidential customer information." This can be dealt with manually by not storing confidential information in the system or it can be handled by password protecting the information. However, if the system is set up so that a clerk entering the customer information automatically will be able to see all customer information, then the business rule cannot be enforced and there is a conflict, which must be identified and resolved. Other business rules which may impact a use case are "Prescription

must be filled within 30 minutes of receiving it" and "The pharmacy must be able to process prescriptions 24 hours per day, 365 days per year."

- Frequency: This is how often this process will be used. It is largely used to gather the nonfunctional requirements of performance. If this process is used 10,000 times per day, performance becomes critical. If it is used once every three months, performance is less of a concern.
- Primary actors: A primary actor is someone or something initiating a use case. It can be a person, a role that a person plays, a group of people, a system, or a time. There can be more than one primary actor. For example, the use case of "Check for interacting drugs" can be initiated by a pharmacy clerk or by a different system. Because a use case must always be initiated from the outside, there will always be at least one primary actor. Sometimes that actor is time. A use case may be initiated by the end of the month, a tax deadline, or some other temporal concept.
- Secondary actors: Secondary actors are needed to complete the use case, but they do not initiate it. If the use case is "Check for interacting drugs," the drug manufacturer would be a secondary actor. They are needed for the successful completion of the use case, but they do not initiate it. There can be two different types of secondary actors. The first type is needed for the use case to be completed; in this case, the drug manufacturer provides drug interaction information. The second type of secondary actor is when they are the indirect trigger of a use case. When the drug maker issues a warning for a newly discovered drug interaction, the pharmacist will enter that into the system and check for potential problems for all patients. In this scenario the pharmacist is the primary actor; interfacing with the system and the drug manufacturer is the secondary actor, triggering the event.
- Security: Again this comes back to the nonfunctional systems requirements. Is there a need for access control? Can all users perform this function? What system audit trail needs to be created?
- Back-up and recovery: Are there any special needs for recovery? Does data need to be accessible 24 hours per day? Is there a manual (or automated) process that can be used if this system is unavailable?
- Assumptions and constraints: List any assumptions that were documented as the use case was developed (such as actor has access to the system) or constraints (must be able to connect to the ABC company credit check network).
- Version control information: This document will go though many changes. Version control will be difficult but critical, especially to ensure that there is no scope creep as the document goes through iterations from high level to detailed requirements.
- Author: Names the person responsible for this document and can include customers and other stakeholders who provided input into the document.

A completed use case template will contain very detailed information. How does the analyst go from some very high-level objectives of a system down to the very precise details contained in the use case template? It is actually an iterative process and one of the advantages of the use case template if it is used correctly. It can be documenting the high-level requirements up front and then gradually be refined into detailed requirements. This document then, after the business analyst has completed it, is turned over to the systems analyst who can add the solution design features to it as well. Done this way, it gives you automatic traceability from the high-level requirements, all the way to the detailed design.

An example of an iterative approach when developing the use cases (for the analysis phase only), which starts with the objectives and finishes with detailed requirements, through gradual expansion of the use cases is:

- High Level
  - Defines scope.
  - Sets the boundaries for the project.
  - Only focuses on main scenario and critical alternative scenarios.
  - Used to get executive commitment.

- Broad
  - Gets a good description of all use cases and actors.
  - Identifies scenarios, but stays at a high level.

- Deep
  - Explores each scenario in detail.
  - Documents nonfunctional requirements.

The high-level iteration should be done with the sponsor, customer management, and other decision makers. Have a clearly defined set of deliverables including the use case diagram and a predefined subset of the use case template. The broad iteration involves the users and focuses on identifying scenarios and user requirements. The final iteration brings in the developers and focuses on the detailed systems requirements, both functional and nonfunctional. This is the session that serves as the translation and hand-off between the business analyst and the systems analyst. The business analyst is responsible for the requirements or the "what," and the systems analyst is responsible for the specification or the "how." Both parties must understand the documentation created here. It is technically owned by the business analyst, but it really should be a collaborative effort.

Strengths of Use Cases
  - Are intuitive for the customer.
  - Concentrate on the purpose of the system.
  - Can see both big-picture business view and detailed systems requirements.
  - Give the foundation for test cases.

Weaknesses of Use Cases
- – Some duplication of requirements, especially data and nonfunctional requirements.
- – May require a lot of alternative paths.
- – The potential of getting into too much detail too fast.

8.4.2.2 Activity Diagrams

The activity diagram (sometimes called swim lane, or work flow diagram) is one of the most frequently used modeling techniques. It is intuitive, the customer relates well to it, and it is excellent in defining communication points between processes and organizations. Although activity diagrams have been around for a long time, they have become more standardized and formalized under the UML notation technique. However, be careful when using a modeling tool for these diagrams. The capabilities of the modeling tool sometimes makes the model more complex than what is needed and the customer may be get lost in the details. Drawing tools like Visio® have the UML notation built into the tool, which helps to enforce the standard, but can make the model look complex. When working on a white board or flip chart, the analyst can simplify the model, making it easier for the customer to understand. There are other standards beside UML for activity diagramming, so don't be surprised if customers or developers are used to a different way of showing the information. Activity diagrams can be shown with or without swim lanes. Figure 8.17 is an example of an activity diagram (it is actually very similar to Figure 3.10). This shows that modeling techniques can often be used at many different stages of the project. The swim lanes add organizational information and bring functional perspective to the diagram; but if that doesn't fit in with the specifics of the project, then just remove the swim lanes and show the activities as they are.

When discussing activity diagrams the main focus is on the flow and the information going from one process to another. Most models discussed earlier in this book are not intended to show sequence, but activity diagrams are, which may make them reflect how the customers view their business.

Some of the key conventions when creating an activity diagram are:

- There can only be one starting point, but there can be multiple ending points.
- People, organizations, and systems can be given their own swim lanes.
- Activity diagrams can be shown following a time-line concept or the sequence can be shown without indicating a specific time for each activity.

A closer look at Figure 8.17 shows some of the strengths of this modeling technique. It shows the steps in the process in a sequential and intuitive mode. Each one of those process steps should have a document attached to it to show the detailed requirements of that process. This is best done using a standard template, similar to

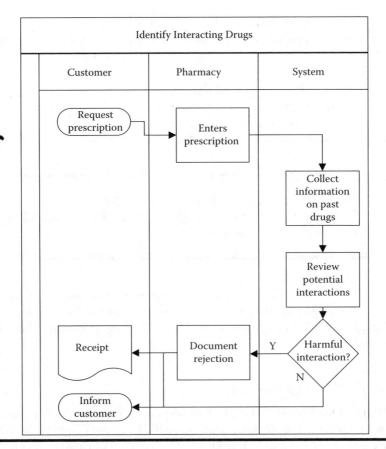

Figure 8.17 Activity diagram.

what was shown earlier for the use case. The diagram also shows any physical manifestation being created by the process. The documents are shown (in this example "Receipt"), and should eventually be defined in detail.

The decision points are the next notable construct. This will allow the process to branch off in different directions based on predefined conditions. Based on those decision points, the process may be sent back to an earlier step (looping back) or forward (skipping steps). There are also examples of a process forking (splitting into two parallel processes and joining (coming back together again).

Of all of the models available, a well-drawn activity diagram is often the most enlightening and understandable one for the customer. For the Prescription Interaction Project, the flow shows the process of checking for drug interaction. The process starts when the customer hands over the prescription and ends with a prescription verified against drug interaction and the customer informed. Note that this is a subprocess of the overall "Fill Prescription" process. It is important to clearly identify the boundaries of what is being modeled. Define the starting point as well as the end point of the process being modeled. This will help the user stay focused during the review. This model then serves as the basis for the detailed requirements gathering. Review the model step-by-step and ask questions about each step:

- What information do you need from the customer?
- Can anyone become a customer?
- How does a customer request a prescription?
- If the customer is on a prescription plan, is there additional information needed?

> Of all of the models available, a well-drawn activity diagram is often the most enlightening and understandable one for the customer.

This form of review will guide the user along the process and minimize excursion into nonrelated areas. Whenever users stray from the step being discussed, put their thoughts on a "to be discussed later" list and gently guide them back to the activity diagram.

8.4.2.3   State Diagrams

State diagrams (also known as state chart diagrams) illustrate the life cycle of an entity within a business. They are part of UML, but state diagrams in different forms have been around long before UML. The intention of the state diagram is to evaluate the behavior of an entity while it is in different states of existence, such as when the entity is created, when it is going through different parts of an organization, and when it is becoming obsolete and no longer needed. State diagrams are not needed for all entities, but for entities which are being processed and changed by an organization, they can be a great tool to clarify requirements. For instance, the entity "Prescription" can have multiple states. It can be a written prescription, an entered prescription, a rejected prescription, an approved prescription, or a filled prescription. Developing the state diagram forces the customer to look at how an entity is viewed, how it can be moved from one state to another, and what some of the unique behaviors are in each state.

Review the state diagram in Figure 8.18. With this example of a state diagram it is easy to see how the model can be used as a part of the customer interview. Walk through the model step by step and ask the customer:

- How is a prescription written?
- Who can approve a prescription?

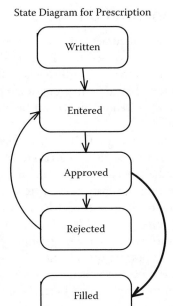

State Diagram for Prescription

Figure 8.18 State diagram.

- How does a prescription get rejected?
- Is there a process to move an approved prescription to a rejected prescription?
- What is the difference between an approved prescription and a filled prescription?
- Should you be able to reject without approval?

Naturally these same questions could be asked without the model, but they would probably appear more disjointed and would be harder to document in a structured fashion.

8.4.3   Interaction Diagrams

Examples of interaction diagrams include collaboration diagrams and sequence diagrams. Although some of these diagrams are used for testing and to increase overall understanding of what a system will do, they tend to fall more in the domain of the systems analyst and the developer rather than the business analyst. Classes (as reviewed earlier) interact with each other and interaction diagrams help identify how the collaboration works and in what sequence things need to happen. However, they are usually defined at too great a level of detail for the customer. As a business analyst, the main use for these diagrams is in discussions with the systems analyst. These models are beyond the scope of this book.

8.5   Matrix Documentation

Somewhere between pure text documentation and models is matrix documentation. It increases readability, can be used to validate information, and is relatively easy to implement. There are some standard matrices that are often used when documenting requirements (such as data dictionaries and use case templates), but in addition much of the textual requirements can be organized in some form of matrix document.

For data models, consider adding a CRUD (create/read/update/delete) matrix as shown in Figure 8.19. On one side of the matrix are all of the data entities identified in the data model. On the other side are the organizational units involved with the project. In each intersection the analysts evaluate whether this is an entity that this organization can create, read, update, or delete. This helps evaluate ownership of data, and also helps identify potential interface needs. If this project does not create an entity, but needs to use it, then the question of who does create it must be answered. Also, instead of putting organizations on one side of the matrix, the analyst can put the business processes which deal with the data. It serves a similar purpose by helping to identify what process creates an entity, what process can change it, and what process can delete it.

Entity Organization	Pharmacy	Inventory	Customer Support
Customer	CRU		RUD
Doctor	CRUD		R
FDA	CRUD		R
Prescription Drugs	R	CUD	R

Figure 8.19 CRUD matrix.

8.6   How to Decide Which Model to Select

The systems development methodologies used will be a driver behind which modeling techniques are selected. If the development organization is more object oriented, the UML diagrams tend to be the favorite choice because they have been developed with that platform in mind. Another big factor is the knowledge and skill level of the team. If no one has experience with use cases and class diagrams, and this is a high-visibility project, then this may not be the time to try to learn these techniques.

However, as a business analyst, the main concern will be what the customer can best relate to. The analyst must find a way, through models or text, to make sure that the customer buys off on the requirements which have been captured. So customer preference must also be involved in the decision process. For the Prescription Interaction Project, it is likely that the customer's experience with systems development is low. The project is an enhancement to an existing system. Based on these two factors, a legacy approach would make sense, "legacy" meaning that the approach will be the same as what the organization has used in the past. This would make sense both for the developers and for the customer.

The analyst must find a way, through models or text, to make sure that the customer buys off on the requirements which have been captured.

8.7 Text Documentation

Very few people enjoy writing down requirements in text form. However, if after meeting with the customer for two hours the end result is a blank sheet of paper, then there are some real problems. It is in the text document that the analyst documents the details of the requirements. When doing that, requirements should be:

- Specific: The requirement should be specific enough to allow for comprehension by all. There is always a question on how far to take this. The example "The system must allow for security" is clearly not specific enough. What type of security? Security of what? By changing the statement to "The system must allow for multiple levels of access to restricted data," it is greatly improved. It becomes a judgment call whether to further define it or to leave it for the design team.
- Unambiguous: Does it mean the same thing to different people? "The system must be fast" could mean different things for the developer and the customer. The statement needs more detail. "The system must have an average response time of three seconds during peak hours, 9 a.m. until 3 p.m. Greenwich Mean Time" would give a much more measurable statement.
- Verifiable: This may be the most important one. All requirements must be verifiable after implementation; if not, they are meaningless. It may be too early to determine exactly how it will be verified, but when looking at the requirement, it should be clear that we can verify that the requirement has been met. The requirement "The system must make the customer happy" is probably not measurable, but the requirement "The system must allow the customer to enter a prescription in less than 1 minute" is.

- Traceable: All requirements must be traceable from a business need to user requirements, to system requirements, to specifications, and finally to the finished product.
- Consistent: All requirements must be consistent with the other requirements. If requirement A asks for a wireless interface and requirement B states no transmission on nonland lines, then there is an inconsistency which must be resolved before the BRD is turned over to the development team.
- Agreed to: Both the customer and the developer must agree to the requirements. It is the customer's prerogative to find a different developer if they see fit, but no developer should take on a requirement that they don't think can be implemented.
- Realistic: Even if the customer wants response time faster than the speed of light, that does not make it realistic.

It is also important to use good writing practices when writing the requirements. Some examples of good writing habits are:

- Use proper grammar and spelling: Sometimes when reading documentation, it is surprising to see that the author has not spell-checked the document. However, spell-check sometimes causes the author to assume that because the tool doesn't flag anything, there are no errors. It is very difficult to catch one's own mistakes. Always have a different person proofread the document before it goes to the customer. A poorly written document will leave a bad impression with the customer and may cause the customer to question the competency and professionalism of the analyst.
- Write in active voice: Don't write "The user would like to be entering order information" but rather "The user enters order information."
- Define terms and abbreviations in a glossary: There may be terms that seem obvious to the person writing the document, but for others, the terms may be totally unknown or have a different meaning. Acronyms like DBA may mean "Database Administrator" in the IT organization and "Doing Business As" for the customer. For the Prescription Interaction Project, something like FDA may cause confusion. Although clearly a related project entity in the United States (Food and Drug Administration), in a different part of the world it could be a different regulatory agency.
- Remove ambiguity: Sometimes a word can mean many things and must be clarified to be understood by all stakeholders. A simple word like "system" can cause confusion: is it the computer system or the business system that is being talked about?
- Use the customer's language: Because the project is likely to eventually lead to a systems development effort, it is easy to start early in the process with technical terms. Avoid this, and talk the customer's language. It is unavoidable

that the customer will need to learn some systems terms, but for the most part it should be the developer learning the customer's language. This is especially important when using development tools. These tools often enforce standards which make sense from a developer's view, but which can be very confusing to the customer. For example, the customer may state a need to track prescription manufacturer. The standard in the data modeling tool could be "Presc_Mfr." This is obviously not intuitive for the customer and should be avoided, except for customers with prior exposure to these formats.

- Organize in single, focused, and short sentences: Rambling, never-ending sentences are difficult to understand. They tend to contain so much information that it is hard to see what the real purpose or focus is. Decompose the requirements so that each requirement has a clear focus and a real purpose. Try to ensure that the successful completion of a requirement can be verified with just a few test cases. There will need to be more test cases for errors and alternative paths, but if there are a large number of test cases needed just to verify successful completion, review the requirements to see if they should be decomposed. For example, the requirement "The system must verify valid zip code, compare against past prescriptions and prompt the customer for other medications not in this system, possibly from other pharmacies and pull the latest drug interaction information from the manufacturer and any controlling government agency" is too long, too complex, and lacks focus. Split it up into short sentences where each requirement has a clear focus.

- Avoid creativity: Writing a BRD is not the same as writing the Great American Novel. The BRD should be a precise document to be used in clear communication. Strive for consistency and avoid synonyms. If it is called "Drug" in one place, use that term consistently. Although "Medication" and "Product" may mean the same thing in the pharmacy, when alternating between the terms in a requirements document, it will cause confusion to the developers when trying to figure out the difference between a "Drug" and a "Medication."

8.8 Validating the Requirements

After weeks of eliciting requirements and days (or more) of documenting them, the final step in the analysis phase must be to validate them. There is a more detailed discussion on validation in Chapter 9 and Chapter 10, including what to include in the review package for the different stakeholders. Both models and text must be validated, and that will normally be done in some type of walk-through. It is especially important for the users to be educated on the models that will be used in the walk-through. Although some of them may have been seen and used during the elicitation of the requirements, be careful not to assume that each reviewer has seen the models before, has been trained on them, or even remembers how to read them.

8.9 Summary

Gathering requirements without creating a model is similar to building a house without a blueprint. It severely limits your chance of developing the right product. The choice of modeling technique is less important than consistent use of that technique. Once the whole organization is trained on a certain technique, the value gained from the technique will greatly increase. Frequent changes of modeling techniques will cause confusion and often produce poor results. Combining different techniques is OK, but be aware of duplication of information. Train all stakeholders on the modeling techniques before using them in requirements sessions. Keep in mind that modeling is primarily a communications technique. If the customer does not relate to it or if it does not help the developer work, then the wrong technique is being used. There may be a need to use different techniques for the customer and the developers. That goes back to the business analyst's role as a translator and liaison.

8.10 Activity

Review the case study section called "Interview with store buyer." If you are using modeling techniques different than the ones used in the exercise, it may be productive to model this business area using those techniques as well.

1. Based on the interview, what use cases are needed for this business area? Identify three to five use cases. Select one of those use cases and fill out the use case template.
2. Identify the key entities that the buyer's business area deals with, identify attributes and relationships for those entities, and outline an entity relationship diagram.
3. "Write a requirements statement for the "Placing special order" requirement. Make the statement specific, measurable, and unambiguous.

Chapter 9

Effective Requirements Communication

England and America are two countries divided by a common language.

—George Bernard Shaw

This chapter concentrates on the communication of the output of the requirements gathering effort, which is only a portion of the overall communication with which the business analyst is involved. However, it is a part of the communication that is often overlooked from a planning standpoint. It includes presenting and making the information available, but also validating and gaining acceptance of the requirements package. Even though the same basic information will be communicated to all stakeholders, the communication needs to be customized to fit the interest and knowledge of each stakeholder.

9.1 Objectives

- Identify stakeholders who need to be aware of the project direction.
- Work with people and organizations who have conflicting views on the direction of the project.
- Determine the best package and review approach for different types of stakeholders.
- Get formal sign-off for the requirements.

9.2 Overview

Although the Business Requirements Document (BRD) should be a complete and comprehensive document used for communication with stakeholders, this does not mean that every stakeholder should be expected to read every part of the BRD. The project manager must understand anything that impacts overall scope, timeline, and budget, but does not need to see detailed requirements. The executives and the sponsor must understand all of the business requirements and the business impact of the product, but they may not need to see the detailed user interface requirements. Too often the stakeholder is handed a document, hundred of pages thick, and asked to review and approve the package. That is an unrealistic expectation.

The BRD review should be customized to fit each stakeholder. It is a good guideline for the business analysts to ask themselves with regard to each piece of documentation presented to the stakeholder, "Why is this stakeholder reviewing this document?" If the answer is something like "For information" or "To keep the stakeholder in the loop," then consider excluding it from the review package for that stakeholder. However, let the stakeholder know that the information is available; the stakeholder will choose to review it if interested. It is always best to let the stakeholders know whenever there is any information excluded from their package.

9.3 Determine the Audience for the Communication

Figure 9.1 is an example that shows the main stakeholders for a BRD and what their main focus areas might be from the requirements package.

Stakeholder	Main focus areas
Customer	Regulatory Requirements Business Requirements Assumption Constraints Risks
User	User Requirements System Requirements Business Rules
Developer	All
Executives	Goals and Objectives Impacts Risk Assumptions Constraints
Internal organizations	Process changes Interface changes
External organizations	Regulatory Requirements

Figure 9.1 Stakeholder focus for the BRD.

- Customer: The primary concerns of the customer are the business requirements, regulatory requirements, assumptions, constraints, and risks. Customer sign-off on the BRD is not going to be based on the detailed user interfaces or the system response time. Those requirements are likely to be left for the actual users of the system.
- User: As long as the customer (the management) is happy with the high-level requirements, the users are unlikely to be concerned about them. Rather, they would be more interested in the usability, efficiency, learning curves, accuracy of data, and other items that are likely to have an impact on their day-to-day job activities. The users are often under time pressure so if they are given too much information, they may not have time to review what will impact them the most.
- The development team: This is the only stakeholder to whom it is recommended that all of the information, the complete BRD, is presented and reviewed. Because this is the team that will take the requirements and create a solution, the development team must have a complete understanding of all categories of requirements, the AS-IS as well as the TO-BE business and system situation, along with information about user profiles, assumptions, constraints, and so on. If the system analyst does not have a clear understanding of both the big picture and the detailed requirements, chances are that the solution will miss the mark.

> If the system analyst does not have a clear understanding of both the big picture and the detailed requirements, chances are that the solution will miss the mark.

- The executives: They are probably the ones hardest to communicate with, or rather to judge how much information to communicate to them. They must be made aware of goals and objectives, impacts to the business, risks to the organization, and any high-visibility assumptions and constraints. The communication to the executives should be concise and allow them to ask questions if they need more information. Also look at each item and see if it is really something that should be reviewed by the executives. Although under-communication is potentially very harmful to the organization, over-communication can also be a serious problem. Stay focused, make it short, and make it clear.
- Other internal organizations: Here the communication effort should be changes to business processes and changes to work flow which may impact other areas. A special highlight should be on the gap analysis between what is done today and what will be done in the future.

- External organizations: There may not be a need to communicate with them at all, but if the system being worked on interfaces with vendors or external customers, there should be some communication, albeit high level, to make them aware of what is going on. They may also need to be aware of any regulatory requirements which might impact them.

9.4   Dealing with Disagreements about Requirements

It is common in a multi-stakeholder environment that there is disagreement between stakeholders regarding requirements, especially in the area of project scope and functionality. What should be in and out of the scope of the product? One stakeholder may prefer more manual processing, while another prefers automation. One stakeholder may prefer outsourcing of a business function; another may want to handle it within the current project. It is not the business analyst's job (nor the project manager's) to determine what is in scope and out of scope. In the stakeholder analysis that was discussed in Chapter 4, each stakeholder should have been prioritized. If there is a difference in priority between the stakeholders, then this is easy, let the higher-priority stakeholder decide. However, often there is no difference in priority. When this type of disagreement occurs, work with the different parties to try to reach a decision. If that does not work, then look at escalating it to the sponsor.

> It is not the business analyst's job (nor the project manager's) to determine what is in scope and out of scope.

There is rarely just one way of performing a job function. Two different users may perform the same job two different ways in today's environment, and they both feel that their way is the best one. This kind of disagreement can be handled through a process like the one just described, but another possible solution might be to build enough flexibility into the product to allow both parties to keep operating their way. This is likely to increase the overall cost of the project (and potentially of the product), so try to minimize the use of this option as a solution.

9.5   Creating the Requirements Review Package(s)

When creating the packages which will be reviewed with the stakeholders, consider both their need for detail and their need for a big-picture understanding. Some of the most common tools to allow for this are:

- Models: Chapter 8 reviewed different modeling techniques, and although models are often used to effectively elicit requirements, they can be just as effective communicating the BRD to a large audience. Some of these diagrams are very intuitive and help to give the reviewer a quick, high-level view of what the system is all about. Models are also great in meetings where the discussion can stay focused by highlighting one area of the model at a time.
- Text: Can be documented in templates or in matrices. Text can often be overwhelming, especially on large projects, so it is important that it is well organized and grouped together based on a well-defined taxonomy (which was discussed in Chapter 6). To make it less overwhelming, try to present the text within the context of a model whenever possible.
- Prototyping: While technically a type of a model, the prototype will allow the simulation of predefined aspects of the system, and is often the most powerful way of reviewing requirements. The business analyst must make sure that the focus is on the requirements of the solution rather than the solution itself. The more high functioning the prototype is, the more difficult it will be for the user to stay focused at a high level.

The *Guide to the Business Analysis Body of Knowledge* (BABOK) published by the International Institute of Business Analysis (IIBA) also discusses that there may be a need to add material to the BRD review which is outside of the actual project documentation. Two especially powerful ways to help ensure that the reviewers understand the material being reviewed are through the use of presentations and storyboards. Presentations can help explain rationale and background of the project and of the requirements of the solution. A good presentation will highlight the most important information and make it easy to understand. For example, when reviewing the BRD with management, it can be best done by a presentation containing:

- Business problem and vision
- Project boundaries
- Impact of solution
- High-level assumptions and constraints
- Business-level requirements
- Key quality-of-service requirements
- Any controversial requirements

By putting the right focuses on the review, what could have been many hours of nonproductive review can now be brief and to the point.

The second way to help with the reviews is to use storyboards (or user stories, which are what IIBA calls them). Storyboards were discussed in Chapter 7 as a way to gather requirements. Here they are used as a way to explain to the stakeholders what the system will do. It is worth noting that this can be done for reviews regardless if storyboards were used to elicit requirements. So instead of using a thick Requirements document to explain all the requirements of the Prescription Interaction Project, a story is used to show what happens when a customer walks into the pharmacy with a prescription for a drug that has a dangerous interaction with another drug the customer has bought in the past. Each step is shown on the "board" (which can be a slide in a PowerPoint presentation). At the draft level, it may look something like the storyboard in Figure 9.2.

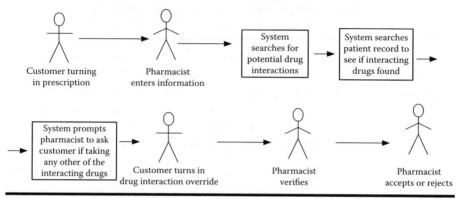

Figure 9.2 Story board for communication.

As seen, the review becomes an intuitive way to discuss a series of steps:

1. Customer presents a prescription.
2. Pharmacist enters information.
3. System searches for potential drug interactions.
4. System searches customer record for interacting drugs.
5. System prompts pharmacist to ask if customer is currently taking any of the interacting drugs.
6. If customer presents a drug interaction override approval, pharmacist verifies with doctor.
7. Pharmacist accepts or rejects prescription.

The business analyst must plan for sufficient time during the analysis phase to create these presentations and storyboards. Although it may be difficult to know the extent to which these will be needed, by evaluating the complexity of the project and the diversity of the stakeholder base, the analyst can make an adequate guess about how much effort to plan for.

Once the determination has been made for who needs to review the package as well as what information each stakeholder should review, verify this with the stakeholders and get an agreement to the package. Depending on the organization, the sponsor will sometimes be the person to determine what a certain stakeholder should see, but whenever possible, it is best to review this with the actual stakeholder. This may already have been decided and, may be a part of the Communication Plan for the project or for the analysis phase. If so, just grab the information from there.

The formality of the package presented will be different, based on whether it is reviewed by an internal or external reviewer. The stakeholder's location can drive how formal the package needs to be. If the reviewer is a development group located somewhere in Asia, the package will need to be much more complete and able to stand on its own than if the developers are sitting right next to the business analyst. Different types of projects will also require different formality in the review package. IIBA has identified four types of projects which will require different types of review packages:

1. Custom-developed software: Review will need to be very comprehensive and detailed. For the most part, the review will be based on the models and text in the BRD.
2. Upgrading to new technology: If the business does not change, then this may be primarily a technical review with limited customer involvement. The customer would primarily need to know what will work differently.
3. Change in a business process: This will need a review of the enterprise impact and business rules as well as reviews of process and data models.
4. Purchasing commercial off-the-shelf software: The review may be focused on the business and user requirements as well as constraints. The detailed functional requirements will often be built into the system, and it will be more a matter of explaining to the user how the package works. Part of the review may be to bring in the package allowing the reviewers to see what they will get. Be aware though that the requirements review session should never be the first time that a stakeholder sees the package; the stakeholder would be likely to start treating that as a requirements gathering session rather than a review session.

Expanding on the last bullet, I can relate a real-life experience about the dangers of assumptions when reviewing requirements. When developing the Saturn dealer system, there had been a number of requirements sessions, including prototypes and text documents. After the main part of the development was done, the dealers were brought back one more time to see what they had created and give it their blessing. Unfortunately, now they had a different opinion. It quickly turned into another requirements session resulting in massive changes to the project. So, make sure that the right level of expectation is set before starting the review.

Most of the review package will be excerpts from the BRD, but there needs to be an introduction section added for each package. This introduction section should include:

- Overview of package
- Timing and location of review meetings
- Expectations of what the stakeholder should do with the package (glance at, analyze, ask questions about, approve)
- List of other reviewers
- Steps and deliverables in the review process

Having this package prior to a review meeting will increase the chance of having a prepared stakeholder going into the session. Although there is no guarantee that the stakeholders will read the package, at least they have been given the opportunity to do so.

9.6   Performing the Review and Getting Sign-Off

Regardless if this is done as a self-guided review by the stakeholders or in a presentation-type format, it is important to guide the stakeholders through the information. If a model is reviewed, do it step by step and focus on one piece of the model at a time. Verify that there is an agreement to each focus area as the review is progressing. It is very difficult for the stakeholders to get comfortable with approving a large review package unless they can see the pieces one at a time and understand them. If the stakeholders get overwhelmed in the review, they are likely to push back and try to delay approval.

Figure 9.3 shows an example of a data model being reviewed with the customer and the way that the review is focusing on one area of the model by shading the

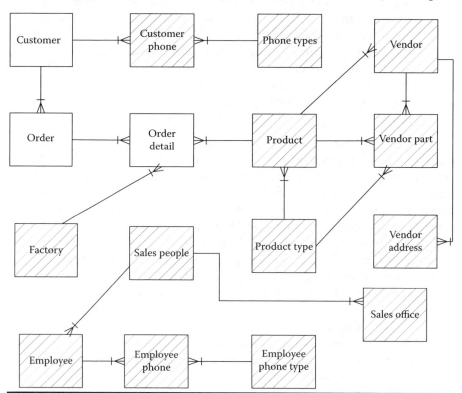

Figure 9.3 Data model for review.

rest. Once this area has been approved, change the focus to a different part of the model and review that. This also allows the reviewers to pay extra close attention to the areas that are most important to them. As an example, if this is a review for the prescription interaction system and the stakeholder is the pharmacist, they are likely to focus on what information is needed for the actual prescription. When reviewing doctor information or the patient information, the pharmacist may be less interested because it may not be a critical part of their job function.

A similar approach can be used when reviewing use cases. Clearly highlight which use case is being reviewed and do a complete review of that use case before moving on to the next. It is common that the stakeholder will start talking about areas of the system other than the part being reviewed. Avoid the temptation to jump over to that other area unless it is clearly essential for the current discussion. A good review takes good facilitation and part of that is to keep the review process focused.

9.7   Summary

Identify who should review the requirements and the best way to present the information to them. Doing this greatly increases the chance of achieving a successful user acceptance of the product down the road and minimizes the risk of the users saying, "I never knew that."

9.8   Activity

1. Document what components you would include for a BRD review with the following case study stakeholders:
   - Sponsor
   - Distribution Center Manager
   - VP of Operations
   - Buyer
   - Developer

2. Document what each one of the stakeholders main areas of focus should be for the requirements package being developed.

Chapter 10

Making Sure the Requirements are Implemented

Facts are the enemy of truth.

—Don Quixote, in *Man of La Mancha*

This chapter looks at the business analyst's involvement with the project after the requirements have been gathered and agreed upon. The level of involvement from the business analyst will vary greatly from organization to organization, but typical activities that the business analyst may be involved with include solution selection, technical proposal analysis, training, impact analysis, and communication.

10.1 Objectives

- Review the importance of exploring alternative solutions.
- Match a solution to the requirements.
- Make sure that the solution is usable.
- Review different types of tests and the role of the business analyst during the testing activities.
- Communicate the impact of the solution to the organization.
- Support the implementation of the solution.

10.2 Overview

The business analyst is responsible for the requirements of the solution, not the solution itself. This means that the business analyst has the responsibility for tracing the requirements through to the product. Obviously this must be done together with the systems analyst and the quality assurance people; nevertheless, it is the business analyst who should have the conversation with the customer on how the requirements have been fulfilled by the solution, what the impact will be on the business environment, and what needs to happen to prepare the users for the implementation. It is also fairly common that there are requirements which cannot easily be implemented or that, if changed, would be significantly easier to implement. The business analyst should be involved with the requirements negotiations that inevitably take place on any complex project.

> The business analyst is responsible for the requirements of the solution, not the solution itself.

10.3 The Importance of Alternative Solutions

The customer is often accused of not being able to think outside of the box and of being too rooted in today's environment to be able to accept creative and innovative solutions. Although that can be true, the same can often be said about the developers and the business analyst. The easy path tends to be that a potential solution is found, it is presented to the customer, and then the team marches to that beat. Then, at the end of the project, the customer comes back with some other solutions such as better ways of doing their job, new processes, new tools, new thinking. By spending a little bit more time up front, brainstorming, doing benchmarking, and just exploring different options, a lot of grief can be avoided later on. Note that this does not mean that the new ideas are always better, but if the new ideas have been reviewed and considered, there will be a higher degree of confidence that the business analyst has been looking out for the customer's best interest.

Some of the categories of options to consider should be:

- Change the business practice. IT people tend to view IT as being the solution to all problems. This is natural. Most professions feel that they have the answers to any problem identified. If you are a surgeon, you will cut; if you are a chiropractor, you will crack; and if you are an IT developer, you will automate. Be wary of this. Many problems will not be solved by implementing a system; the system will only give a faster way to reach the problem.

- Enhance the existing system. If the current environment basically is working, don't redo everything. Often a simple enhancement solves a problem faster and cheaper.
- Write a new solution. This tends to be the default approach, at least for a large problem. It does mean that there are fewer constraints based on the current environment, but it also means higher risk.
- Outsource writing a new solution. Similar to the previous item, but the project outsources development to mitigate risk.
- Buy an existing solution. Don't reinvent the wheel unless there is a reason. If a package meets the requirements, then this is often the best approach.
- Do nothing. This should always be considered. What will happen if nothing is done? How bad is the problem? How bad will the solution be?

Some of these options can also be sub-categorized. For example, to write a new solution or buy an existing solution may have sub-categories reflecting different technology alternatives. Does the customer want to focus on existing technology? Or should it be more of a leading edge initiative, where new technology will be implemented?

Once a number of potential solutions have been identified, these solutions should be evaluated based on a selected set of criteria. Work together with the customer, the sponsor, and the organization to determine what the driving factors should be. Also look at what weight should be assigned to each one of those factors. Typical factors may include:

- Timeliness: If there is a strong urgency to solving the problem, enhancing an existing system or buying off-the-shelf software may be more realistic.
- Cost: If cost is a major driver behind the decision, changing the business practice or doing nothing may be options.
- Organizational competencies: If the organization is short on technical expertise or there are competing business priorities, then look at outsourcing or changing the existing system.
- Available products: Are there products available for this area? If not, the option of buying off the shelf goes away.
- Competitive business practice: If this problem deals with the core of the customer's business and there is a need for a competitive advantage, it is more likely that the organization will need to develop the product.

Once a comprehensive list of evaluation criteria has been identified, they should be assigned weights. This can be done as a subjective process by just asking the customer to give each criterion a weight from 1 to 10. Or, if there is a need for deeper analysis, use a technique like forced pair ranking. The example of this, used earlier in Chapter 7, is shown again here in Figure 10.1.

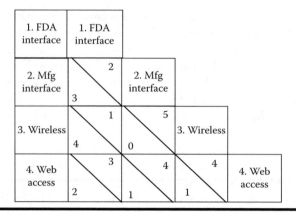

Figure 10.1 Forced pair filled in.

Based on this the total weights for the four requirements are:

1. FDA Interface: 6
2. Manufacturer Interface: 12
3. Wireless: 8
4. Web Access: 4

The weights created out of the forced pair matrix can then be used to evaluate potential alternatives. The business analyst may be asked to evaluate some package solutions against the requirements to see which one would fit the best. This time a matrix is created where the requirements (or selection criteria) goes on top of the columns and each row represents a potential solution, as seen in Figure 10.2.

Solution\Requirement	FDA Interface Weight = 6	Manufacturer Interface Weight = 12	Wireless Weight = 8	Web Access Weight = 4	Total
Buy Product ABC	0	0	1	1	12
Buy Product DEF	1	1	0	1	22
Build Product	1	1	1	1	30

Solution score: 0 = Does not meet, 1= Meets

Figure 10.2 Alternative solutions.

Each requirement carries the ranking weight from the forced pair ranking in Figure 10.1. Each alternative solution is then evaluated to see how well it meets the requirement. In this case the evaluation consists of:

- 0 = Solution does not meet requirement.
- 1 = Solution does meet requirement.

That evaluation can be made more sophisticated with objective criteria for what it takes to get a certain rating. For example, if one of the requirements is, "Must cost less than \$100,000," a solution costing \$100,000 or less may get a 3, a solution costing \$100,000 to \$125,000 gets a 2, a solution costing \$125,000 to \$150,000 gets a 1, and anything above \$150,000 gets a 0. This allows for more granularity in the selection process. By predetermining the scales used, the process tends to become more transparent and objective.

The process of identifying and evaluating the alternative solutions should result in a formal document, presented to the decision makers, documenting each alternative, with an evaluation of how well it meets the selection criteria as well as with an overall analysis of impact to the business and to the project. Some of the decisions made here may have a long-lasting impact to the organization. As an example, deciding to go with a package solution for a significant business area is likely to drive other development efforts later on, both from a positive and negative standpoint. From a positive view, it may make it easier to implement other packages from the same vendor down the road; from a negative standpoint it may limit development flexibility later on, tying the organization into functionality and integration limitations of the package.

Each one of the solution criteria also has a different risk ranking associated with it. Figure 10.3 shows where on the risk spectrum the different criteria discussed would fall.

Requirement	Organizational risk	Project Risk
FDA Interface	Low – Well defined	High – External dependency
Manufacturer Interface	Low – Well Defined	Medium – External dependency
Wireless	Medium – Infrastructure not in place	Low
Web Access	Medium – Limits access control	Medium – Low internal skill set

Figure 10.3 Requirements and risk.

The risk analysis should be done from two perspectives: (1) organizational risk which is the domain of the sponsor and the executives, and (2) project risk, which is the domain of the project manager.

Many alternative solutions will be based on different technologies and as such would not fall directly in the domain of the business analyst. It is often emphasized that the business analyst should focus on "what" the product should do and leave the "how" it will do it to the systems analyst or the infrastructure group. However, it is still the responsibility of the business analyst to evaluate the impacts and risks of each solution option and clearly communicate those to the customer. Some of the factors that the business analyst may need to bring back to the customer are:

- Gap analysis between the requirements and the capabilities of the technology selected
- Short- and long-term cost impact from technology selection
- Potential organizational value of different technologies (both within the project boundaries and throughout the organization)
- Organizational constraints

> ... it is still the responsibility of the business analyst to evaluate the impacts and risks of each solution option and clearly communicate those to the customer.

Although business analysts are not the drivers of selecting a technology, they do need to be able to discuss and inform the customer about it. So again, it can be seen that the job of the business analyst is very broad. The analysts will need to have an understanding of most aspects of the project, even the areas that they are not directly involved with.

10.4 Selecting a Solution

Once the analysis of the alternatives has been completed, a decision package should be assembled for each of the parties. This can often be done effectively by using a matrix like the one seen earlier in Figure 10.2

This type of matrix is best presented to the stakeholders in a meeting, because different people looking at the matrix will have different questions and different assumptions. If the reviewer analyzes the matrix unilaterally, they might make a decision which may be hard to change later. If the information is presented in a meeting, the decision makers can see other reactions to the information and any questions and concerns can be dealt with real-time. Similar to what has been discussed earlier, decisions are often better when they are made through an interactive review process.

Looking at Figure 10.2, there is a certain flow to how the information should be presented. Start with the criteria for the selection and review the process of how the requirements were weighted. If there is no agreement that these are the right criteria and that the weighting accurately reflect the stakeholders' view, then the rest of the evaluation will be unreliable. After this is reviewed, discuss the alternatives, including any that may already have been rejected with a rationale for the rejection. Then finally review how each alternative matches up against the selection criteria.

By this time the stakeholders should have a clear picture of the pros and cons of each alternative and should be able to make a decision. A frequent concern with this approach is that the customer wants to change the criteria and the weights of the criteria until the matrix shows the solution that the customer likes. Don't be too concerned about this. What will often happen is that intuitively the customer feels that there is something wrong with the selection. And in all honesty, despite the best effort of all involved, this process is subjective in nature. By allowing the discussion and the changing of weights, the process helps by adding structure to the discussion. As with so many tools discussed in this book, it is not the tool that is important, it is the discussion generated by the tool. The end result will still be subjective, but there has been solid discussion and increased understanding of the problem and the solution. This is one of the business analyst's most important and difficult job functions; to generate and facilitate communication.

10.5 Matching the Solution to the Needs of the Customer

Once the solution has been selected, there must be a mapping of the solution back to the requirements. The main concern is to identify requirements which have not been met by the solution or have only partially been met. All of these "missed" requirements must be evaluated, brought back to the customer, and a decision must be made on what to do about them. Maybe the package can be customized, maybe the customer can live without that requirement, or maybe there is a different system or business process that can provide this capability. It is rarely realistic to expect that all of the customer's requirements will be met, and in most cases the customer understands this as well. Customers expect that some things will happen, some things will be deferred, and some things will be dropped. They may not act like they understand this, but often it is necessary to make trade-offs with time, cost, or other factors to come up with an acceptable product. An acceptable product doesn't always mean meeting all the customer's requirements. This is a time when the negotiation skill of the business analyst, the project manager, and other stakeholders is put to the test.

There is also a need to evaluate what excess functionality the customer will get from this solution, especially if it is a package solution. This part of the evaluation is easy to forget because there is a tendency to think that excess functionality is at best positive, giving customers more than they asked for, or at worst is neutral because the customers will not use it anyway. In reality though, excess functionality can be a real negative. It may be duplicating functionality already existing elsewhere, which could confuse the customers or cause duplication of work. It may also prove to be more expensive to support and maintain this extra functionality, which typically is not included in training and testing plans. So carefully evaluate this side of the equation as well and decide how to approach and handle the extras.

10.6 Support Testing and Quality Assurance

Quality assurance is more than just testing; it also includes making sure that the process is being followed and that a well-thought-out business strategy is developed. Many times a test plan is created without considering the entire strategy. Just writing test cases and running through them during the project's testing cycle may be catching the defects, but it will probably not create great customer confidence. The purpose of the test strategy is to look at what, when, how much, where, and who. It should be a formal document which is signed off by the customer or sponsor or both. Figure 10.4 shows an example of a test strategy document for the Prescription Interaction Project.

Section	Example
Overview	This document outlines the testing approach for the user acceptance test for the Prescription Interaction Project.
Intended audience	Business analysts, Developers, Users
Operational environment	The system test will involve pharmacy, accounting, and customer support
Test environment	The corporate training facility for pharmacists will be used for the test
Testing resources	Three pre-selected pharmacists Business Analyst
Tolerance to defects	Low, there's a high liability risk if the product does not catch dangerous drug interactions
Test types	Stress Test Usability Test Functionality Test
Critical test success factors	All potential drug interactions caught in test cases
Sign-off	_____

Figure 10.4 Test strategy.

The key sections to include are:

- Overview: High-level description of project and of the purpose of this document.
- Intended audience: Who will receive this document and what should they do with it?
- Operational environment: Which organizations will be impacted by this product and where are they located?
- Test environment: What setup will be used for the test?
- Testing resources: Who will perform the test and what equipment will they need?
- Tolerance to defects: What will happen if there are errors after testing is done?
- Test types: What special situations will be tested for?
- Critical test success factors: What will it take to get sign-off?
- Sign-off: Signature of decision maker.

The test plan for a project should be initiated as soon as the requirements are captured and documented. In many organizations, it is the role of the quality assurance function to create and execute test plans, but it is also common that some or all of the responsibility falls on the business analyst. The testing topics that will be covered in this section are:

- Validation versus verification
- Planning for the test
- Types of tests: Black box, regression, usability, stress
- Evaluating customer satisfaction
- Acceptance test

10.6.1   Validation versus Verification

Most testing done is for product verification, which means making sure that the system does what the requirements said it should do. It is primarily a tool to see if the developers correctly understood and implemented the Business Requirements Document. Traditionally, if the product passed the test, but the customer is not satisfied, the developer (and business analyst) can go back to the customer and say, "You got what you asked for." That may be a valid argument, but it is no longer good enough when developing a product. If an organization is to be successful in the long run, it must not only give the customers what they ask for, but also give the customers a product that will solve the problem they had in the first place.

There is a general shift in the industry today away from product verification being the main goal, even though it is still important, and toward product validation, which is much more difficult, but also more critical and much more rewarding. To validate a product, the original objectives must be evaluated and a determination made if the product met those objectives. Were the problems and constraints dealt with effectively? Were the cost savings achieved? Did the market share increase? Did the organization become Sarbanes–Oxley[1] compliant? Organizations that successfully verify and validate their products will have a strong competitive advantage and are likely to win more business from their customers.

> Organizations that successfully verify and validate their products will have a strong competitive advantage and are likely to win more business from their customers.

Look at the following example based on the Prescription Interaction Project. The customer has a need to minimize lawsuits and unnecessary deaths or illness resulting from prescription drug interactions. To do this, the customer stated the requirement, "All new prescriptions must be checked against other prescriptions on record for the customer in order to identify interaction problems." Although this sounds good, the business analyst must dig deeper. How severe is the problem today? What causes the problem? How much of the problem will go away if this requirement is implemented? The business analyst must go to work quantifying the problem. Some causes may be due to either a customer using a spouse's prescription or the customer having old medication from a different pharmacy. Neither of those two scenarios would be resolved with the requirement as stated. So, in this case while verification may be met, validation will not be.

What would be a better requirement? There may need to be an industrywide database which will show prescriptions across all pharmacies. Maybe the requirement needs to be expanded to include checks against family members. Maybe there needs to be a checklist added for questions that the pharmacist asks the customer. The point here is that what looks like a good idea initially may not actually solve the customer's problem. If the customer has just spent a large amount of money without having the problem fixed, that is ultimately going to have an impact on customer satisfaction.

10.6.2 Planning for the Test

A Test Plan consists of many components. It should reference the test strategy document created earlier (who, what, when, etc.), it should outline test types (user

---

[1] Sarbanes–Oxley is legislation coming out of the fall of Enron and has been a major driver of many IT projects over the last few years.

test, stress test, etc.), and it should have test cases. While the test strategy document is for organizational commitment, the Test Plan is a more detailed document outlining the testing process for the project team. The first portion of the plan should be developed during the analysis phase of the project, often by the business analysts or least with significant input from them. Although a detailed test case with well-defined test data may not be possible until the system design is done, the vast majority of test cases should be identified, at least at a summary level, during the analysis phase of the project. In general, a good testing approach follows the V cycle of testing as shown in Figure 10.5.

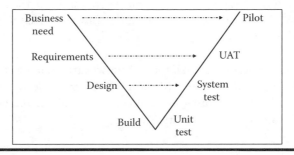

Figure 10.5 V testing cycle.

The strength of this visual is that it shows that you start developing the test plans for Business Need, Requirements, Design, and Build during those phases and then execute the actual test cases during the testing phase. It encourages the business analyst to start developing the test plans early. Obviously the business analyst is not responsible for all of this. Design and build testing should be done by the systems analyst and the developers, or possibly by quality assurance if that is the way the organization is structured. Regardless, the business analyst should be aware of all the testing going on because any potential errors or questions that arise during the testing may need to be discussed with the customer and often results in new requirements being discovered. Typical sections of a Test Plan include:

- Introduction/Overview: Stating what this document contains, the intended audience, and a brief description of the project.
- Testing types covered by this document: Could be all types of tests or those focused specifically on acceptance, integration, or usability testing, etc. These types are covered in more detail in Section 10.6.3. Note that there will be sub-documents outlining the detailed plan for each type of test.
- Roles and responsibilities: Who will be involved with the testing? Who is responsible for what portion of the testing effort?
- Authority: Who can sign off on the test plan and who can approve each individual test result?

- Test scenarios: The scenarios describe the tests that need to happen without going down to the details of what data to input and what data to expect out. Each test scenario will lead to multiple test cases as seen in Figure 10.6.

The test scenario describes what should be tested: "Customer attempting to fill a prescription for a drug which has a negative interaction history with another drug that the patient is taking." This scenario may have test cases involving incorrect data, patient no longer taking the previous drug, patient overriding the warning, etc. The business analyst should identify at least one test scenario for each requirement identified. It is often good to consider one successful scenario and one unsuccessful scenario. Some of the details of each test case may need to wait until the design phase of the project.

- Test cases: The test cases take the testing scenario and add input data and expected output data. There will normally be multiple test cases for each scenario, at least one leading to a successful completion and normally many leading to different error conditions.

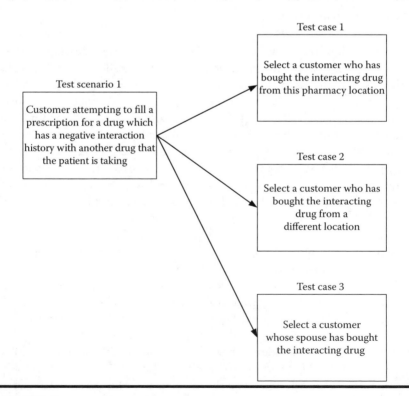

Figure 10.6 Test scenarios and test cases.

- Test schedule: The test activities should be included in the Project Plan from the beginning of the project. Sufficient time must be planned for all the different types of testing as well as recovery time from expected errors found during the test. It is common to see a project schedule containing unit test, system test, integration test, and user acceptance test, followed by implementation, without having any time set aside between the tests to evaluate and act upon the test results. There is a natural hesitation to do this because it implies that errors are anticipated. However, by not setting aside the time, the project is creating a risk of not implementing on time. To determine how much time should be set aside, the best guideline is to look at history. What is the normal level of defects found for each test and how much time is normally spent correcting them? This will at least provide a rough guidance for the plan.
- Testing environment: The most difficult part about performing a test is to create a realistic copy of the "live" environment. Creating a setup with system interfaces, realistic historical data, and valid user inputs can be very time consuming and, even in the best of circumstances, will be a compromise. Some organizations have a "Model Office" environment that allows them to set up an adequate environment. Other organizations will need to spend time creating data, simulating interfaces, and creating user inputs. This effort must be accounted for in the Project Plan and should start early in the project.
- Test reporting: Describes how the test results will be reported, the report format, and who needs to see the reports.
- Assumptions, issues, and risks: What are the open items at this time? What risks are discovered using the selected testing approach?
- Version control: This is a document that will go through numerous changes during the project cycle. It is important that every affected stakeholder has access to the most recent version.

10.6.3 Types of Tests

There are many types of tests done and even more names for them, such as regression, stress, and usability. Not all of them fall within the domain of the business analyst, but the analyst should at least be aware of them. There can often be synergy between the different tests, especially in the area of setting up the test environment and identifying testing scenarios. Be aware though that using the same testing environment and test scenarios for all the tests increases the chance of overlooking certain conditions. It may be beneficial to have a different environment for the integration test and for the system test, for example. By comparing the results from both, the value of each test is enhanced.

The business analyst should be familiar with all of these types of testing:

- Unit test: This test, typically done by the development team, makes sure that the system was programmed according to specifications. It is recommended that the developer of the actual unit being tested does not test their own work to avoid a situation where the developer only tests what they already knows is working. Rather, have a peer on the team do the testing.
- System test: The primary purpose of this test is to test that the design is implemented correctly. This can be done in layers, with first testing subsystems and then gradually going to a higher level of testing. Does the flow reflect the design? Is the right data available? Although this is normally the responsibility of the systems analyst (or quality assurance), there is a real benefit for the business analyst to be involved. It may point out surprises in how a requirement was implemented and will give a head start in addressing potential issues with the users.
- Integration test: This if often a very difficult test to set up and often needs involvement from other organizations. The purpose is to make sure that the system being developed correctly communicates with other systems and organizations. The business analysts and the systems analysts will normally need to work closely together to plan and execute this test, not only within the project team, but also with other organizations that may not even be interested in this project. There is a lot of negotiation and relationship building needed to successfully complete an integration test. Start early with ongoing communication with both the management and the support team for the areas with which the project will interface.
- Regression test: This test is really looking to answer the question, "Did something unrelated break due to this system being developed?" Although this is part of the business analyst's job, it is not done in the analysis phase. This is not a test based on requirements, but rather a test of the areas supposedly unaffected by the requirements. Some organizations have automated testing tools that will run predefined testing scripts to see if a system works. This is a great way to do regression testing because it already has the test cases built in and requires a minimum amount of customer involvement. If this option doesn't exist, then at a minimum identify the high-visibility functions within the business and schedule a user to run through a few key transactions. Even though this is not guaranteed to stop all errors, it gives a reasonable chance to identify any glaring mistakes.
- Usability test: A system can be meeting all functional requirements, but when the user sits down to use it, it's just not user friendly. Or, while it is performing the right functions, it is not practical in the user's work environment. The business analyst is often the person primarily responsible for usability testing, both to define it and to work on executing it. Things to look for in usability testing are:

  - Is the user interface consistent with other systems that the user uses on a daily basis? If the customers are used to a certain look and feel of their application, based on it being a commercial off-the-shelf product or based on standardized designs within the organization, it is important that this system has the same look and feel.

- – Is the equipment and user interface practical in the work environment? As an example, voice recognition may be great for a phone answering system, but may not work in a busy or loud office environment. If the system is to be carried around by the user while doing work, such as an inventory system, there are weight and size considerations that may make a system impractical.
- – Is the flow through the system consistent with the way work should be done? It is not enough to test that the functions can be done; the product must also provide the ability to do them in a logical flow, sometimes one that is flexible, based on the user's situation. If the system does not flow properly, there is a great chance that although the system will pass the test, it will run into problems when a larger number of users start using it in a production environment.

- Stress test: This is often a difficult test to create and execute, but there are tools that will help in some environments. The purpose here is to determine the level of activity on a system at peak times, and then create that scenario to ensure that the system remains viable. Although it is realistic to expect some degradation in performance, it is important to define what an acceptable level of degradation is. Most estimates for peak activity levels are based on analysis of the current situation, so always build in extra capacity to account for unexpected growth. The business analyst should be heavily involved with defining the criteria for the stress test, but the execution of it is often done by the systems analyst.

- Acceptance test: This is the users' time to verify that everything was implemented based on requirements and that the system is ready for production. The basis for this test should have been developed during the analysis phase, and the business analyst is responsible for being the driving force behind this test. However, the business analysts should not actually do all the testing by themselves, but should have the users heavily involved at this stage. If they are not, it will be too easy for them to disassociate themselves from any responsibility for the system. One important goal that the business analyst must have throughout the development process is to have the customer take ownership of the product. The acceptance test is part of that process, and if that is delegated to the analyst, it is likely to cause problems down the road.

- Beta/pilot testing: Refers to a limited production release of a system (or a part of the system) to a small portion of the organization. Although the terms themselves are not used consistently in the industry, the intent of the Beta or pilot testing is to allow the customer to use the product for a while to test how well it is functioning. It will also help evaluate any implementation and training issues. One of the great risks with implementing a system is the impact on the user environment. It is a good risk mitigation strategy to do a gradual rollout of the system to allow for lessons learned and process improvements. Be aware that there are some down sides because the support staff must support both the old and the new system, and any external interfaces must also be duplicated. However, for a large complex project, it can still be a good idea to perform these types of tests.

10.6.4 Evaluating Customer Satisfaction

Beyond the testing itself, there should also be a long-term evaluation of how well the product has been received by the customers. The business analyst should plan on multiple surveys to verify this. One can be done shortly after implementation (one to three months) to evaluate training, implementation, support, and process issues. A second one can be done with a long-term view (12 to 18 months) to determine how well the product actually solved the business problem, basically asking the question, "If we could start over, would we do it again?" or "Was it worth the effort?" Make sure to request feedback from the paying customers, internal management, and of course, the users. The results of the evaluation, which become a lessons learned document, can be used for future process improvements as well as for reaffirming with the customer that this was a successful project. "Here's what the problem was, here's how it was fixed, and here's the final result." This should be part of the sales job for the development organization. The best time to ask for more business or to promote an organization is after it has successfully implemented a new product.

10.7 Implementing and Supporting the Solution

Often when the original Project Plan is created, there is a lack of detail on implementation and support issues. This is partly because these activities often occur after the project manager is officially done with the project and also because they seem so distant on the horizon. There are a number of factors to consider in this area such as:

- Conversions: The conversion effort should start in the analysis phase when creating the AS-IS and the TO-BE data model. Based on these models, a conversion process must be developed to decide what data gets converted and how it is mapped to the new system. This process is not trivial and must involve both the business analyst and the customer. Some of the conversion may be automated (hopefully most of it) but some of it (especially exceptions) may need to be manually reviewed and decided upon.
- Business transitions: What needs to change on the business side to take advantage of the new system? This can include user training on business processes, process changes, changed job descriptions, and elimination of job functions

as well as creation of new ones. While this must be led by the business, the business analyst will often be involved.

- Communication of the implementation plan to the users: It may seem obvious, but sometimes the users do not know how a system will be implemented, what functionality goes away from an old system, and what new functionality is added. This is extra important for those stakeholders who may not have been closely involved with the development effort. This step may include training on the system and provide documentation.
- Communication with other affected organizations: It is rare that a new product is only impacting the organization that it was developed for. Most of the time there are interfaces, both from a systems view and from an organization's view, and those interfaces must still be working on implementation day. Although it is mostly the system analyst who will verify the pure system interfaces, the business analyst should communicate with the affected organizations and make them aware of what may change when a new system is being implemented and to watch out for any abnormalities. It can be difficult enough for an outside organization to be impacted, but if they are not told ahead of time about any potential impact, it will be an even more frustrating experience for them.

10.8 Summary

Although the business analysts do not own the design, development, or implementation of the solution, they are heavily involved with it. Make sure that the roles and responsibilities reflect this, and have the business analysts plan their activities not only for the analysis phase, but for all their involvement on the project. A good business analyst is able to discuss all aspects of the product development with the customer. Although the project manager owns the project areas of cost, schedule, and scope, the business analyst owns the product aspect, the ability to trace the product in use by the customer back through the testing, the design, the requirements, and ultimately all the way back to the business problem that initiated the need for the product. This takes a set of skills and characteristics which are hard to find, but when found, are invaluable to the business.

10.9 Activity

1. Describe three parts of the case study where the customer is likely to have a very low risk tolerance.
2. The following requirement was documented for the case study: The system must verify that the customer has sufficient credit to place an order if the order is above $1,000 and if the customer does not have an existing line of credit with us.
3. Write two test scenarios that would help verify this requirement.

Chapter 11

Swede-Mart Case Study

The following description of a fictitious retailer called Swede-Mart is to be used to complete the Activity section at the end of each chapter, applying the concepts discussed therein. Sample solutions for each of the activities are given in Chapter 12.

11.1 Introduction

Swede-Mart is a rapidly expanding clothing store headquartered in Gothenburg, Sweden, with 300 stores across the globe, 200 of which are in Europe. The retailer targets affluent families who want fashionable clothing, but who are also concerned about price.

Swede-Mart has a three-year plan to greatly expand its presence in Asia and North America. The goal is to become the largest clothing store in the world in the market of upper-middle-class, young families, as measured by number of stores and revenue.

Swede-Mart offers high-quality products, competitive prices, and a trendy image. Holding on to this image will be key as the company expands. The target market is very finicky and will jump ship quickly if the company's image does not match their lifestyle.

11.2 Strategy

Swede-Mart has recently gone through a business planning effort and formulated its mission and vision; however, a SWOT (strengths–weaknesses–opportunities–threats) analysis has not yet been done.

The initial focus of the strategic plan is ensuring customer retention and growth through inventory management, which will allow Swede-Mart to have the right products available at the right location, at the right time, and for the right price. This has been a major part of the company's marketing campaign. This means setting up regional distribution centers which can ship efficiently to the local stores. The company will need to make sure that it can execute this as well at a global level as it has in Sweden.

The goal is to reach less than 1 percent out of stock of an advertised product over the duration of advertising. Year-round inventory should turn eight times per year; currently it is only six times.

Successful improvement of the inventory management system will allow Swede-Mart to increase its rate of growth across the globe, and will also provide cash flow for acquisitions and store growth.

11.3   Industry Background

The retail clothing industry has always been a high-risk industry with frequent turmoil. It is a very competitive market. Whomever has a successful product line can make good profits, but any missteps will be paid for dearly through lower margins and unused inventory. Some products sold can also be bought in many other stores, although some brands are unique to Swede-Mart. The discount market for clothing operates on very thin margins and counts on high volumes and unsold merchandise from other companies. Swede-Mart is considered a mid-range clothing store, competing with the likes of Gap and H&M.

The key functions of the business are purchasing products from designers, sourcing the manufacturing of the products, managing the inventory process, and marketing and selling the products to the customer.

The selection of the right products based on recent trends and finding the right price point is key to success in this industry. Competition is fierce and each company must find its image to sell. Swede-Mart's is fashionable and available in a fun and well-laid-out store. That puts the company's success in the hands of the buyers and the inventory management system.

The largest costs are space, inventory, and staff. Not only must the product be there at the right time, there must also be enough staff there to support the sales. Swede-Mart is famous for having friendly but not overbearing staff.

11.4   Project Background

Joe Jones is the sponsor of this initiative to enhance the inventory and order processing functions for the distribution centers. Joe has 20 years with Swede-Mart and has been in charge of the distribution centers for the last three years. He is widely assumed to be the next president of the company.

Joe is known to want frequent, informal communications. He is OK with bad news, but he wants it early and he wants ideas on how to fix it. In his general directions to the team he asked not to be surprised. He's always willing to get involved and help, but he is not a micro-manager, so he will assume that things are OK unless he is told otherwise.

11.5 Distribution Center/Inventory Operations

The initial focus from the strategic plan will concentrate on reviewing the inventory-management and order-taking areas. Distribution centers are organized in regions with each region containing one or more distribution centers. Each distribution center has up to 25 stores that it supports. This may need to be adjusted as the business grows. Optimizing the inventory levels between the distribution centers and quickly recognizing increased demand will be a driver of success.

11.6 Product Lines

There are three main product lines:

- Seasonal: These products will change every season, but they are pretty much standard for the season (shorts, winter coats, etc.). There are good statistics for use, but any unusual weather patterns will cause huge fluctuations.
- Special fashion: Changes on a nonseasonal basis. Is often related to a special event or new fashion. Could be for a sporting event, New Year's Eve, or just a brand-new fashion trend. These are short-term events, with not much residual value of the product. Leftover products go to clearance.
- Year-round: Always in stock, always in demand. Socks, underwear, suits. Predictable volumes, competition mainly focused on pricing. The inventory for these items turns over frequently.

Products are identified by a product code. Each manufacturer has unique product codes, so Swede-Mart must use its own product codes internally. Each store has a buyer who can order from the Swede-Mart product catalog. Not all products will be in stock during all seasons. The distribution center is responsible to determine stock levels. Some products can be special ordered, with a longer lead time. This can be done for products not stored by the distribution centers (typically high-priced items), or for items out of season. Naturally, the delivery time will be much longer for these types of items.

Although many items are purchased directly from the manufacturer, often there is a third party involved, especially for low volume products.

11.7 Purchasing

Buyers are assigned to product lines and to vendors. Where a vendor is providing multiple product lines, there is a primary buyer who is responsible for the price negotiations and the general vendor relationship. Each buyer buys for all the distributions centers. Most of the buyers are at the headquarters in Sweden, but some are located at the distribution centers around the world. This is likely to increase with the global expansion over the next few years.

The buyer will get sales and predicted demands from the stores and distribution centers, and then do a sales forecast based on that data. The buyer will negotiate prices with the vendors and look out for special discounts or sales from the vendors to take advantage of opportunities as they arise.

Stocked items will have a reorder level. This level is set for each stocked product, for each store, and for each distribution center. When a product reaches a reorder level, an automatic order will be generated by the system. This reorder level is updated by the distribution center as order patterns change.

11.8 Receiving

Vendor shipments typically will be shipped to the distribution centers. Occasionally, special orders may be shipped directly to the stores. Receiving will match the shipments to purchase orders to make sure the shipment is correct and that it has arrived at the right location. After that, items that are to be stocked in the center are entered into inventory and stored in their bins.

Products which are to be reshipped directly to the stores get sent over to Shipping and combined with any other shipments being sent. On average the distribution centers send one large shipment per week to each store.

The term "bin" in the distribution center refers to a specific location where a product is stored. It could be a shelf, a bin, a corner of the warehouse. Each bin is described by its type and size and also has information on location (floor number, part of building). Any changes to a bin location must be immediately reflected to make sure that the warehouse will operate efficiently. A product may be stored in multiple bins and in some cases multiple products will share one bin.

11.9 Accounts Payable

Vendor invoices are matched to a purchase order. The purchase order is updated by Receiving when a shipment is received and no invoice will be approved for payment until the shipment has arrived and been approved. The invoice price is compared to the purchase order price, and the payment terms are compared as well. If there are discrepancies, those are forwarded to the buyer for resolution. Once all of this is approved the invoice is marked as payable.

The payment date will be based on the terms from the invoice. If there are discounts offered for early payments, or penalties for late payments, then those discounts or penalties are annualized and compared to the organization's cost of funds to determine whether there should be an early or late payment.

There must be an ability to find previously paid invoices, to know their status, including knowing what the cost of funds were at the time of payment.

11.10 Order Processing and Shipping

When the stores place orders with the distribution center, products can be shipped to the store for retail sales. Typically, orders are placed once per week and then shipped the following week. A store can place an emergency order, which will sometimes happen when there's been an unusual weather pattern or a new product is more successful than expected. This type of order can be placed at any time, and is typically shipped out the same day if received before 3 p.m. local time. Depending on the cost of shipping and any other shipments going out, the shipment may be delayed to make it financially viable. The store will always be involved in that decision process and will be responsible for all shipping charges.

When an order is received from a store, the distribution center checks the inventory levels to see if there's enough inventory. All items that are in stock are confirmed and a notice is sent back to the store with the expected shipping date. If there is not enough quantity in stock, then a partial confirmation will be made. If no stock is available, that line item will be cancelled. The store will have to try to reorder the following week if the product is still wanted. If there is a special need to get a product earlier, then the store needs to place a special order.

If the store order is for a product that isn't carried in inventory, then a special order to the supplier is placed. Once a delivery date is received from the supplier, this information is passed on to the store. These products are typically shipped directly to the store. All store orders will typically be from their primary distribution center. On rare occasions they can place an order with a different distribution center, but that will continue to be handled manually.

Stores can continuously check on the status of an order and will frequently call before placing an order to find out about the inventory situation. Often they will ask for similar products if the one that they were interested in ordering is not available. The distribution center will invoice the store for the orders shipped, as a way of auditing financial discipline.

11.11   Reporting

There are a number of reports that must be created for this business area. Some of the key reports are:

- Invoice report: Shows payable invoices and payment due date.
- Inventory report: Complete list of products and quantities.
- Store order report: Shows all stores for a distribution center and what they have ordered. This report must be available in multiple sorting sequences.

All reports will be in English, the corporate language.

11.12   Summary

The new order management system that will be created for Swede-Mart must be state of the art and must be able to support the aggressive growth goals of the company. Although a timely solution is needed and cost is important, this project is really focused on doing the right thing. The solution must be flexible, accurate, and very responsive. The last few decades are filled with stories of retail companies who have not been able to get the right product to the right place in the right time frame. Swede-Mart is determined not to be another one of those stories.

11.13   Interview with Store Buyer

I will use the system to check on the status of system-generated orders. Sometimes there may be an issue with them and I'll have to call the distribution center to make changes. I normally check if there were any line items that were not in inventory and if there are any expected delays in ship dates. I also need to be able to look up a product and see the inventory levels in our store, at the primary distribution center, and at other distribution centers. This should be displayed so I see the centers in sequence of expected shipping times.

I must be able to place special orders; this normally happens when demand increases unexpectedly or when the system-generated order is not correct. A special order is also placed for products which we carry in our catalogue, but which are not available in our stores. These items are typically high priced and have a very low sales volume.

Chapter 12

Activity Solutions for Swede-Mart Case Study

12.1 Chapter 1 Activity Solution

The most common answers are:

1. Changing requirements
2. Customers not available
3. Customers not knowing what they want
4. No repeatable process
5. Lack of management buy-in
6. Lack of resources
7. Lack of skilled business analysts
8. No common language
9. Developers do not understand the business
10. No tools

Actions

• Changing requirements	– Implement a formal change control process – Educate team on the process
• Customers not available	– Give customers as much lead time as possible – Get buy-in from customers to requirements gathering

• Customers not knowing what they want	– Showcase similar products – Create prototypes
• No repeatable process	– Define and implement templates and a simple process to start with – Research what other organizations do
• Lack of management buy-in	– Review charter and scope with management – Review requirements plan with management

Meeting

This can be the start of what the Software Engineering Institute (SEI) calls a "Software Engineering Process Group," which would become the owner of the processes adopted.

12.2 Chapter 2 Activity Solution

Organization	Standard	Process Owner	In Use Since
IT	System Specification	IT	At least 5 years
Finance	Project Justification Form	Director of Finance	1990
Steering committee	Project Charter	Not sure	Five years
IT	Enhancement Request Form	Director of IT	1990

Note that this will provide a starting point of forms and templates for the organization. It will also identify potentially overlapping forms and activities and help clarify roles and responsibilities.

12.3 Chapter 3 Activity Solution

Project Charter	
Project Name: Swede-Mart Inventory	Customer: VP Operations
Project Manager: Sven Svenson	Project Sponsor: Distribution Center Manager
Business need/issue	With Swede-Marts expansion globally and the focus on increasing market share and customer loyalty, a new order and inventory control system must be created. This will support Swede-Mart's vision of the right product at the right place at the right time.
Project justification	This market is increasingly competitive. Many competitors carry the same brands as we do. If we don't have them in stock when the customer needs them, the customer will go elsewhere and probably keep going there.
Critical success factors	• Never run out of inventory on year round items • Less than 1 percent out of inventory of advertised products • Ability to tell customers when an out of inventory item will be available • Minimize cost of inventory
Key product deliverables and milestones	• Order processing system • Inventory management system
Organizational assumptions	• No other systems will change • Corporate language is English, no multi-lingual support
Organizational constraints	• Must be completed in 18 months • Must use existing infrastructure

12.4   Chapter 4 Activity Solution: Requirements Plan

1. Project overview and background.
   Swede-Mart is expanding globally and as they move into new markets they have an increasing need to control material flow. This project will replace the existing inventory and order system with a state-of-the-art model that will maximize product availability while minimizing cost.

2. Scope and deliverables. Identify three examples of exclusions.
   The Analysis phase scope includes:

   - Create a plan for the analysis phase and obtain approval
   - Collect requirements from the stakeholders
   - Create a Business Requirements Document (BRD)
   - Validate and get approval of the BRD

   The following areas are excluded:

   - Requirements related to multi-lingual support
   - User training
   - Test cases

3. Stakeholder analysis. Fill out the stakeholder analysis for Joe Jones.

Stakeholder Analysis	
Project Name: Swede-Mart Inventory project	Date: July 1, 2007
Project Manager: Sven Svenson	Project Sponsor: Joe Jones
Stakeholder organization:	Distribution centers
Stakeholder name and contact information:	Joe Jones (121) 555-1212
What will this stakeholder provide to the project?	Approve changes to the cost and schedule of the analysis phase Escalation point to obtain the correct stakeholders in the requirements sessions
What will the project provide to this stakeholder?	Status reports BRD Product
What is the impact to this stakeholder if the project succeeds or fails?	Very important for the success of the stakeholder's organization as well as for his personal career.
Hot issues for this stakeholder	Bad news early No surprises Bring ideas not problems Frequent communication

4. Communications plan. Fill out with two sample communication items.

What	Who (Responsible)	Who (Audience)	Why	When	Where	How
Weekly Status Reportrt	Lead analystst	Sponsor, PM	Informational, continued support	Monday am	Joe's office	In person
Team meeting	Project Manager	Project team	Status, issues, upcoming milestones	Friday am	Team room	In person, conference call

5. Project activities. Create a WBS with three layers (top layer being analysis phase) and a total of 15-18 activities at the lowest level.
6. Roles and responsibilities. Assign responsibilities to the activities from step 5 (Figure 12.1).

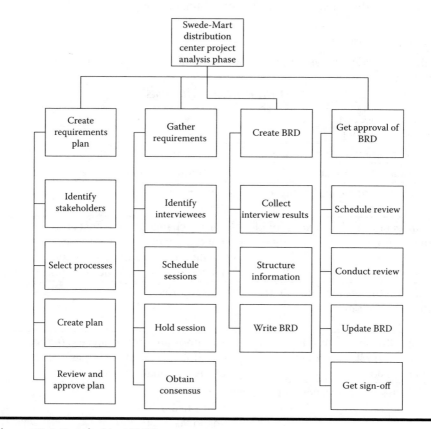

Figure 12.1 Swede-Mart WBS.

Task	Responsible
Create Requirements Plan	Lead Analyst
Gather Requirements	Business Analysis Team
Create BRD	Lead Analyst
Get approval of BRD	Project Manager, Lead Analyst, Lead Systems Analyst

7. Resource Plan. Create a list of potential non-human resources and Subject Matter Experts you may need.

Resource Need	Comment
Facilitator	No internal candidate, must have superior communication skills
Documentation tool	Must support modeling techniques selected
SME	Need expert in inventory optimization

8. Requirements Risk Plan. Brainstorm requirements related risk, either to the requirements gathering effort or to the product being developed. Select the top one and create a risk handling plan.

Risk Assessment Form (Type: Prod = Product Risk, Req = Requirements gathering risk)					
Risk ID	Type	Risk	Probability	Impact	Comment
1	Prod	Local legal restriction may make the system not usable	L	H	
2	Prod	Hardware cost may be too much for some stores	L	M	
3	Prod	Some stores may not have English speaking staff	M	H	
4	Req	May not be able to interview stakeholders from other countries	M	H	

Risk Handling Form	
Risk ID: 4	Business Area: Distribution Centers
Raised By: Analysis Team	Project Name: Swede-Mart Distribution Center Project
Date Raised: July 1, 2007	Assigned to: Lead Analyst
Risk Description: If we cannot interview users in other countries, we are likely to miss local legal restrictions and different nuances in how business is conducted.	
Likelihood: M	Impact: H
Impact Description: The acceptance of the product when rolling it out internationally could be jeopardized and the users may resist using the system, instead resorting to manual orders	
Recommended Preventative Actions: Bring in a user from each continent to the requirements sessions Send prototypes to each distribution center for review	
Recommended Contingent Actions: Prepare to send trainers out at implementation time	

9. Identify who will be responsible for approving changes.
   - There is a customer change control board that will approve product scope changes.
   - The customer sponsor will approve project scope changes.
   - The IT change control board will approve infrastructure changes.

12.5 Chapter 5 Activity Solution

Approach	*Risks*	*Mitigations*
Waterfall	• Customer is not clear on requirements • Organization has not done anything similar in the past • Must be international consensus	• Verify with prototype • Formal review of all deliverables • Add outside expertise team
Iterative	• Scope continuously changing • Can get analysis paralysis	• Clearly define purpose and deliverables for each iteration
Agile	• Requirements continually changing • May be difficult to sub divide project into manageable components	• Clearly define the boundaries of the effort • Identify pieces which can be done agile and combine with a more traditional approach for larger modules

Based on the complexity and size of this project, a waterfall approach would be the best option. Portions of the requirements gathering can be done in an iterative approach.

12.6 Chapter 6 Activity Solution

Sample requirements for the case study:

> **External:** Swede-Mart must operate in accordance to local labor laws.
>
> **Business—strategic:** Increase inventory turn rate to 8 times per year.
>
> **Business—tactical:** The distribution centers must be able to do daily trend analysis on inventory to forecast any increase (or decrease) in demand.
>
> **Business—operational:** The store manager must be able to override default shipping in case of near out of inventory condition.
>
> **User:** The buyer in the store must be able to place a special order for a product not carried in inventory.
>
> **Quality of service:** A distribution center must be able to process orders from up to 50 stores each day.
>
> **Assumption:** Users will be able to dedicate four hours to a training program for the system.
>
> **Constraint:** All order history will be converted to the new system.
>
> **Implementation:** The turnover from old to new system must be completed in 12 hours or less.

12.7 Chapter 7 Activity Solution

Activity 7.1

Stakeholder	Elicitation Approach	Special Actions
Joe Jones – Sponsor	Interview	Prepare list of questions Obtain sign-off on scope and requirements
Buyer in Store	Job shadowing 1 or 2 Survey the rest	Explain goals of project Create a survey for post-project evaluation
Distribution center inventory staff	Discovery session	Meet with each person prior to session Hire a JAD facilitator Select modeling techniques
Shipping	Focus group	Select participants who are well respected Brief participants before session Follow-up with decisions after the session

Activity 7.2
Discovery Session for Distribution Center Inventory Staff

Attendees: Inventory managers from each continent
                Inventory optimization SME
                IT group supporting current inventory system

Agenda: Kick-off by Joe Jones
                Team building activity
                Review goals and objectives
                Establish ground rules
                Review modeling techniques to be used
                Model the inventory flow
                Capture detail requirements
                Validate information captured
                Decide next steps

12.8 Chapter 8 Activity Solution

Use Case Identification

1. Place special order
2. Inquire on order status
3. Inquire on inventory levels
4. Order from nonprimary distribution center

Use Case #1

General Characteristics	
Intent	To place an order which was not automatically identified and generated by the system.
Scope	Store buyer placing special order
Author	Sven Svenson
Last Update	July 15, 2007
Status	Under development
Primary Actor	Store buyer
Secondary Actors	Distribution center inventory manager
Preconditions	System generated order has been created and transmitted
Assumptions	Buyer needs to modify system order
Trigger	Out of stock at store, special order at store, forecast changed
Success Condition	Special order is confirmed for shipping with a ship date
Failed Post Condition	Product can not be ordered, no inventory available or special shipping cost prohibitive
Models	Workflow model store purchasing process
Overview	A buyer needs to try to make sure that the store does not run out of inventory. If the risk for this is high, they will need to place special orders. Special orders can also be placed when a customer orders a nonstocked item.

Happy Path	
Step	*Action*
S	Successful order is placed for product in inventory at distribution center
1	The buyer decides to place special order
2	System asks for product
3	Buyer enters product
4	System displays available inventory
5	Buyer enters quantity
6	System confirms order and provides shipping date

Alternatives	
Step	*Branching Action*
4	No inventory available
	Buyer reviews all distribution centers Buyer evaluates shipping cost from closest distribution center with available inventory Buyer accepts or rejects alternative distribution center

Related Information	
Performance	Must be able to perform happy path in less than 30 seconds
Frequency	20 times per day per buyer
Concurrency	Many buyers will be performing this concurrently
Open issues	Approval of orders from non primary distribution centers
Future considerations	None
Due date	2008
Additional information	N/A

1. Identify the key entities that the buyer's business area deals with and identify attributes and relationships for those entities and outline an entity relationship diagram (Figure 12.2).
2. Take the requirement of "placing a special order." Write a sample requirements statement for this which is specific, measurable, and unambiguous. There will be many requirements statements for this use case, right now just do one as an example: "The system must support 50 buyers per distribution center, entering an order at the same time, and be able to complete those orders (assuming happy path) in 30 seconds."

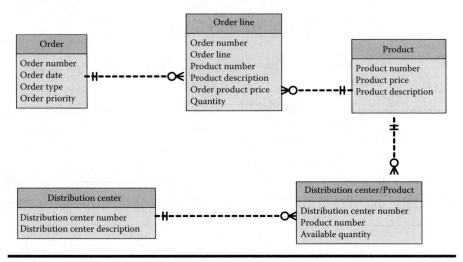

Figure 12.2 Swede-Mart data model.

12.9   Chapter 9 Activity Solution

Key stakeholders and their focus during BRD review:

- Sponsor: Scope, business requirements, assumptions, and constraints
- Distribution center manager: Business requirements and high level user requirements
- Vice President of Operations: Store requirements, assumptions and constraints, and use cases
- Buyer: Use Cases, User requirements, and functional requirements
- Developer: All documents

12.10 Chapter 10 Activity Solution

1. Describe three parts of the case study where the customer is likely to have a very low risk tolerance.

   - Communication between store and distribution center
   - Accurate tracking of inventory levels
   - Any condition increasing out of stock on advertised products

2. The following requirement was documented for the case study: The system must verify that the customer has sufficient credit to place an order, if the order is above $1,000, and if the customer does not have an existing line of credit with us.

   Write 2 test scenarios that would help verify this requirement.

   - Existing customer with line of credit placing an order for above $1,000
   - New customer placing an order for above $1,000

Appendix A: Acronyms

AHP: Analytical Hierarchy Process
BABOK®: IIBA's *Guide to the Business Analysis Body of Knowledge*
BRD: Business Requirements Document
CASE: Computer-Aided Systems Engineering tools
CMMI™: SEI's Capability Maturity Model Integrated
COTS: Commercial off-the-shelf Software
CRUD: create/read/update/delete
DFD: Data Flow Diagram
DSDM: Dynamic Systems Development Methodology
ERD: Entity Relationship Diagram
ERP: Enterprise Resource Planning
FDD: Functional Decomposition Diagram
I-CASE: Integrated CASE tools
IIBA®: International Institute of Business Analysis
IPO: Input/Process/Output model
ISO: International Organization for Standardization
IT: information technology
JAD: Joint Application Development (or Joint Application Design)
JIT: Just In Time
OMG: Object Management Group
OO: object oriented
OPM3: PMI's Organizational Project Management Maturity Model
PMBOK™: *Guide to the Project Management Institute's Body of Knowledge, Third Edition*
PMI™: Project Management Institute
RAD: Rapid Application Development
RUP™: Rational Unified Process
SDLC: Systems Development Life Cycle
SEI: Carnegie Mellon University's Software Engineering Institute

SME:	subject matter expert
SOW:	Statement of Work
SWAT:	skilled with advanced tools
SWOT:	strengths-weaknesses-opportunities-threats
UML:	Unified Modeling Language
WBS:	Work Breakdown Structure
XP:	Extreme Programming

Appendix B: Business Requirements Document Templates

The following templates have been included as reference material. All templates should be customized to fit the organizational and project environments in which they will be used.

1. Business Requirements Document (BRD) Comprehensive (Courtesy ESI International)
2. Business Requirements Document (BRD) Simple

B1. Business Requirements Document (BRD) Comprehensive (Courtesy of ESI International)

This document is used by ESI International in their Business Analysis Curriculum and has kindly been allowed to be included in this book.

Business Requirements Document for [insert Project Name here]	
Prepared by	
Prepared for	
Date submitted	
Project Sponsor	
Client Acceptor	
Project Manager	
Business Analyst	
Filename	
Document Number	
Last edit	
Comments	Important notice: This template includes instructional summaries at the beginning of each section. They use a style called instructions, which has been configured as hidden text. This means you can choose to display and print them, at will. Under normal circumstances, these should be hidden when you distribute your actual reports, unless you judge that the instructions themselves provide value to your readers. Please see the last section in this template for step-by-step instructions on how to see and print hidden text, along with shortcut keys for the various styles used in the template.

Table of Contents

Section Zero: Positioning of the Business Requirements Document

The Goal: Common Understanding through Structured Business Analysis and a Standard Business Requirements Document

The Business Requirements Document is a major deliverable representing the achievement of the Business Analysis milestone in a typical project management methodology. As such it requires formal review and sign off by the Client Acceptor (representing the interests of business area stakeholders). Under normal circumstances, the Business Requirements Document is created by the Senior Business Analyst delegated to a project.

This Business Requirements Document template conforms to industry best practices in business analysis, and is the primary tool for structuring requirements-gathering activities. Interim feedback loops and approvals for Business Requirements Document sections are achieved in an iterative manner, as requirements become clear over successive meetings with project stakeholders, primary and secondary users. This facilitates the final review and approval of the overall document, which by then will contain "no surprises."

A Word of Caution about Removing/Adding Sections

Do not arbitrarily add or remove sections within your Business Requirements Document. To do so raises the risk of diluting the standard, as future teams may look to your documents for guidance in building their own reports. That being said, please use the following guidelines.

Adding Sections: Although all project Business Requirements Documents begin with the standard template sections, the unique nature of each project may require additional sections and information. These are organized as Appendices.

Removing Sections: Because the Business Requirements Document template has been designed as a comprehensive study, removal of specific sections of the standard template is not recommended. Doing so represents requirements detail that will not be covered, and therefore can create project risk. Whoever authorizes removal of standard sections is accountable for ownership of that risk, and any consequences that emerge as a result. This is a key point that must be understood by all members of the project team. Document the sections that have been removed, and under whose direction, within the Risk section of the Business Requirements Document.

Final Note: Balance brevity with completeness, quality with quantity. You cannot document everything down to the tiniest detail and thereby eliminate all project risk. The Project Sponsor needs to have sufficient understanding to create an acceptable level of risk in proceeding. This will vary based on project importance and urgency, as well as the business environment within which your project lives.

Different Types of Requirements

Functional requirements can only be derived following elicitation and documentation of business and user requirements. The distinctions between these different requirements levels are important.

1. Business Requirements: Place the business at the center of focus, and tie the project to documented regulatory, strategic, tactical, and operational goals. If you are developing products or services for sale, customer requirements will also need to be documented. Customer requirements are covered at a high level in this section, then in detail under User Requirements.
2. User Requirements: Place the user at the center of focus, and describe, with flow charts, use case diagrams, use case scenarios, line of vision, and other process models, the TO-BE user experience with the new system. In some cases, especially where business processes are being modified, it may also be necessary to document the AS-IS state of user experience with the current system.
3. Functional Requirements: Place the proposed system at the center of focus, and provide a prioritized list of capabilities the system must demonstrate to satisfy business and user requirements.
4. Nonfunctional Requirements: Refer to needs that must be fulfilled related to things like the user interface, access security, availability, robustness, system failure, integration, migration, and documentation. As such, they do not deal with the actual functionality of the system, but represent key project success factors nevertheless.

Prioritizing Requirements

Ensure that your users are aware of the following interpretations regarding the prioritization of requirements:

- Must Have: Will be included in this release. These items represent core functionality and must be present. Absence of any Must Have functionality represents project failure.
- Should Have: Will be included in this release provided all Must Have requirements have been met and sufficient project resources and time remain.
- Nice to Have: Will be included in this release provided all Must Have and Should Have requirements have been met and sufficient project resources and time remain.

Section One: Glossary

This section identifies any industry or line of business jargon, acronyms, common words used in special context, and special terms that are used within the project and the Business Requirements Document itself. Pay particular attention to acronyms that may have multiple meanings: a commonly used one and a meaning that has special significance to the business area. For example, PMO is an industrywide acronym for Project Management Office. It may also stand for Prime Minister's Office or Preventive Maintenance Optimization. The project and business context determine the meaning.

Enter content here.

Section Two: Project Scope and Objectives Summary

This section is used to restate, in summary form, the project vision and scope statements from prior project documentation such as the Project Charter or an Opportunity Analysis. It reconfirms the understanding of project objectives, and allows for clarification of those statements that may be required due to the passage of time.

However, the Business Requirements Document is not a project scope change device. Should scope have changed, previous project activities must be reopened, because the reality represented by the official documentation and the signatures they contain are no longer valid.

Use this section to document high level project deliverables (what is needed), without drilling down into details or straying into solution specifications (how we will do this).

Enter content here.

Section Three: Technology Infrastructure and Information Architecture Compliance

It is important that all project initiatives and their requirements comply with existing technology standards. Use this section to position this project within that framework. Remember that specific technologies are not normally a part of requirements. If presented as such, they often become constraints. For example, a user might state "the solution must use a Microsoft SQL Server™ database." Because this might be a violation of the approved information architecture and technology infrastructure of your company, you must verify compatibility, documenting any variance here. Note also that the only reason the existing infrastructure exists is that some prior project with a strong enough business case pushed the envelope. Your project may do the same.

Do not prejudge approval or disapproval of technology constraints that are presented as requirements. Simply raise the red flag, providing information to support a decision. However, if the decision is made during business analysis activities, document the requirement and the decision here, indicating parties involved and when the decision was made. Don't lose the history.

Enter content here.

Section Four: Intended Audience

Both readers and approvers of the Business Requirements Document are identified here. Organizational titles and functional project roles for each individual are included. An organizational chart is very helpful in complex reader/approver environments.

Enter content here.

Section Five: Decision Making and Approval Process for the Business Requirements Document

In some cases, projects will have a number of key stakeholders who must discuss and provide interim approval for all or for specific sections of the Business Requirements Document. However, there must always be a single Client Acceptor who will ultimately approve the document, representing the requirements viewpoint of the business area addressed by the project.

Within project management and business analysis, the identification of the Client Acceptor is a key delegation. The delegation of Client Acceptor may be awarded to the same individual who serves as Business Area Project Sponsor.

Pay particular attention to cultural or behavioral norms within the organization that may affect the decision making process. This includes standard intervals for getting together (the monthly meeting), and the in-place approval and conflict resolution approach of the group.

Enter content here.

Section Six: Approach

This section describes:

1. The overall project management approach for the project, including all organizations, such as service providers, system integrators and external vendors, and the roles they will play.
2. The approach that will be used for business analysis activities within this project. These may include, but are not limited to, interviews, focus groups, Requirements Joint Application Design sessions, surveys, and questionnaires. These components comprise the Requirements Work Plan.

Section 6.1 – Overall Project Management Approach

Enter content here.

Section 6.2 – Business Analysis Approach

Enter content here.

Section Seven: Background, Historical, and Prior Project Information

Projects exist as development or sustainment efforts within the Product Life Cycle of systems and solution applications. Use this section to document the positioning of your project within that context. Diagrams are often helpful here.

Enter content here.

Section Eight: Business-Level Requirements: Goals, Value Proposition, and Benefits

All project initiatives exist within the organizational context of your company and consume organizational resources. As such, they must be justified by tying them to strategic, tactical, and operational goals. In some cases, there may also be regulatory governance considerations that must be taken into account. When present, regulatory requirements are documented first. Documenting business level requirements is a critical exercise, because:

1. Regulatory requirements often provide clear, non-negotiable project constraints and quantitative success factors.
2. It assists in budgeting when there are specific moneys pre-allocated to business goals.
3. It facilitates prioritization according to the varying priorities of business goals.
4. It serves as a gauge regarding the ongoing importance of a project. That is, if the business goals or their relative priorities change during the project, your project's goals and priorities will likewise change.

Section 8.1 – Regulatory Requirements

Enter content here.

Section 8.2 – Related Strategic Goals (Organization Level)

Enter content here.

Section 8.3 – Related Tactical Goals (Division or Department Level)

Enter content here.

Section 8.4 – Related Operational Goals (Staff Level)

Enter content here.

Section Nine: User Class Profiles and Key Delegations

Users are categorized by functional groups, then by job titles as appropriate. Actual names of key individuals are supplied. The following groups are identified and described:

1. Sponsorship and stakeholders
2. Primary Users: Those who will interact with the proposed system on a daily or regular basis, and whose job functions are directly involved with it
3. Secondary Users: Organizations, groups, departments and individuals who benefit from, provide input to, or derive output from the proposed system without direct involvement in its daily processes. This group also involves business or system administration personnel who must support the proposed system.

Section 9.1 – Sponsors and Stakeholders

Enter content here.

Section 9.2 – Primary Users

Enter content here.

Section 9.3 – Secondary Users

Enter content here.

Section Ten: User and Functional Level Requirements

This section provides detailed user and functional requirements information through text and process modeling. Your company will have standard tools that have been approved for use. These may include:

- Flowcharts
- Context-level data flow diagram

- UML-based use case diagrams and scenarios
- Swim lane process work flow diagrams
- IDEF0 process models

Clear description of functional requirements defines success factors for the project. As such, functional requirements are closely tied to the project's Quality Plan. It is critical to understand that Quality is conformance to documented and approved requirements and specifications. It is therefore not the same as Excellence or Perfection. Excellence is a moving target representing the highest level of quality achievable within the timeframe of the project. Perfection is zero defects. In addition, quality has a cost expressed as follows:

Cost of Quality = Cost of Conformance + Cost of Nonconformance

Nonconformance of deliverables is frequently tied to insufficient levels of detail in the documentation of requirements. In light of this, the real focus of the Business Requirements Document can be expressed as the establishment of project quality standards for project deliverables. An overall focus on the identification, definition, elicitation and documentation of quantitative measures versus qualitative descriptions is a key element of functional requirement definition. You may begin your descriptions using qualitative language such as "improved" or "faster," but follow this with actual metrics.

Enter content here.

Section Eleven: Additional Information Regarding Functional Requirements Related to Output and Reporting

This section describes the requirements of primary and secondary users related to screen, transmitted, and hardcopy output from the proposed system. This includes but is not limited to:

- Ad hoc queries
- Scheduled/batch reports
- Audit or control reports

Also included here are:

- Recipient information maps: Who gets what information (need to know, should know, wants to know)
- Business rules that govern output generation: Who, what, where, when, why, how much

Enter content here.

Section Twelve: Conceptual Data Model

This is a very high level, requirements oriented set of diagrams that will be elaborated upon by database analyst personnel during solution design. This section may be limited to simply identifying database systems and their interactions with project applications. Alternatively, it may include actual database schema diagrams and descriptions. The amount of detail will vary by project and company policy.

Enter content here.

Section Thirteen: Nonfunctional Requirements

This section documents requirements that are not directly related to the functionality of the proposed system. Like functional requirements, the clear, quantitative definition of these requirements feeds the project's Quality Plan. Please be conscientious in your investigation of nonfunctional requirements, as these are often overlooked or given insufficient attention.

Section 13.1 – Operational Environment

Enter content here.

Section 13.2 – User Interface Requirements

Enter content here.

Section 13.3 – User Access/Security Requirements

Enter content here.

Section 13.4 – Service Level/Performance/ Capacity Requirements

Enter content here.

Section 13.5 – Data Requirements (Input, Correlative)

Enter content here.

Section 13.6 – Business Continuity and Recovery Requirements

Enter content here.

Section 13.7 – Integration/Migration Requirements

Enter content here.

Section 13.8 – Administrative/Backup/Archive Requirements

Enter content here.

Section 13.9 – Expected Life Span Requirements

Enter content here.

Section 13.10 – Documentation Requirements

Enter content here.

Section 13.11 – Training Requirements

Enter content here.

Section 13.12 – Other Nonfunctional Requirements

Enter content here.

Section Fourteen: Assumptions, Dependencies, and Constraints

Assumptions: All projects operate in a less-than-perfect world. Not everything can be officially verified as existing or available ahead of time. These "unknowns" are documented in project assumptions. An example might be "The project assumes the continued availability of funding following the upcoming merger."

Dependencies include, but are not limited to the availability of project resources, applications and systems that interact with this one, hardware, facilities, equipment, business processes and regulatory approvals. Of particular importance is the dependency on the availability of project stakeholders and users, and conformance to approval and change management processes.

Constraints are those regulatory, technological or business realities that legitimately constrain solution development. An example might be "The new system must be built in Oracle™." Although this example might sound, on the surface, like a specification (and therefore not part of a Business Requirements Document) it becomes a constraining requirement when stated up front. It is for this reason that users must be cautioned against careless statement of constraints.

In essence, this section allows you to document that which cannot be ascertained in advance. These items may feed the Risks and Risk Management section, which follows.

Section 14.1 – Assumptions

Enter content here.

Section 14.2 – Dependencies

Enter content here.

Section 14.3 – Constraints

Enter content here.

Section Fifteen: Risks and Risk Management Process

This section documents project risks:

1. That have been uncovered as a result of business analysis activities
2. Related to the business analysis itself (such as not having adequate time to perform required analysis and nonavailability of key requirements voices)

In addition, this section documents:

1. Risk mapping: Likelihood versus impact potential
2. Who owns risks, and deadlines for risk resolution
3. Contingency plans.

Enter content here.

Section Sixteen: Solution Options

As a business analysis vehicle, the Business Requirements Document focuses on requirements, not specifications nor solutions. Nevertheless, as requirements are elicited and documented, discussion around solution options will occur. This section is used to document those options which have been considered to date, rejected, or approved for further investigation. It is important to include rejected entries for the historical record of the project, and to pre-empt future readers who may ask "did they consider such-and-such?"

Remember that solution options must be derived based on clear understanding of project requirements, assumptions, dependencies and constraints.

Section 16.1 – Short List Solution Options

Enter content here.

Section 16.2 – Information Regarding Pilot

Note: this section is included only if a pilot has, in fact, been proposed. It will cover the specific target user groups, subset of requirements to be addressed, funding, timing and key personnel required. Do not use this section as a project plan for a pilot, although it will identify the pilot's key personnel.

Enter content here.

Section 16.3 – Rejected Solution Options

Enter content here.

Section Seventeen: Change Management Process

Because business analysis activities are exploratory and iterative up to the approval of the Business Requirements Document, it is likely that some requirements will evolve throughout the process. This consumes project resources and so must be governed by change management. For example, a requirement that takes one day to elicit, document and approve, but that changes 30 times during business analysis will consume 30 project days worth of appropriate resources.

This section provides information, normally documented in official policy, regarding the change management process to be used for this project. It also includes details regarding any additional change management that must be applied due to the special needs or unique nature of this project.

If there is an official change management policy that is documented elsewhere (such as in the Project Plan), you may simply reference it here.

Enter content here.

Section Eighteen: Business Requirements Document Revision Log

This section documents requirements that have changed over the course of successive documentation iterations during business analysis activities. Pay particular attention to requirements with ongoing adjustment. These are high risk areas that may represent:

1. Lack of clear business process definition
2. Unclear reporting requirements
3. Areas of regulatory flux
4. Unclear secondary user hand-off points
5. Unclear governance related to specific requirements

If you find that a majority of must have requirements cannot be nailed down, you may have a situation where the project itself must be reassessed at a scope level.

Enter content here.

Section Nineteen: Appendices

Each Appendix must have:

- A separate header, numbered A through Z, with an appropriate descriptive title. For example: APPENDIX A – REGULATORY REQUIREMENTS.
- Note: Use the Heading 1 Style for each Appendix Header. This style will automatically insert a page break.
- A lead in paragraph that states the importance of the data to this report.
- A closure, centered on a separate line, that repeats the header, such as End of Appendix A – Regulatory Requirements.

Enter content here.

Section Twenty: Approval

This section documents the approvals required for sign off of the Business Requirements Document and establishment of the Requirements Analysis milestone. Each signatory is described by both organizational title and project functional role. Required signatories are the Business Analyst and the Client Acceptor. Other signatories may be required by your company policy.

This document has been approved as the official Business Requirements Document for the [name of project] project, and accurately reflects the current understanding of business requirements. Following approval of this document, requirements changes will be governed by the project's change management process, including impact analysis, appropriate reviews and approvals, under the general control of the Project Plan and according to company policy.

Prepared by

_____

Business Analyst   Date

Approved by

_____

Client Acceptor   Date

All products, services and company names used within this template are trademarks or registered trademarks of their respective owners.

B2. **Business Requirements Document (BRD) Simple**

Business Requirements Document

XYZ Product

1. As-Is Scenario
    a. Background
    b. Context diagram
    c. Business Processes
    d. Business Rules
    e. Business Objectives
    f. Business Constraints
    g. Regulatory Constraints
    h. Process models
    i. Data models
    j. Data Flow Diagrams

2. Product Vision and Scope
    a. Vision statement
    b. Key features
    c. Exclusions
    d. Impacted stakeholders
    e. Context diagram
    f. Assumptions
    g. Constraints

3. Business Requirements
    a. Business Processes
    b. Business Rules
    c. Business Objectives
    d. Business Constraints
    e. Regulatory Constraints

4. User Requirements
    4.x Use Case 1

5. Nonfunctional requirements
    a. Performance
    b. Safety
    c. Security
    d. Quality attributes
    e. User documentation

6. Data Requirements
    a. Entity Relationship Diagram
    b. Data Flow Diagram

Appendix A: Glossary
Appendix B: Issues lists

Use Case Template

Use Case

General Characteristics	
Intent	[a summary statement of the purpose of the use case]
Level	[one of: business level , system level, or component]
Author	[name of use case author(s)]
Last Update:	[date last updated/change history]
Status	[one of: incomplete, under review, finalized, etc.]
Primary Actor	[role name for the primary actor, <optional description>]
Secondary Actors	[role names of other actors (could be systems) relied upon to accomplish use case]
Preconditions	[what we expect is already the state of the world]
Assumptions	[any assumptions relative to this use case]
Trigger	[the event that starts the use case]
Success Post Condition	[the state of the world upon successful completion]
Failed Post Condition	[the state of the world if use case abandoned]
Overview	[description in words that encompasses all scenarios]

Main Success Scenario	
Step	Action
S	[description in words of the main success scenario]
1	["This use case starts when …" followed by the trigger.]
2	[step description… <"included" use case pointer>]
3	[step description… <"included" use case pointer>]
4	["This use case ends when …" the final step in main success scenario.]

Extension Scenarios	
Step	Branching Action
1	[description in words of the extension scenario]
	[any scenario other than the main scenario. Could be valid but less common path or error path]

Related Information	
Performance	[process and/or system performance]
Frequency	[how often it is expected to happen]
OPEN ISSUES	[list of issues awaiting decision]
Future Considerations	[list of all requirements or possible requirements that have been deferred to future increments]
Comments	

Appendix C:
United Nations
Organizational Chart

The United Nations System

Principal Organs

Trusteeship Council	Security Council	General Assembly	Economic and Social Council	International Court of Justice	Secretariat

Trusteeship Council

Security Council

Subsidiary Bodies

Military Staff Committee

Standing Committee and ad hoc bodies

International Criminal Tribunal for the former Yugoslavia (ICTY)

International Criminal Tribunal for Rwanda (ICTR)

UN Monitoring, Verification and Inspection Commission (Iraq) (UNMOVIC)

United Nations Compensation Commission

Peacekeeping Operations and Missions

General Assembly

Subsidiary Bodies

Main committees

Human Rights Council

Other sessional committees

Standing committees and ad hoc bodies

Other subsidiary organs

Advisory Subsidiary Body

United Nations Peacebuilding Commission

Programmes and Funds

UNCTAD United Nations Conference on Trade and Development

   ITC International Trade Centre (UNCTAD/WTO)

UNDCP [1] United Nations Drug Control Programme

UNEP United Nations Environment Programme

UNICEF United Nations Children's Fund

UNDP United Nations Development Programme

   UNIFEM United Nations Development Fund for Women

   UNV United Nations Volunteers

   UNCDF United Nations Capital Development Fund

UNFPA United Nations Population Fund

UNHCR Office of the United Nations High Commissioner for Refugees

WFP World Food Programme

UNRWA [2] United Nations Relief and Works Agency for Palestine Refugees in the Near East

UN-HABITAT United Nations Human Settlements Programme

Research and Training Institutes

UNICRI United Nations Interregional Crime and Justice Research Institute

UNITAR United Nations Institute for Training and Research

UNRISD United Nations Research Institute for Social Development

UNIDIR [2] United Nations Institute for Disarmament Research

INSTRAW International Research and Training Institute for the Advancement of Women

UNU United Nations University

UNSSC United Nations System Staff College

UNAIDS Joint United Nations Programme on HIV/AIDS

Other UN Entities

OHCHR Office of the United Nations High Commissioner for Human Rights

UNOPS United Nations Office for Project Services

UNDEF United Nations Democracy Fund

Other UN Trust Funds [7]

UNFIP United Nations Fund for International Partnerships

Economic and Social Council

Functional Commissions

Commissions on:

   Narcotic Drugs

   Crime Prevention and Criminal Justice

   Science and Technology for Development

   Sustainable Development

   Status of Women

   Population and Development

Commission for Social Development

Statistical Commission

Regional Commissions

Economic Commission for Africa (ECA)

Economic Commission for Europe (ECE)

Economic Commission for Latin America and the Caribbean (ECLAC)

Economic and Social Commission for Asia and the Pacific (ESCAP)

Economic and Social Commission for Western Asia (ESCWA)

Other Bodies

Permanent Forum on Indigenous Issues (PFII)

United Nations Forum on Forests

Sessional and standing committees

Expert, ad hoc and related bodies

Related Organizations

WTO World Trade Organization

IAEA [4] International Atomic Energy Agency

CTBTO Prep.Com [5] PrepCom for the Nuclear-Test-Ban-Treaty Organization

OPCW [5] Organization for the Prohibition of Chemical Weapons

International Court of Justice

Specialized Agencies [6]

ILO International Labour Organization

FAO Food and Agriculture Organization of the United Nations

UNESCO United Nations Educational, Scientific and Cultural Organization

WHO World Health Organization

World Bank Group

   IBRD International Bank for Reconstruction and Development

   IDA International Development Association

   IFC International Finance Corporation

   MIGA Multilateral Investment Guarantee Agency

   ICSID International Centre for Settlement of Investment Disputes

IMF International Monetary Fund

ICAO International Civil Aviation Organization

IMO International Maritime Organization

ITU International Telecommunication Union

UPU Universal Postal Union

WMO World Meteorological Organization

WIPO World Intellectual Property Organization

IFAD International Fund for Agricultural Development

UNIDO United Nations Industrial Development Organization

UNWTO World Tourism Organization

Secretariat

Departments and Offices

OSG [3] Office of the Secretary-General

OIOS Office of Internal Oversight Services

OLA Office of Legal Affairs

DPA Department of Political Affairs

DDA Department for Disarmament Affairs

DPKO Department of Peacekeeping Operations

OCHA Office for the Coordination of Humanitarian Affairs

DESA Department of Economic and Social Affairs

DGACM Department for General Assembly and Conference Management

DPI Department of Public Information

DM Department of Management

OHRLLS Office of the High Representative for the Least Developed Countries, Landlocked Developing Countries and Small Island Developing States

DSS Department of Safety and Security

UNODC United Nations Office on Drugs and Crime

UNOG UN Office at Geneva

UNOV UN Office at Vienna

UNON UN Office at Nairobi

Published by the United Nations Department of Public Information

06-39572—August 2006—10,000   0—DPI/2431

NOTES: Solid lines from a Principal Organ indicate a direct reporting relationship; dashes indicate a non-subsidiary relationship.

1 The UN Drug Control Programme is part of the UN Office on Drugs and Crime

2 UNRWA and UNIDIR report only to the GA

3 The United Nations Ethics Office and the United Nations Ombudsman's Office report directly to the Secretary-General

4 IAEA reports to the Security Council and the General Assembly (GA)

5 The CTBTO Prep.Com and OPCW report to the GA

6 Specialized agencies are autonomous organizations working with the UN and each other through the coordinating machinery of the ECOSOC at the intergovernmental level, and through the Chief Executives Board for coordination (CEB) at the inter-secretariat level

7 UNFIP is an autonomous trust fund operating under the leadership of the United Nations Deputy Secretary-General. UNDEF's advisory board recommends funding proposals for approval by the Secretary-General.

Sources and Bibliography

Ahern, Dennis M., Aaron Clouse, Richard Turner, *CMMI® Distilled*, 2nd Edition, A practical Introduction to Integrated Process Improvement, Pearson Education, Inc, Boston, MA, 2004.

Andrews, Dorine C., Naomi S. Leventhal, *Fusion, Integrating IE, CASE, and JAD: A Handbook for Reengineering the Systems Organization*, Prentice Hall, Englewood Cliffs, NJ, 1993.

BABOK™, *A Guide to the Business Analysis Body of Knowledge*, version 1.6 (DRAFT), International Institute of Business Analysis, Toronto, CA, 2006.

Chrissis, Mary Beth, Mike Konrad, Sandy Shrum, *CMMI® Guidelines for Process Integration and Product Improvement*, Pearson Education, Inc, Boston, MA, 2003.

Glib, Tom, *Principles of Software Engineering*, Addison-Wesley, 1988.

Hall, Elaine M., *Managing Risk, Methods for software systems development*, Addison-Wesley, Upper Saddle River, NJ, 1998.

Kulak, Daryl and Eamonn Guiney, *Use Cases, Requirements in Context*, Second Edition, Pearson Education, Inc, Boston, MA, 2004.

Managing Negotiation, Situation Management Systems, Inc, Hanover, MA, 1996.

Martin, James, *Rapid Application Development*, Macmillan Publishing Company, New York, NY, 1991.

McConnell, Steve, Rapid Development, Microsoft Press, Redmond, WA, 1996.

PMBOK®, *Guide, A Guide to the Project Management Body of Knowledge*, Third Edition, Project Management Institute, 2004.

Pilone, Dan, *UML 2.0 Pocket Reference*, O'Reilly Media, Inc, Sebastopol, CA, 2006.

Scholtes, Peter R., and others, *The Team Handbook*, Joiner Associates, Inc, Madison, WI, 1988.

Schwaber, Ken, *Agile Project Management with Scrum*, Microsoft Press, Redmond, WA, 2004.

Scott W. Ambler – *Detailed Requirements Specifications: Possible a Worst Practice?* ISSIG Review 2006 Vol X No. 2.

Software Engineering Institute – CMU/SEI –93-TR-6.

Stephens, Ryan K., and Ronald R. Plew, *Database Design*, Sams Publishing, Indianapolis, IN, 2001.

Ward, J. LeRoy, *Project Management Terms – A working glossary*, ESI International, Arlington, VA, 2000.

Webster's New Collegiate Dictionary, G. & C. Merriam Co, Springfield, MA, 1981.

Wiegers, Karl E., *Software Requirements*, 2nd Edition, Microsoft Press, Redmond, WA, 2003.

Wiegers, Karl E., *More about Software Requirements*, Microsoft Press, Redmond, WA, 2006.

Wilkie, George, *Object-Oriented Software Engineering – The Professional Developer's Guide*, The MARI Group, Great Britain, 1993.

Wood, Jane, Denise Silver, *Joint Application Development*, 2nd Edition, John Wiley & Sons, INC, 1995.

Index